FARMING LIFE IN ANOTHER WORLD ④

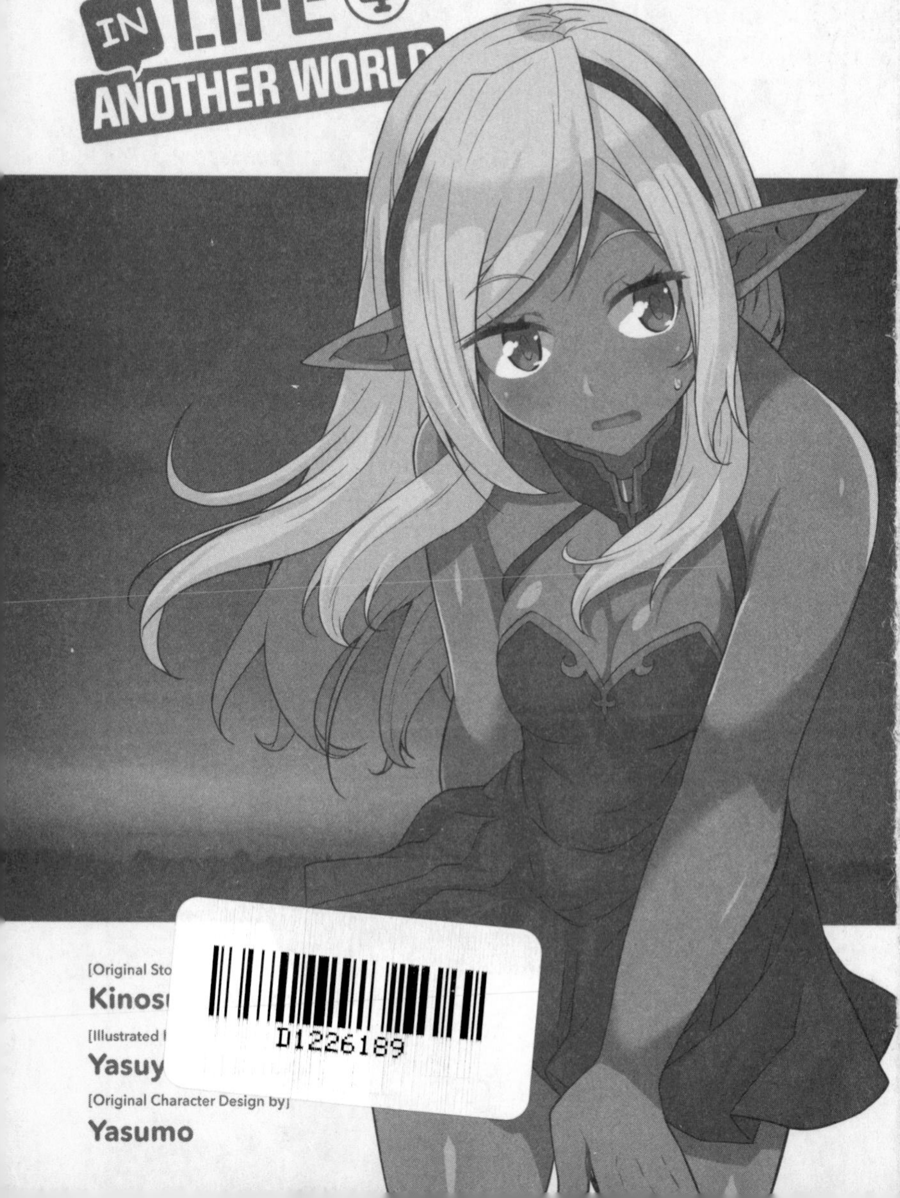

[Original Sto

Kinos

[Illustrated

Yasuy

[Original Character Design by]

Yasumo

CHAPTER 59: THE FESTIVAL PLANNING COMMITTEE AND THE INSTRUMENTS PART 1

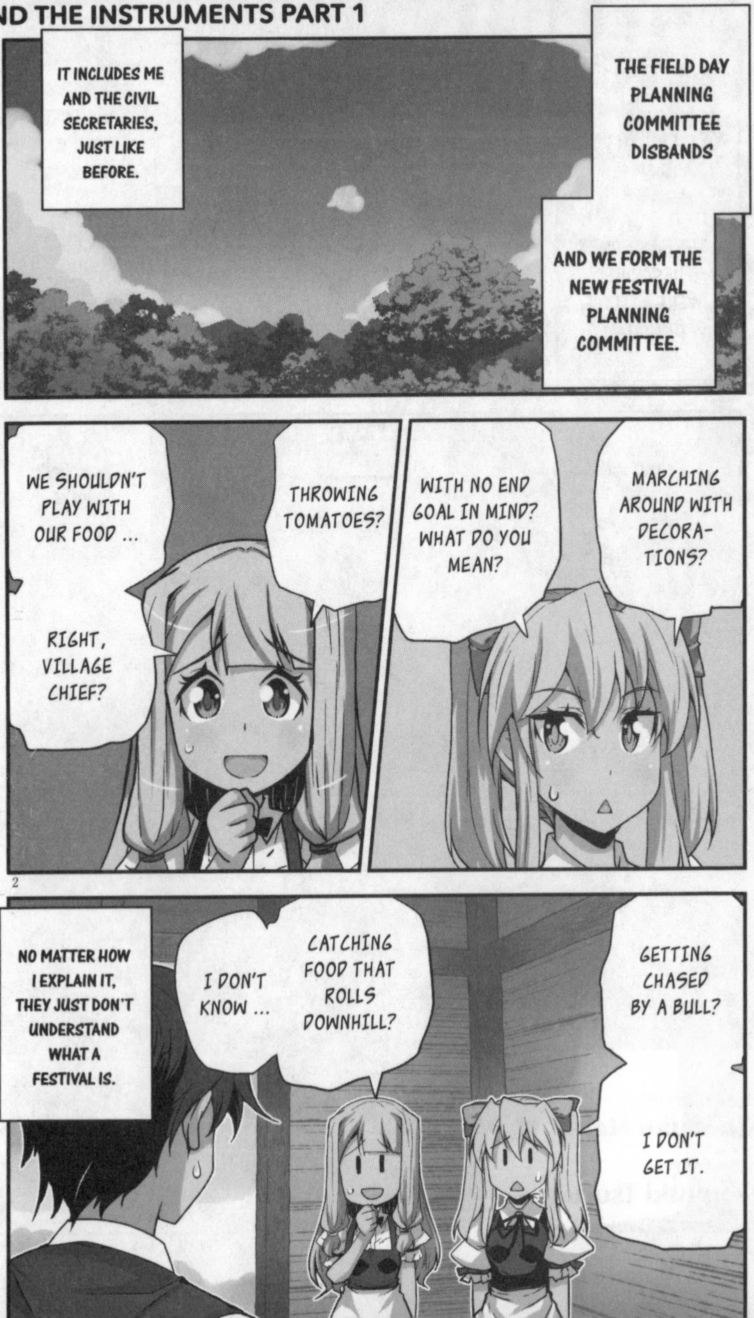

THE FIELD DAY PLANNING COMMITTEE DISBANDS
AND WE FORM THE NEW FESTIVAL PLANNING COMMITTEE.
IT INCLUDES ME AND THE CIVIL SECRETARIES, JUST LIKE BEFORE.
MARCHING AROUND WITH DECORA- TIONS?
WITH NO END GOAL IN MIND? WHAT DO YOU MEAN?
THROWING TOMATOES?
WE SHOULDN'T PLAY WITH OUR FOOD ...
RIGHT, VILLAGE CHIEF?
GETTING CHASED BY A BULL?
I DON'T GET IT.
CATCHING FOOD THAT ROLLS DOWNHILL?
I DON'T KNOW ...
NO MATTER HOW I EXPLAIN IT, THEY JUST DON'T UNDERSTAND WHAT A FESTIVAL IS.

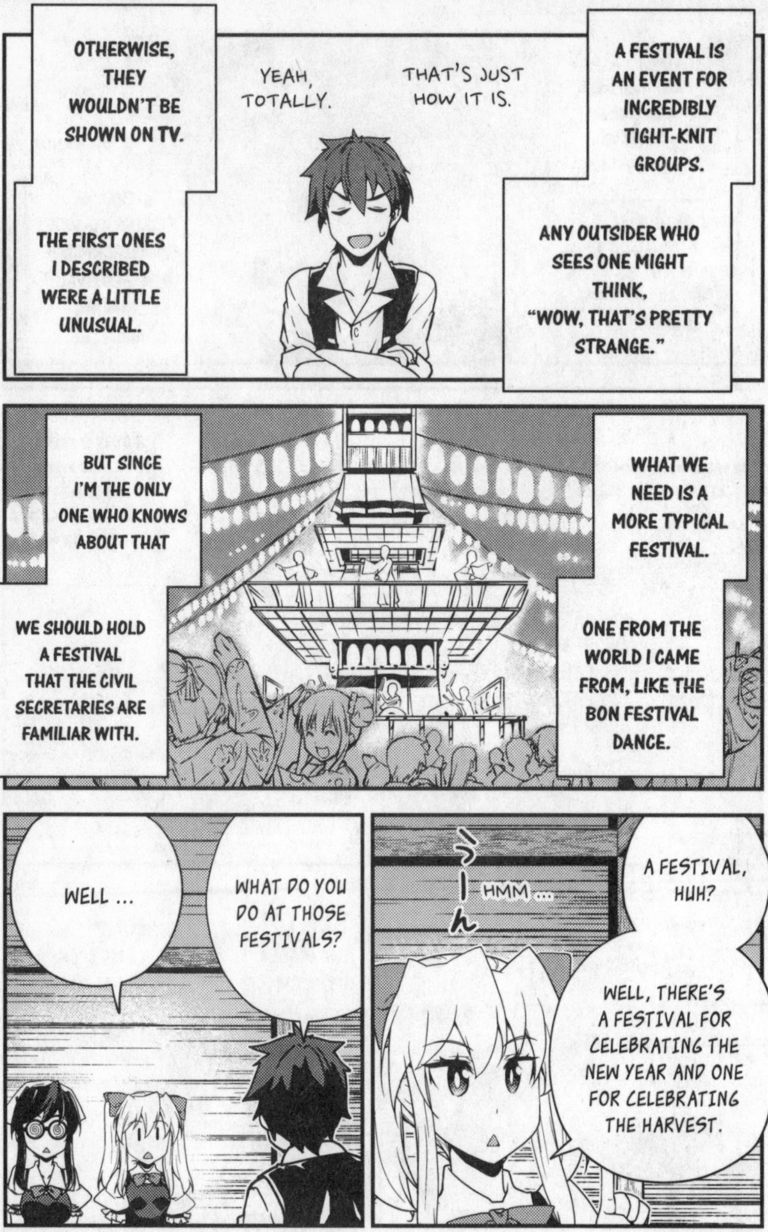
A FESTIVAL IS AN EVENT FOR INCREDIBLY TIGHT-KNIT GROUPS.
ANY OUTSIDER WHO SEES ONE MIGHT THINK, "WOW, THAT'S PRETTY STRANGE."
THAT'S JUST HOW IT IS.
YEAH, TOTALLY.
OTHERWISE, THEY WOULDN'T BE SHOWN ON TV.
THE FIRST ONES I DESCRIBED WERE A LITTLE UNUSUAL.
WHAT WE NEED IS A MORE TYPICAL FESTIVAL.
ONE FROM THE WORLD I CAME FROM, LIKE THE BON FESTIVAL DANCE.
BUT SINCE I'M THE ONLY ONE WHO KNOWS ABOUT THAT
WE SHOULD HOLD A FESTIVAL THAT THE CIVIL SECRETARIES ARE FAMILIAR WITH.
A FESTIVAL, HUH?
うーん
HMM ...
WELL, THERE'S A FESTIVAL FOR CELEBRATING THE NEW YEAR AND ONE FOR CELEBRATING THE HARVEST.
WHAT DO YOU DO AT THOSE FESTIVALS?
WELL ...

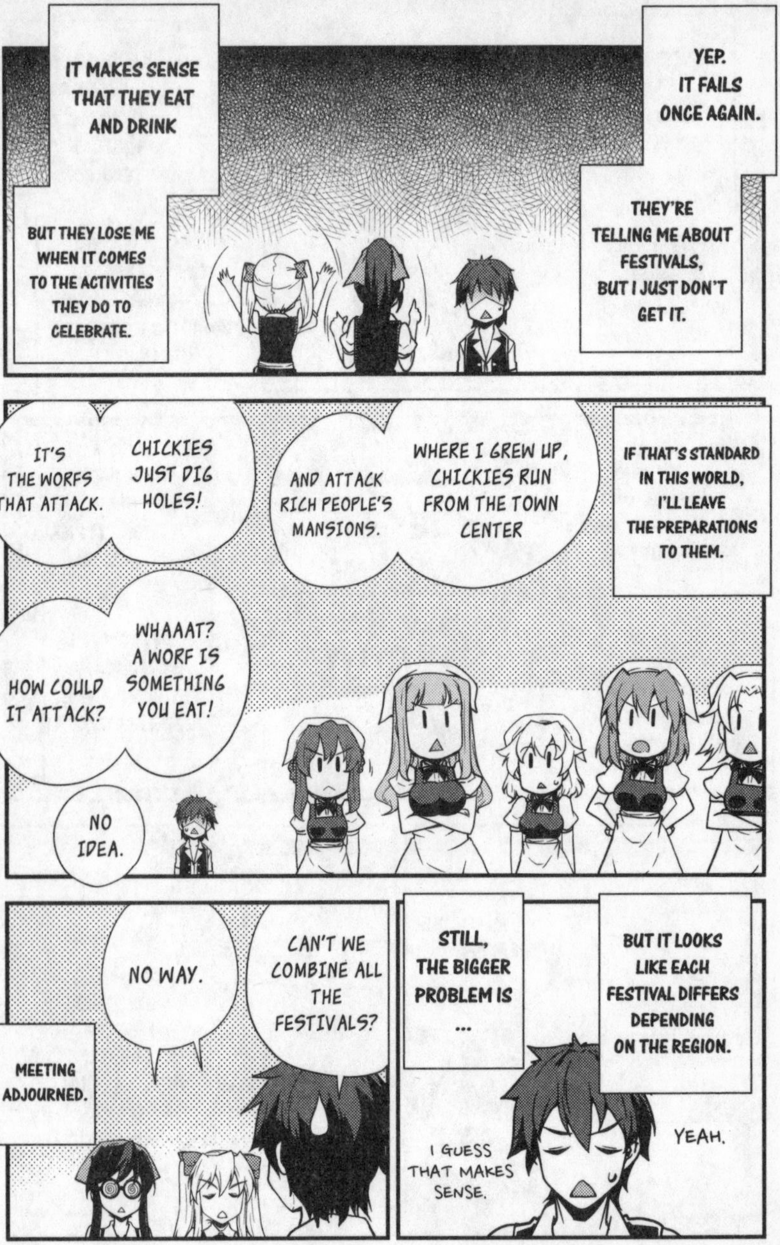
YEP. IT FAILS ONCE AGAIN.
THEY'RE TELLING ME ABOUT FESTIVALS, BUT I JUST DON'T GET IT.
IT MAKES SENSE THAT THEY EAT AND DRINK
BUT THEY LOSE ME WHEN IT COMES TO THE ACTIVITIES THEY DO TO CELEBRATE.
IF THAT'S STANDARD IN THIS WORLD, I'LL LEAVE THE PREPARATIONS TO THEM.
WHERE I GREW UP, CHICKIES RUN FROM THE TOWN CENTER
AND ATTACK RICH PEOPLE'S MANSIONS.
CHICKIES JUST DIG HOLES!
IT'S THE WORFS THAT ATTACK.
WHAAAT? A WORF IS SOMETHING YOU EAT!
HOW COULD IT ATTACK?
NO IDEA.
BUT IT LOOKS LIKE EACH FESTIVAL DIFFERS DEPENDING ON THE REGION.
STILL, THE BIGGER PROBLEM IS ...
YEAH.
I GUESS THAT MAKES SENSE.
CAN'T WE COMBINE ALL THE FESTIVALS?
NO WAY.
MEETING ADJOURNED.

A DAY IN THE LIFE OF A CAMBION

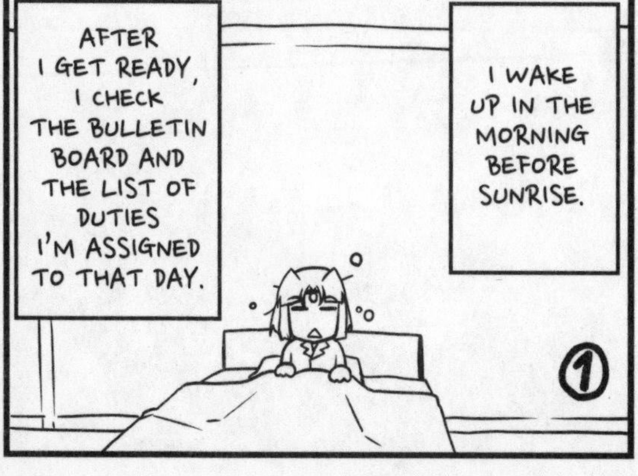
I WAKE UP IN THE MORNING BEFORE SUNRISE.
AFTER I GET READY, I CHECK THE BULLETIN BOARD AND THE LIST OF DUTIES I'M ASSIGNED TO THAT DAY.
1

Farming life in another world.

CHAPTER 60: THE FESTIVAL PLANNING COMMITTEE AND THE INSTRUMENTS PART 2

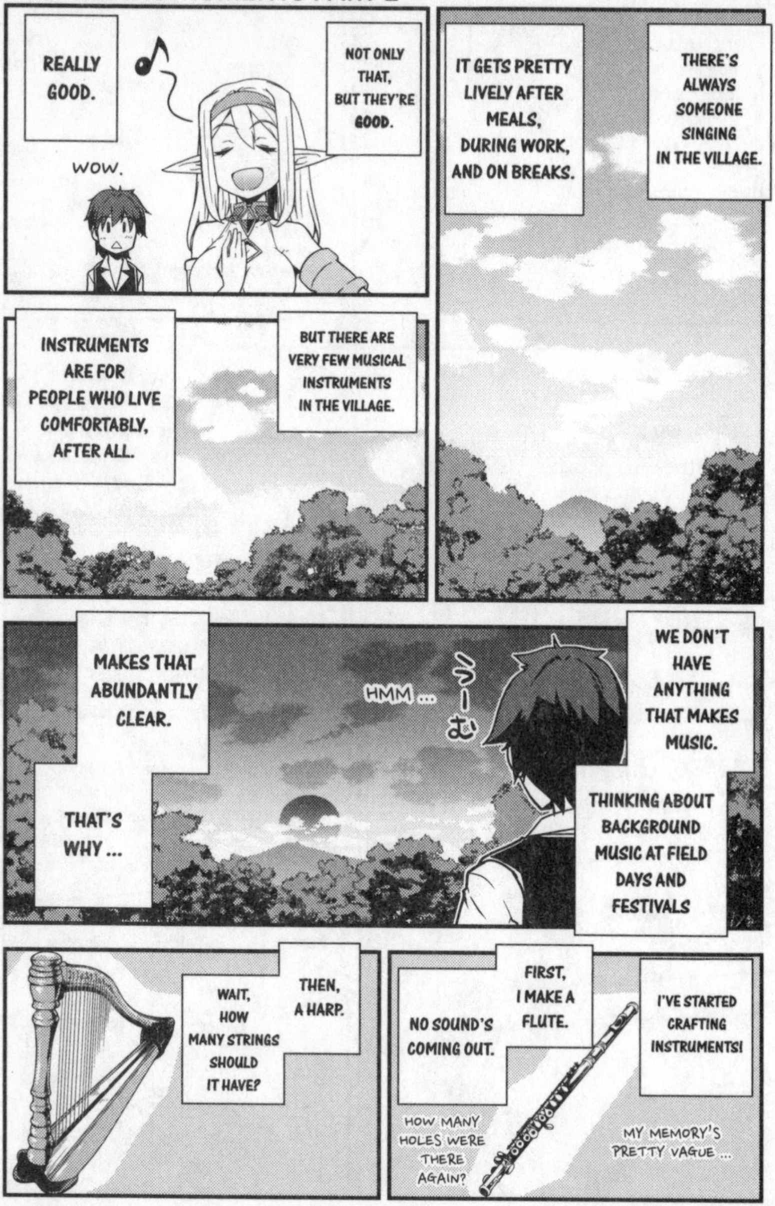
THERE'S ALWAYS SOMEONE SINGING IN THE VILLAGE.
IT GETS PRETTY LIVELY AFTER MEALS, DURING WORK, AND ON BREAKS.
NOT ONLY THAT, BUT THEY'RE GOOD.
REALLY GOOD.
WOW.
BUT THERE ARE VERY FEW MUSICAL INSTRUMENTS IN THE VILLAGE.
INSTRUMENTS ARE FOR PEOPLE WHO LIVE COMFORTABLY, AFTER ALL.
WE DON'T HAVE ANYTHING THAT MAKES MUSIC.
THINKING ABOUT BACKGROUND MUSIC AT FIELD DAYS AND FESTIVALS
HMM ...
うーむ
MAKES THAT ABUNDANTLY CLEAR.
THAT'S WHY ...
I'VE STARTED CRAFTING INSTRUMENTS!
FIRST, I MAKE A FLUTE.
NO SOUND'S COMING OUT.
MY MEMORY'S PRETTY VAGUE ...
HOW MANY HOLES WERE THERE AGAIN?
THEN, A HARP.
WAIT, HOW MANY STRINGS SHOULD IT HAVE?

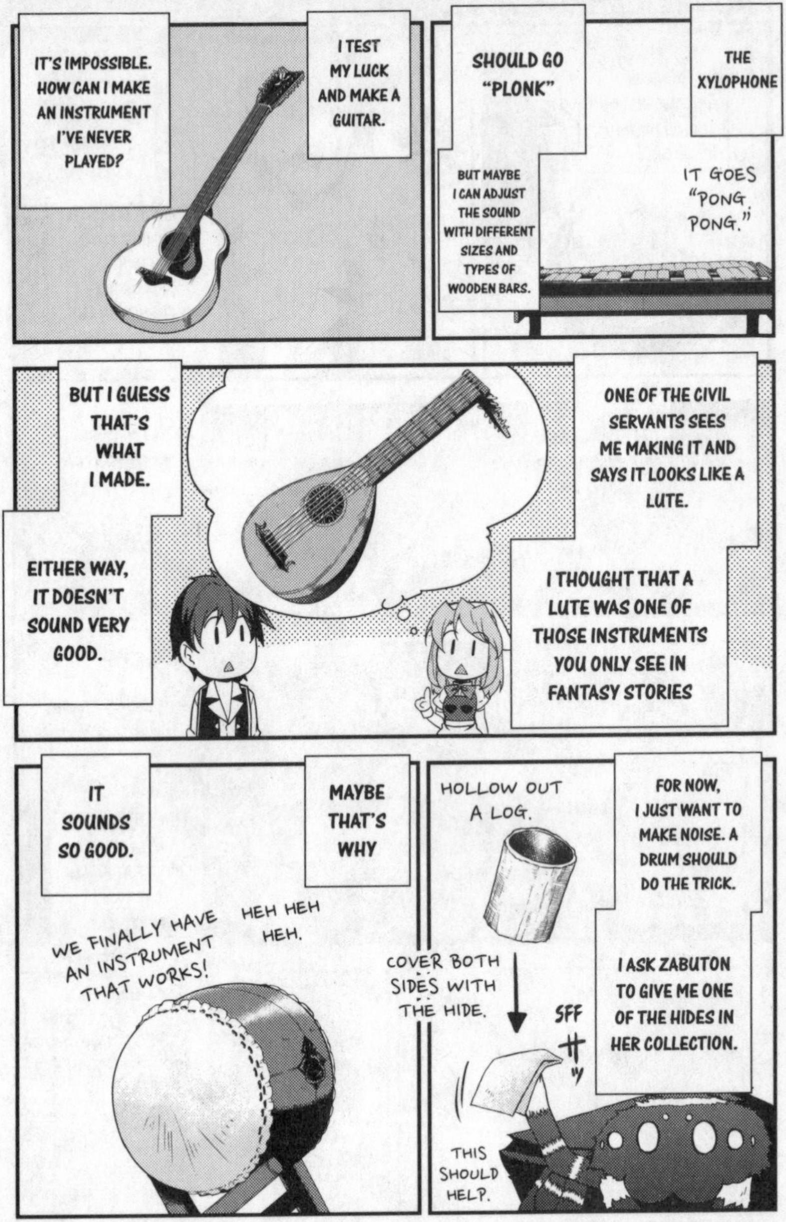

THE XYLOPHONE
SHOULD GO "PLONK"
IT GOES "PONG PONG."
BUT MAYBE I CAN ADJUST THE SOUND WITH DIFFERENT SIZES AND TYPES OF WOODEN BARS.
I TEST MY LUCK AND MAKE A GUITAR.
IT'S IMPOSSIBLE. HOW CAN I MAKE AN INSTRUMENT I'VE NEVER PLAYED?
ONE OF THE CIVIL SERVANTS SEES ME MAKING IT AND SAYS IT LOOKS LIKE A LUTE.
BUT I GUESS THAT'S WHAT I MADE.
I THOUGHT THAT A LUTE WAS ONE OF THOSE INSTRUMENTS YOU ONLY SEE IN FANTASY STORIES
EITHER WAY, IT DOESN'T SOUND VERY GOOD.
FOR NOW, I JUST WANT TO MAKE NOISE. A DRUM SHOULD DO THE TRICK.
HOLLOW OUT A LOG.
I ASK ZABUTON TO GIVE ME ONE OF THE HIDES IN HER COLLECTION.
COVER BOTH SIDES WITH THE HIDE.
SFF
THIS SHOULD HELP.
MAYBE THAT'S WHY
IT SOUNDS SO GOOD.
HEH HEH HEH.
WE FINALLY HAVE AN INSTRUMENT THAT WORKS!

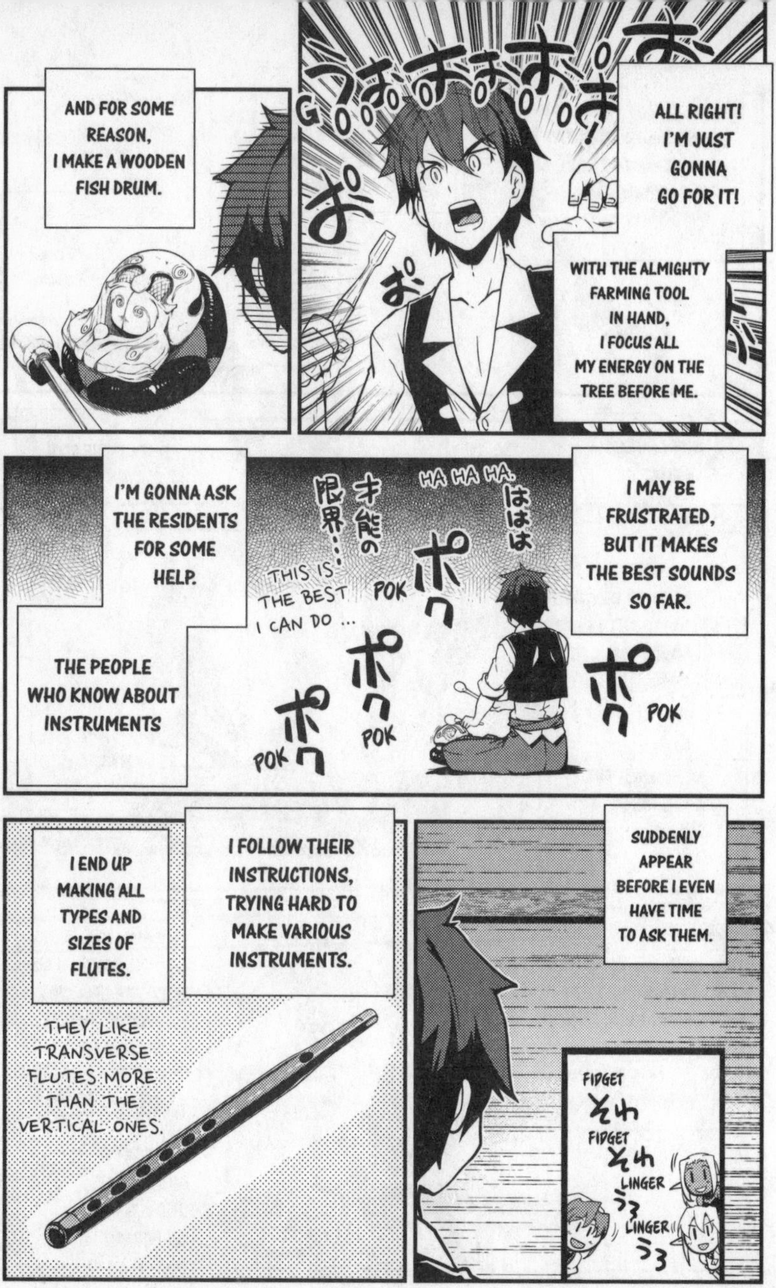
ALL RIGHT! I'M JUST GONNA GO FOR IT!
GOOOOOOOOO!
WITH THE ALMIGHTY FARMING TOOL IN HAND, I FOCUS ALL MY ENERGY ON THE TREE BEFORE ME.
AND FOR SOME REASON, I MAKE A WOODEN FISH DRUM.
I MAY BE FRUSTRATED, BUT IT MAKES THE BEST SOUNDS SO FAR.
HA HA HA.
POK
POK
THIS IS THE BEST I CAN DO ...
POK
POK
I'M GONNA ASK THE RESIDENTS FOR SOME HELP.
THE PEOPLE WHO KNOW ABOUT INSTRUMENTS
SUDDENLY APPEAR BEFORE I EVEN HAVE TIME TO ASK THEM.
FIDGET
FIDGET
LINGER
LINGER
I FOLLOW THEIR INSTRUCTIONS, TRYING HARD TO MAKE VARIOUS INSTRUMENTS.
I END UP MAKING ALL TYPES AND SIZES OF FLUTES.
THEY LIKE TRANSVERSE FLUTES MORE THAN THE VERTICAL ONES.

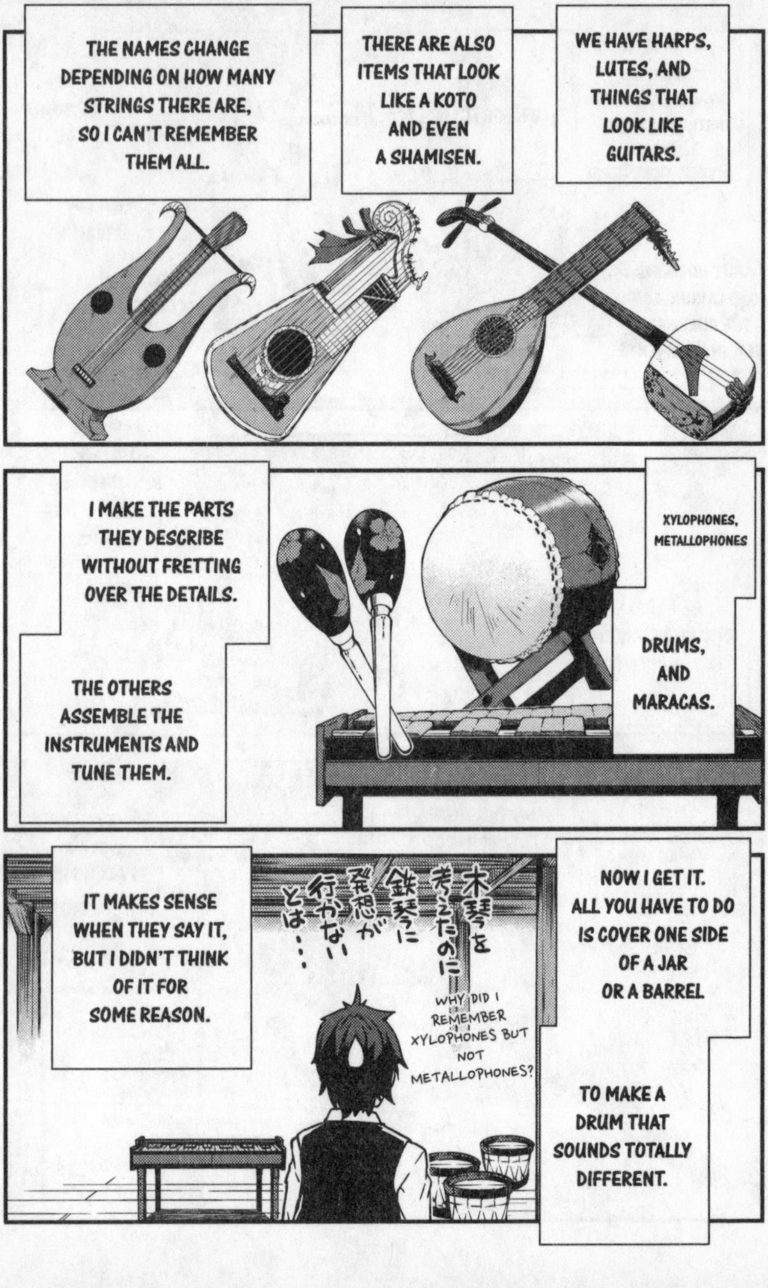

WE HAVE HARPS, LUTES, AND THINGS THAT LOOK LIKE GUITARS.
THERE ARE ALSO ITEMS THAT LOOK LIKE A KOTO AND EVEN A SHAMISEN.
THE NAMES CHANGE DEPENDING ON HOW MANY STRINGS THERE ARE, SO I CAN'T REMEMBER THEM ALL.
XYLOPHONES, METALLOPHONES
DRUMS, AND MARACAS.
I MAKE THE PARTS THEY DESCRIBE WITHOUT FRETTING OVER THE DETAILS.
THE OTHERS ASSEMBLE THE INSTRUMENTS AND TUNE THEM.
NOW I GET IT. ALL YOU HAVE TO DO IS COVER ONE SIDE OF A JAR OR A BARREL
TO MAKE A DRUM THAT SOUNDS TOTALLY DIFFERENT.
木琴を考えたのに鉄琴に発想が行かないとは…
WHY DID I REMEMBER XYLOPHONES BUT NOT METALLOPHONES?
IT MAKES SENSE WHEN THEY SAY IT, BUT I DIDN'T THINK OF IT FOR SOME REASON.

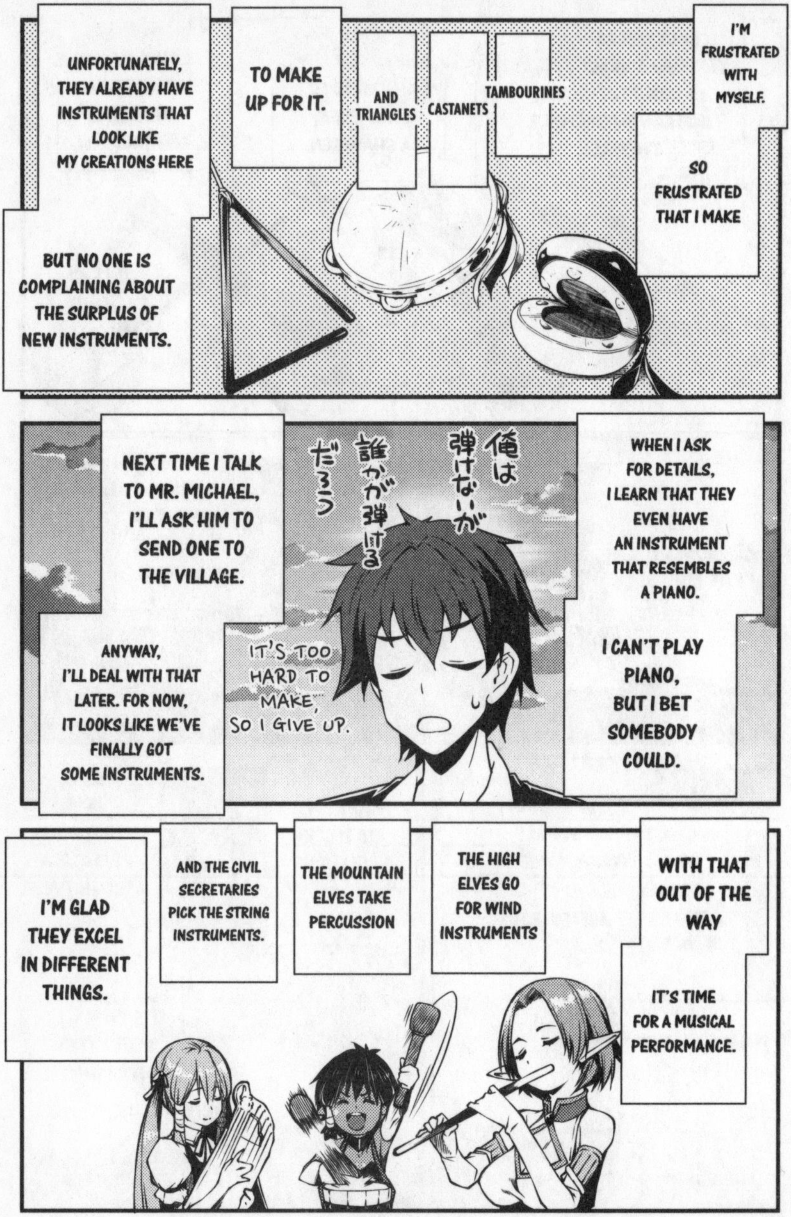
I'M FRUSTRATED WITH MYSELF.
SO FRUSTRATED THAT I MAKE
TAMBOURINES
CASTANETS
AND TRIANGLES
TO MAKE UP FOR IT.
UNFORTUNATELY, THEY ALREADY HAVE INSTRUMENTS THAT LOOK LIKE MY CREATIONS HERE
BUT NO ONE IS COMPLAINING ABOUT THE SURPLUS OF NEW INSTRUMENTS.
WHEN I ASK FOR DETAILS, I LEARN THAT THEY EVEN HAVE AN INSTRUMENT THAT RESEMBLES A PIANO.
I CAN'T PLAY PIANO, BUT I BET SOMEBODY COULD.
俺は弾けないが
誰かが弾けるだろう
NEXT TIME I TALK TO MR. MICHAEL, I'LL ASK HIM TO SEND ONE TO THE VILLAGE.
IT'S TOO HARD TO MAKE, SO I GIVE UP.
ANYWAY, I'LL DEAL WITH THAT LATER. FOR NOW, IT LOOKS LIKE WE'VE FINALLY GOT SOME INSTRUMENTS.
WITH THAT OUT OF THE WAY
IT'S TIME FOR A MUSICAL PERFORMANCE.
THE HIGH ELVES GO FOR WIND INSTRUMENTS
THE MOUNTAIN ELVES TAKE PERCUSSION
AND THE CIVIL SECRETARIES PICK THE STRING INSTRUMENTS.
I'M GLAD THEY EXCEL IN DIFFERENT THINGS.

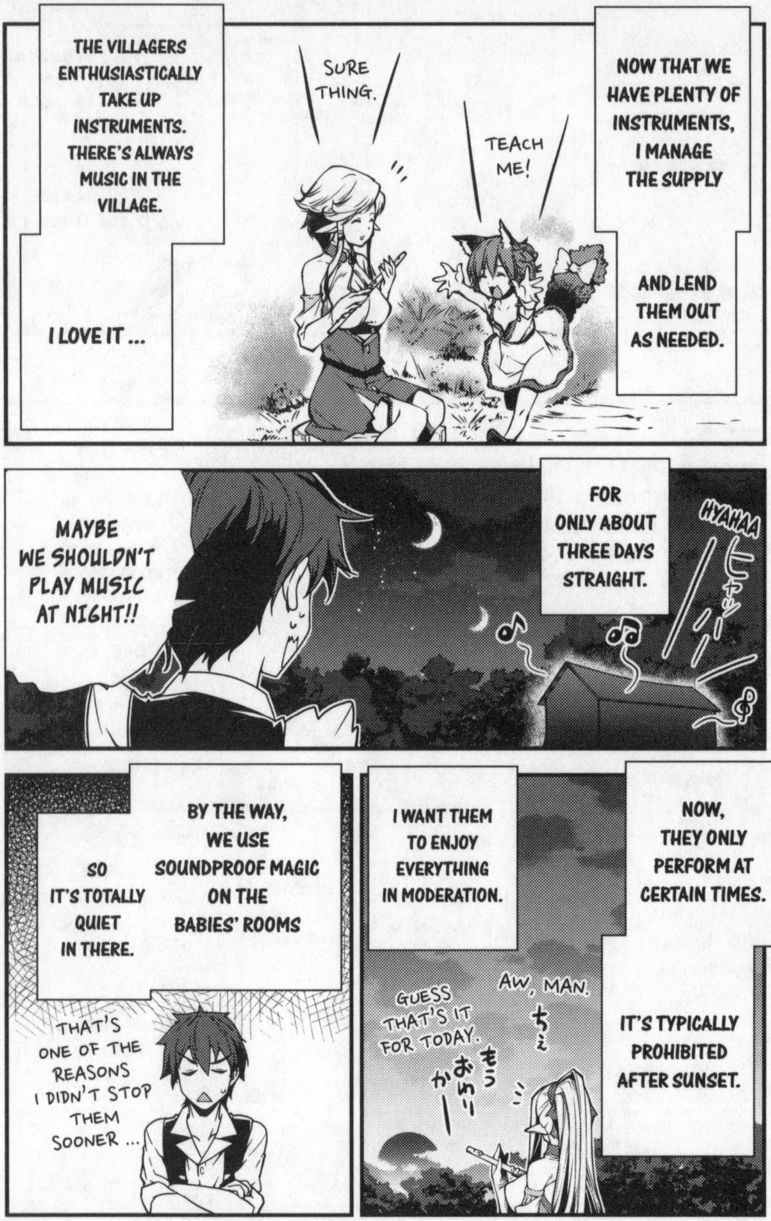
NOW THAT WE HAVE PLENTY OF INSTRUMENTS, I MANAGE THE SUPPLY
AND LEND THEM OUT AS NEEDED.
TEACH ME!
SURE THING.
THE VILLAGERS ENTHUSIASTICALLY TAKE UP INSTRUMENTS. THERE'S ALWAYS MUSIC IN THE VILLAGE.
I LOVE IT ...
FOR ONLY ABOUT THREE DAYS STRAIGHT.
HYAHAA
MAYBE WE SHOULDN'T PLAY MUSIC AT NIGHT!!
NOW, THEY ONLY PERFORM AT CERTAIN TIMES.
I WANT THEM TO ENJOY EVERYTHING IN MODERATION.
IT'S TYPICALLY PROHIBITED AFTER SUNSET.
AW, MAN.
ちぇ
GUESS THAT'S IT FOR TODAY.
もうおわりかー
BY THE WAY, WE USE SOUNDPROOF MAGIC ON THE BABIES' ROOMS
SO IT'S TOTALLY QUIET IN THERE.
THAT'S ONE OF THE REASONS I DIDN'T STOP THEM SOONER ...

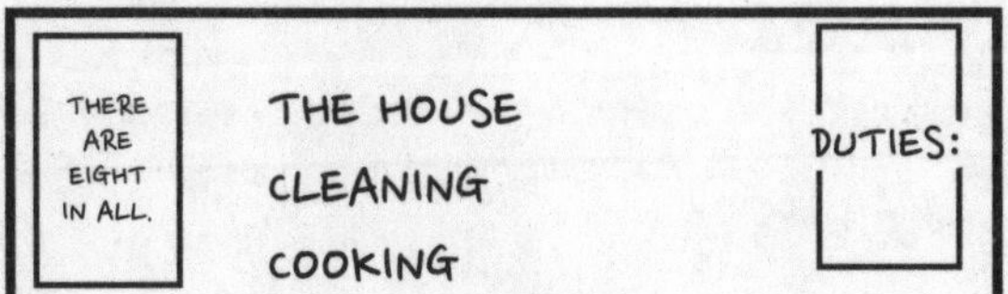

DUTIES:		
THERE ARE EIGHT IN ALL.	THE HOUSE CLEANING COOKING THE VILLAGE VILLAGE CHIEF MASTER ALFRED MASTER TIZZEL BREAK	 

Farming life in another world.

CHAPTER 61: THE DWARF WAY OF LIFE AND A NEW GUEST

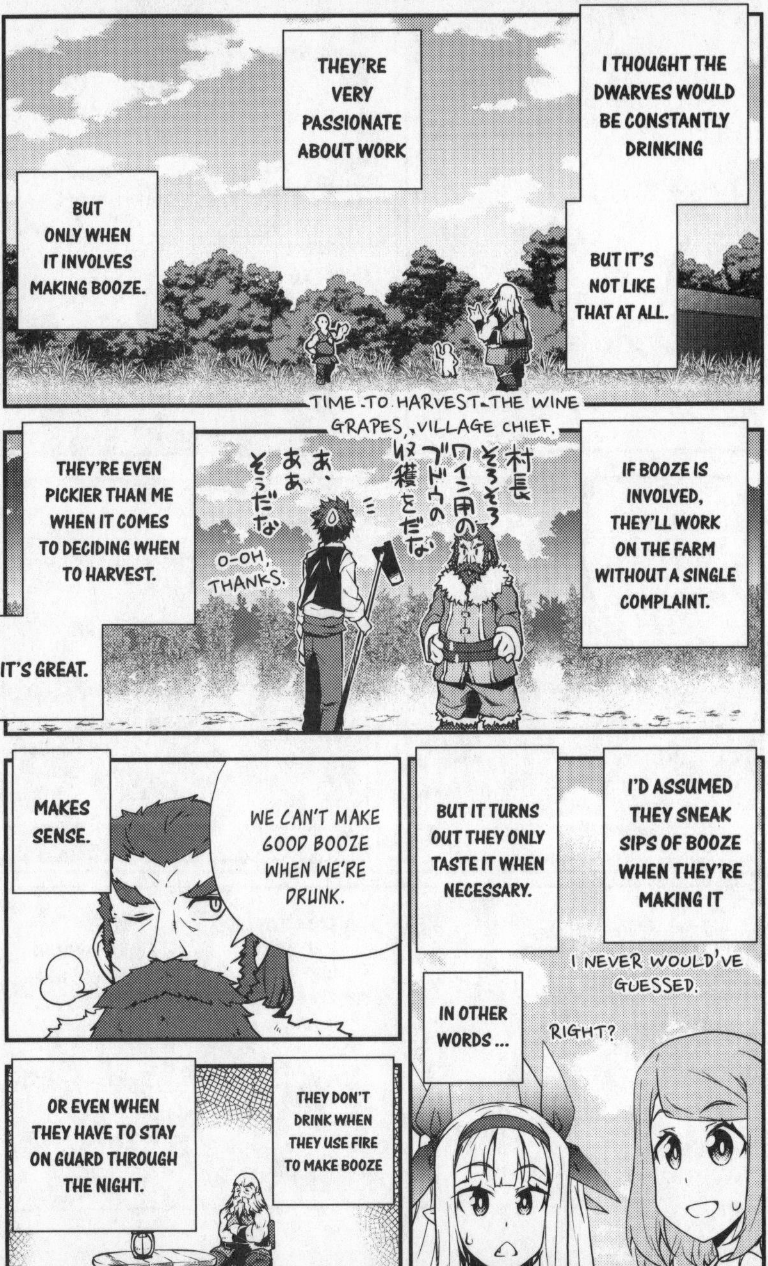

I THOUGHT THE DWARVES WOULD BE CONSTANTLY DRINKING
BUT IT'S NOT LIKE THAT AT ALL.
THEY'RE VERY PASSIONATE ABOUT WORK
BUT ONLY WHEN IT INVOLVES MAKING BOOZE.
TIME TO HARVEST THE WINE GRAPES, VILLAGE CHIEF.
村長そろそろワイン用のブドウの収穫をだな
IF BOOZE IS INVOLVED, THEY'LL WORK ON THE FARM WITHOUT A SINGLE COMPLAINT.
あ、ああそうだな
O-OH, THANKS.
THEY'RE EVEN PICKIER THAN ME WHEN IT COMES TO DECIDING WHEN TO HARVEST.
IT'S GREAT.
I'D ASSUMED THEY SNEAK SIPS OF BOOZE WHEN THEY'RE MAKING IT
BUT IT TURNS OUT THEY ONLY TASTE IT WHEN NECESSARY.
I NEVER WOULD'VE GUESSED.
IN OTHER WORDS ...
RIGHT?
WE CAN'T MAKE GOOD BOOZE WHEN WE'RE DRUNK.
MAKES SENSE.
THEY DON'T DRINK WHEN THEY USE FIRE TO MAKE BOOZE
OR EVEN WHEN THEY HAVE TO STAY ON GUARD THROUGH THE NIGHT.

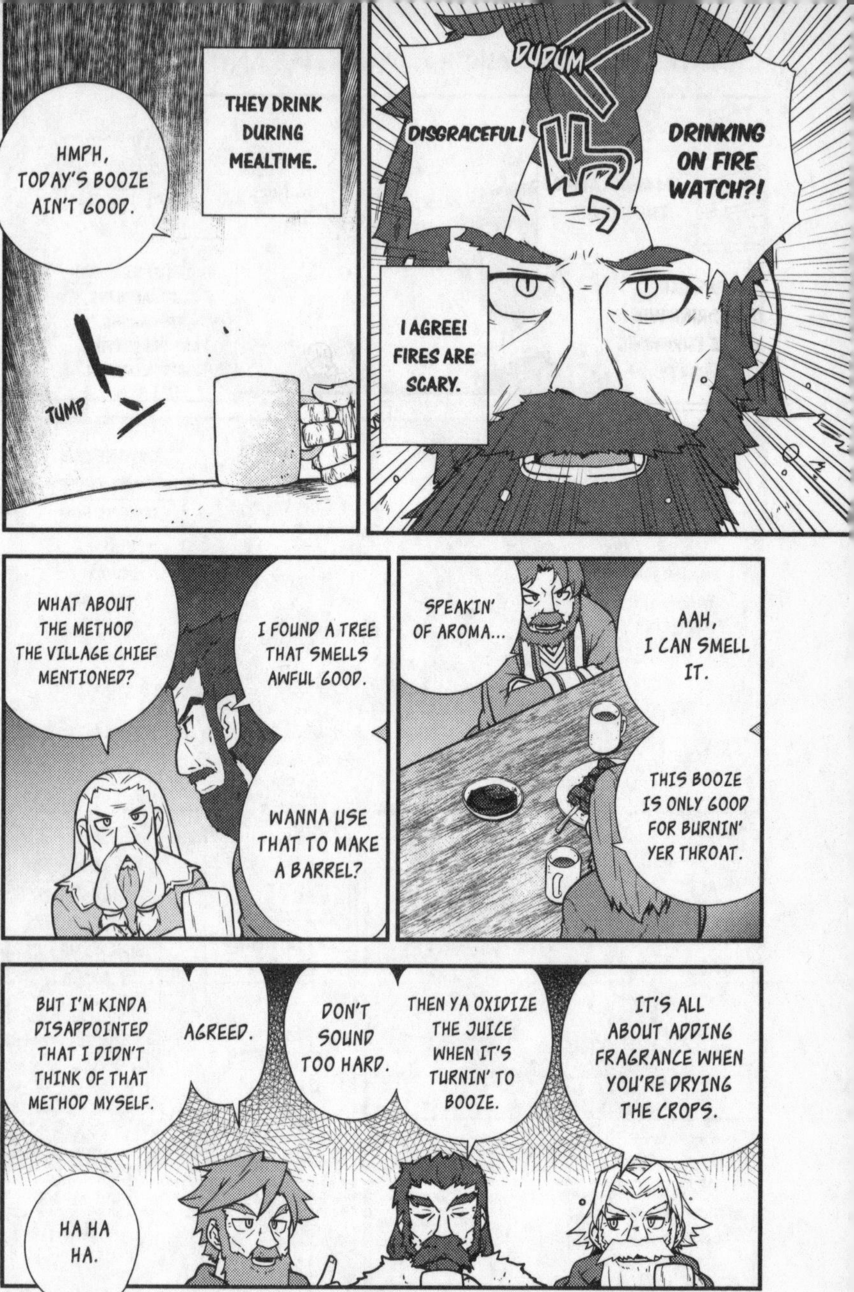
DUDUM
DRINKING ON FIRE WATCH?!
DISGRACEFUL!
I AGREE! FIRES ARE SCARY.
THEY DRINK DURING MEALTIME.
HMPH, TODAY'S BOOZE AIN'T GOOD.
TUMP
AAH, I CAN SMELL IT.
SPEAKIN' OF AROMA...
THIS BOOZE IS ONLY GOOD FOR BURNIN' YER THROAT.
I FOUND A TREE THAT SMELLS AWFUL GOOD.
WHAT ABOUT THE METHOD THE VILLAGE CHIEF MENTIONED?
WANNA USE THAT TO MAKE A BARREL?
IT'S ALL ABOUT ADDING FRAGRANCE WHEN YOU'RE DRYING THE CROPS.
THEN YA OXIDIZE THE JUICE WHEN IT'S TURNIN' TO BOOZE.
DON'T SOUND TOO HARD.
AGREED.
BUT I'M KINDA DISAPPOINTED THAT I DIDN'T THINK OF THAT METHOD MYSELF.
HA HA HA.

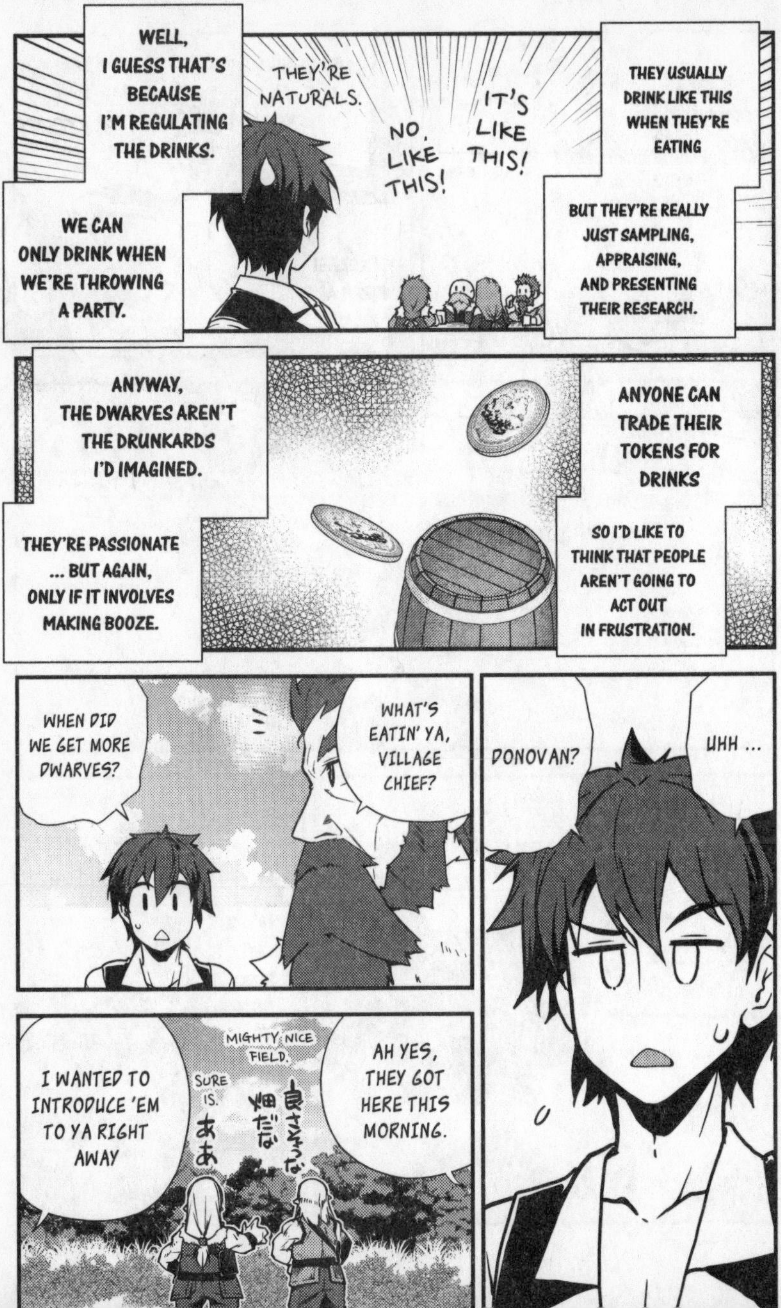
THEY USUALLY DRINK LIKE THIS WHEN THEY'RE EATING
BUT THEY'RE REALLY JUST SAMPLING, APPRAISING, AND PRESENTING THEIR RESEARCH.
IT'S LIKE THIS!
NO, LIKE THIS!
THEY'RE NATURALS.
WELL, I GUESS THAT'S BECAUSE I'M REGULATING THE DRINKS.
WE CAN ONLY DRINK WHEN WE'RE THROWING A PARTY.
ANYONE CAN TRADE THEIR TOKENS FOR DRINKS
SO I'D LIKE TO THINK THAT PEOPLE AREN'T GOING TO ACT OUT IN FRUSTRATION.
ANYWAY, THE DWARVES AREN'T THE DRUNKARDS I'D IMAGINED.
THEY'RE PASSIONATE ... BUT AGAIN, ONLY IF IT INVOLVES MAKING BOOZE.
UHH ...
DONOVAN?
WHAT'S EATIN' YA, VILLAGE CHIEF?
WHEN DID WE GET MORE DWARVES?
AH YES, THEY GOT HERE THIS MORNING.
良さそうな畑だな
MIGHTY NICE FIELD.
ああ
SURE IS.
I WANTED TO INTRODUCE 'EM TO YA RIGHT AWAY

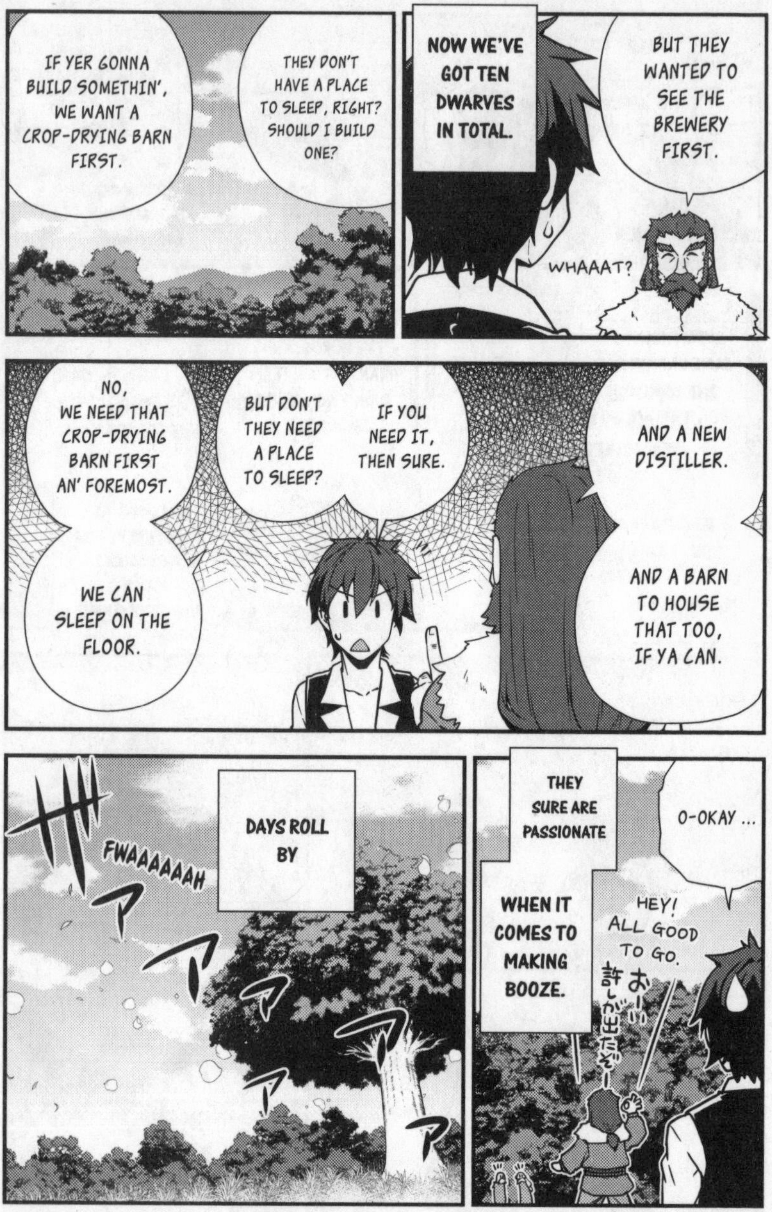
BUT THEY WANTED TO SEE THE BREWERY FIRST.
NOW WE'VE GOT TEN DWARVES IN TOTAL.
WHAAAT?
THEY DON'T HAVE A PLACE TO SLEEP, RIGHT? SHOULD I BUILD ONE?
IF YER GONNA BUILD SOMETHIN', WE WANT A CROP-DRYING BARN FIRST.
AND A NEW DISTILLER.
AND A BARN TO HOUSE THAT TOO, IF YA CAN.
IF YOU NEED IT, THEN SURE.
BUT DON'T THEY NEED A PLACE TO SLEEP?
NO, WE NEED THAT CROP-DRYING BARN FIRST AN' FOREMOST.
WE CAN SLEEP ON THE FLOOR.
O-OKAY ...
THEY SURE ARE PASSIONATE
WHEN IT COMES TO MAKING BOOZE.
HEY! ALL GOOD TO GO.
おーい
許しが出たぞー
DAYS ROLL BY
FWAAAAAAH

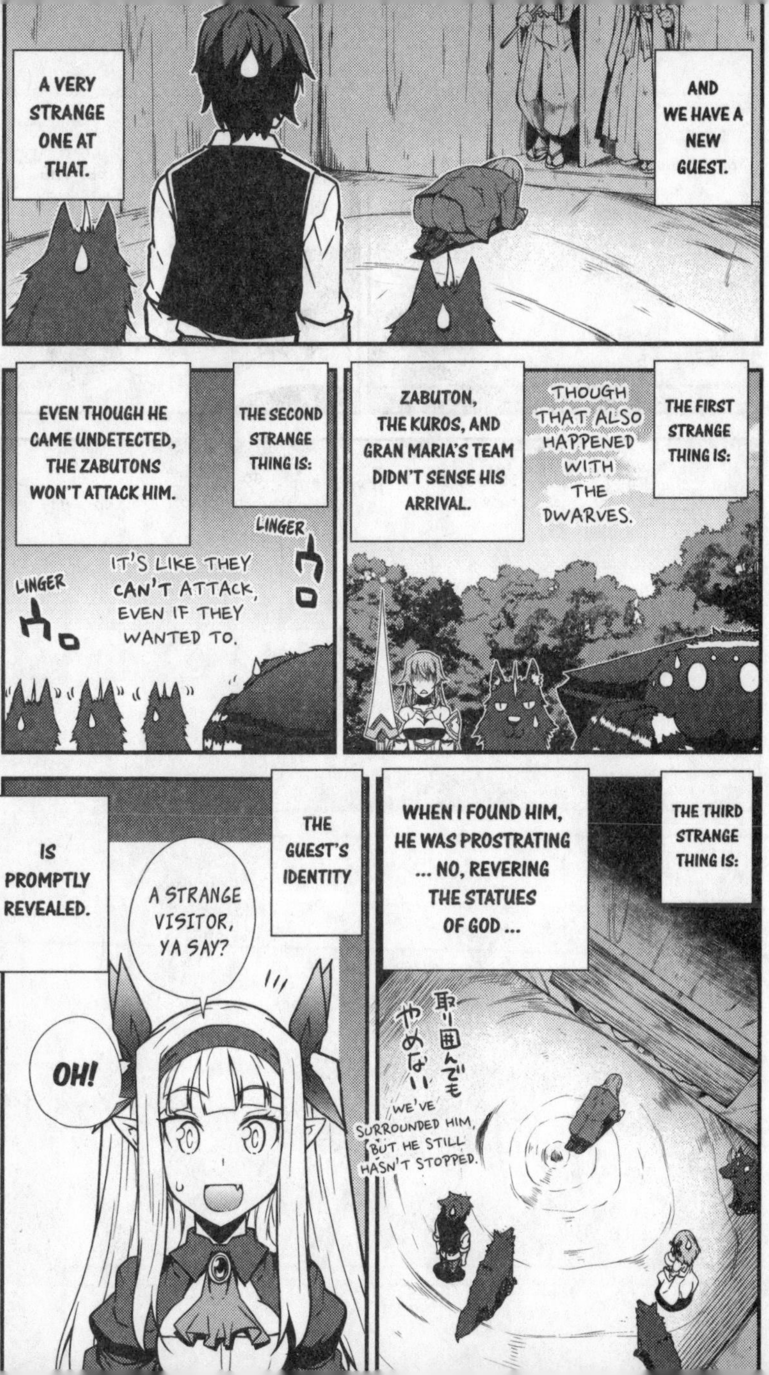
AND WE HAVE A NEW GUEST.
A VERY STRANGE ONE AT THAT.
THE FIRST STRANGE THING IS:
THOUGH THAT ALSO HAPPENED WITH THE DWARVES.
ZABUTON, THE KUROS, AND GRAN MARIA'S TEAM DIDN'T SENSE HIS ARRIVAL.
THE SECOND STRANGE THING IS:
EVEN THOUGH HE CAME UNDETECTED, THE ZABUTONS WON'T ATTACK HIM.
LINGER
IT'S LIKE THEY CAN'T ATTACK, EVEN IF THEY WANTED TO.
LINGER
THE THIRD STRANGE THING IS:
WHEN I FOUND HIM, HE WAS PROSTRATING ... NO, REVERING THE STATUES OF GOD ...
取り囲んでもやめない
WE'VE SURROUNDED HIM, BUT HE STILL HASN'T STOPPED.
THE GUEST'S IDENTITY
IS PROMPTLY REVEALED.
A STRANGE VISITOR, YA SAY?
OH!

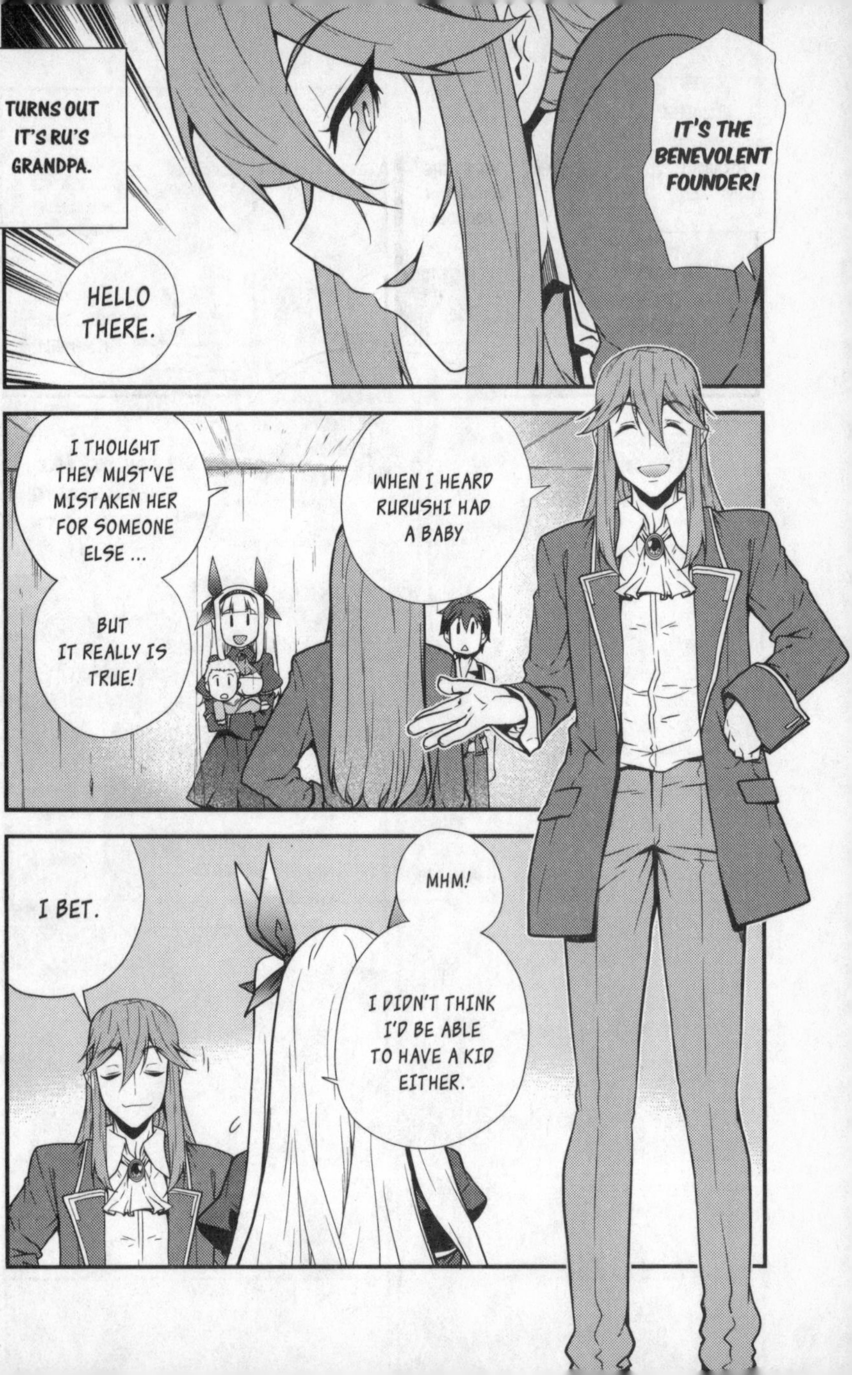

IT'S THE BENEVOLENT FOUNDER!
TURNS OUT IT'S RU'S GRANDPA.
HELLO THERE.
WHEN I HEARD RURUSHI HAD A BABY
I THOUGHT THEY MUST'VE MISTAKEN HER FOR SOMEONE ELSE ...
BUT IT REALLY IS TRUE!
MHM!
I DIDN'T THINK I'D BE ABLE TO HAVE A KID EITHER.
I BET.

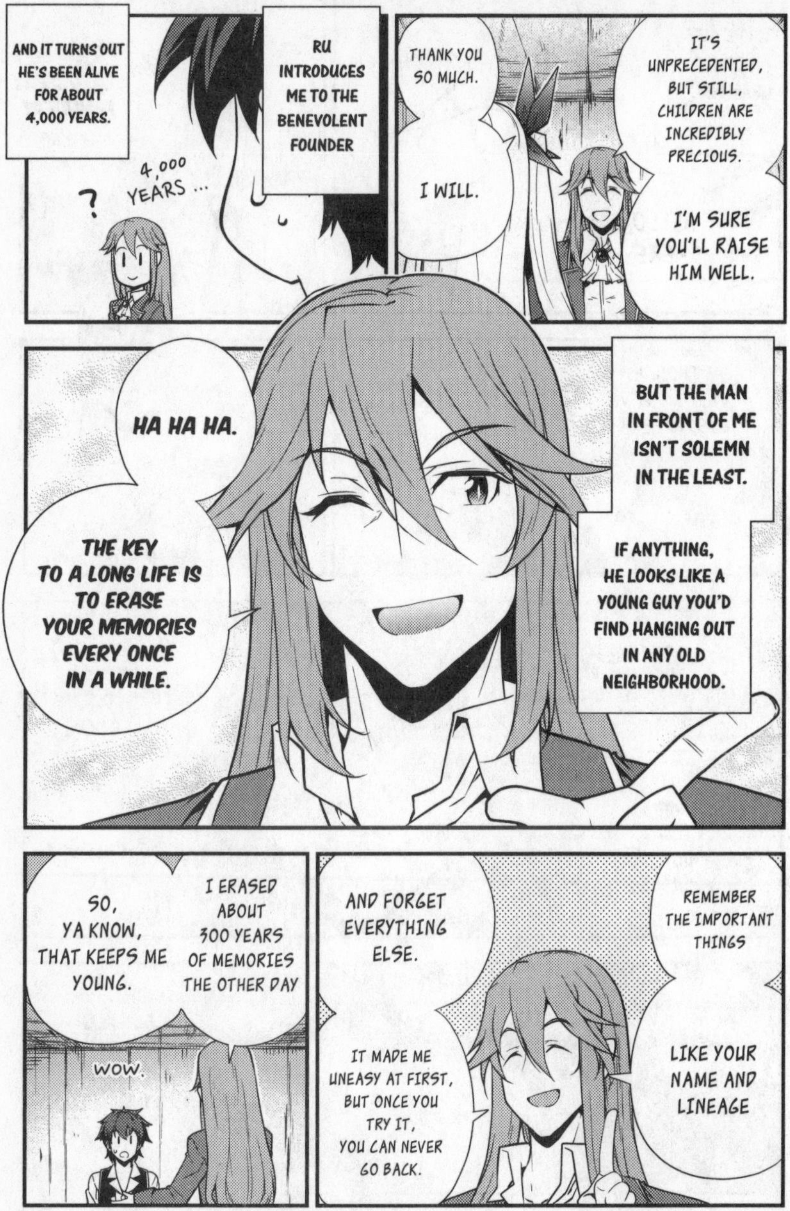
IT'S UNPRECEDENTED, BUT STILL, CHILDREN ARE INCREDIBLY PRECIOUS.
I'M SURE YOU'LL RAISE HIM WELL.
THANK YOU SO MUCH.
I WILL.
RU INTRODUCES ME TO THE BENEVOLENT FOUNDER
AND IT TURNS OUT HE'S BEEN ALIVE FOR ABOUT 4,000 YEARS.
4,000 YEARS ...
?
BUT THE MAN IN FRONT OF ME ISN'T SOLEMN IN THE LEAST.
IF ANYTHING, HE LOOKS LIKE A YOUNG GUY YOU'D FIND HANGING OUT IN ANY OLD NEIGHBORHOOD.
HA HA HA.
THE KEY TO A LONG LIFE IS TO ERASE YOUR MEMORIES EVERY ONCE IN A WHILE.
REMEMBER THE IMPORTANT THINGS
LIKE YOUR NAME AND LINEAGE
AND FORGET EVERYTHING ELSE.
IT MADE ME UNEASY AT FIRST, BUT ONCE YOU TRY IT, YOU CAN NEVER GO BACK.
I ERASED ABOUT 300 YEARS OF MEMORIES THE OTHER DAY
SO, YA KNOW, THAT KEEPS ME YOUNG.
WOW.

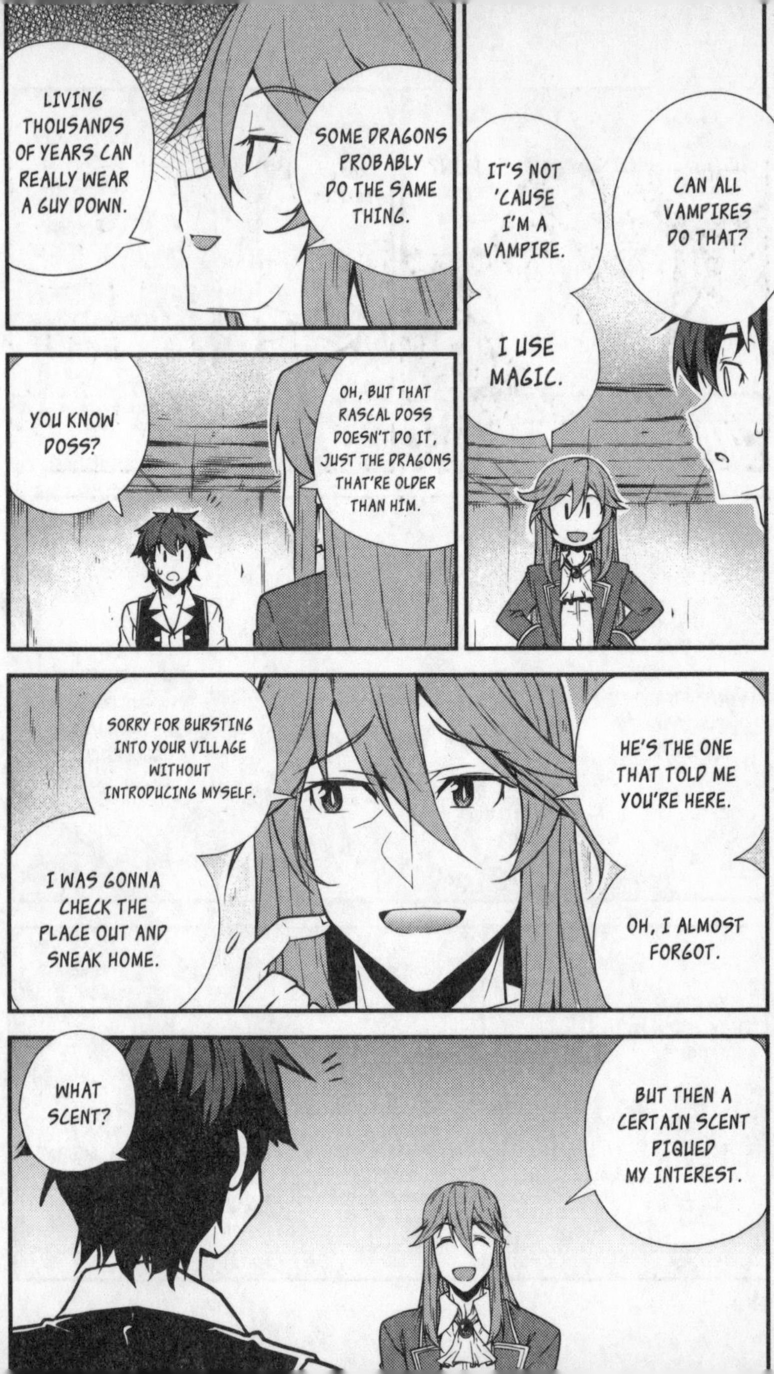
CAN ALL VAMPIRES DO THAT?
IT'S NOT 'CAUSE I'M A VAMPIRE.
I USE MAGIC.
SOME DRAGONS PROBABLY DO THE SAME THING.
LIVING THOUSANDS OF YEARS CAN REALLY WEAR A GUY DOWN.
OH, BUT THAT RASCAL DOSS DOESN'T DO IT, JUST THE DRAGONS THAT'RE OLDER THAN HIM.
YOU KNOW DOSS?
HE'S THE ONE THAT TOLD ME YOU'RE HERE.
OH, I ALMOST FORGOT.
SORRY FOR BURSTING INTO YOUR VILLAGE WITHOUT INTRODUCING MYSELF.
I WAS GONNA CHECK THE PLACE OUT AND SNEAK HOME.
BUT THEN A CERTAIN SCENT PIQUED MY INTEREST.
WHAT SCENT?

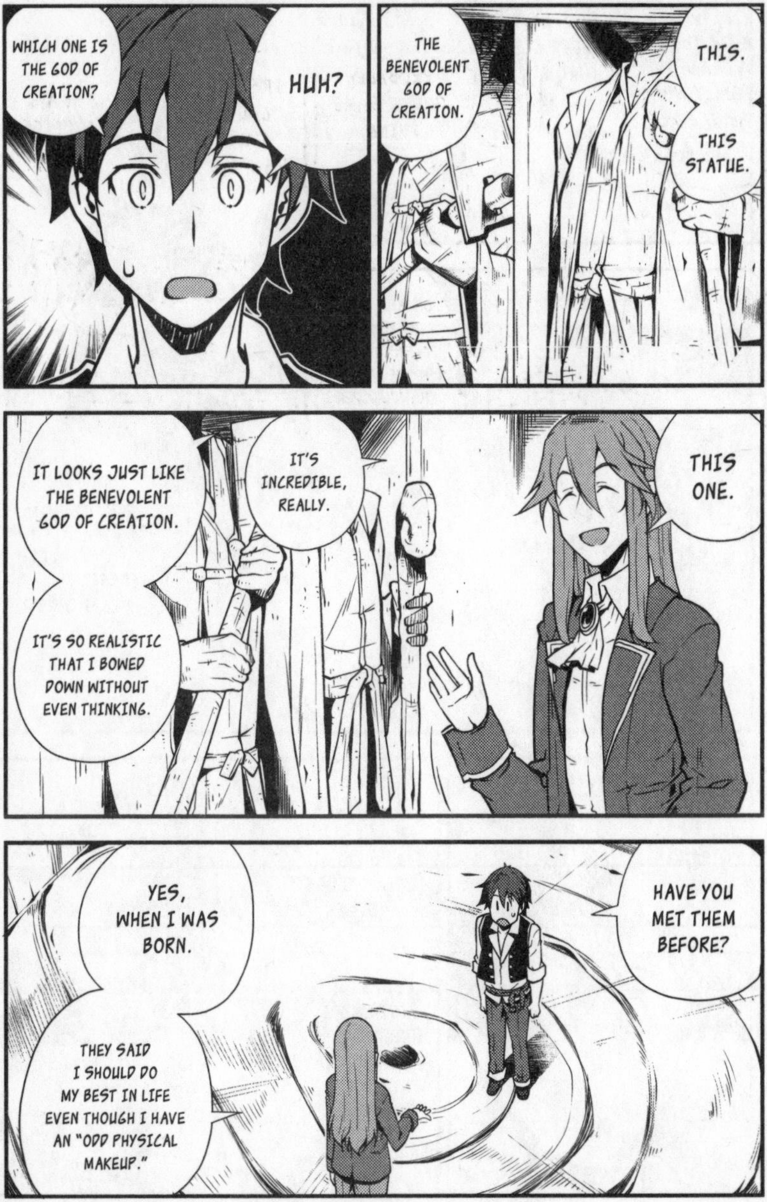
THIS.
THIS STATUE.
THE BENEVOLENT GOD OF CREATION.
HUH?
WHICH ONE IS THE GOD OF CREATION?
THIS ONE.
IT'S INCREDIBLE, REALLY.
IT LOOKS JUST LIKE THE BENEVOLENT GOD OF CREATION.
IT'S SO REALISTIC THAT I BOWED DOWN WITHOUT EVEN THINKING.
HAVE YOU MET THEM BEFORE?
YES, WHEN I WAS BORN.
THEY SAID I SHOULD DO MY BEST IN LIFE EVEN THOUGH I HAVE AN "ODD PHYSICAL MAKEUP."

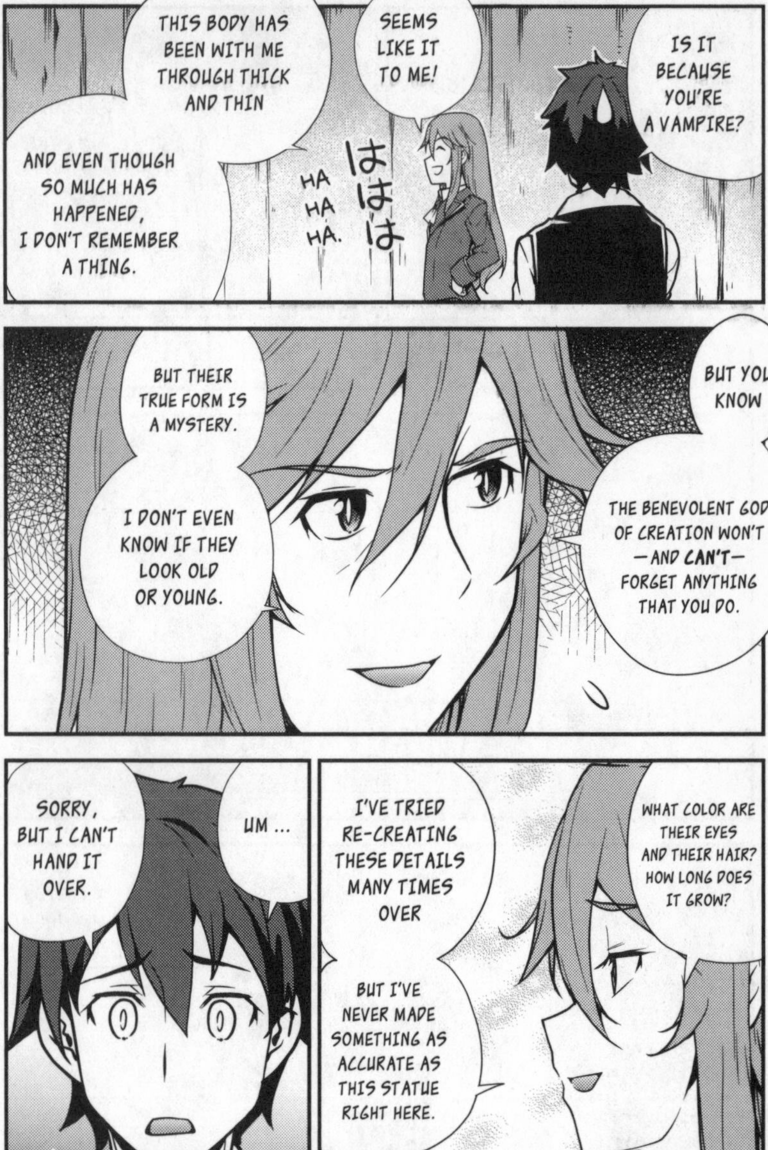
IS IT BECAUSE YOU'RE A VAMPIRE?
SEEMS LIKE IT TO ME!
HA HA HA.
ははは
THIS BODY HAS BEEN WITH ME THROUGH THICK AND THIN
AND EVEN THOUGH SO MUCH HAS HAPPENED, I DON'T REMEMBER A THING.
BUT YOU KNOW
THE BENEVOLENT GOD OF CREATION WON'T —AND **CAN'T**— FORGET ANYTHING THAT YOU DO.
BUT THEIR TRUE FORM IS A MYSTERY.
I DON'T EVEN KNOW IF THEY LOOK OLD OR YOUNG.
WHAT COLOR ARE THEIR EYES AND THEIR HAIR? HOW LONG DOES IT GROW?
I'VE TRIED RE-CREATING THESE DETAILS MANY TIMES OVER
BUT I'VE NEVER MADE SOMETHING AS ACCURATE AS THIS STATUE RIGHT HERE.
UM ...
SORRY, BUT I CAN'T HAND IT OVER.

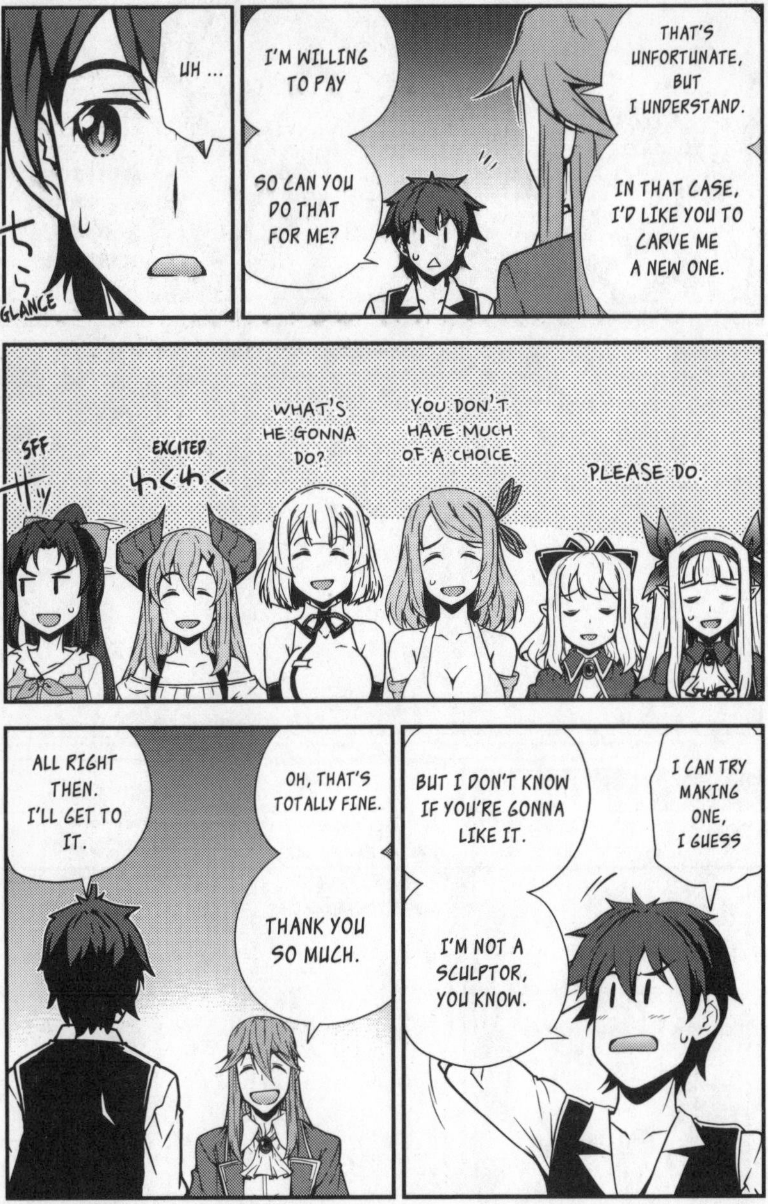
THAT'S UNFORTUNATE, BUT I UNDERSTAND.
IN THAT CASE, I'D LIKE YOU TO CARVE ME A NEW ONE.
I'M WILLING TO PAY
SO CAN YOU DO THAT FOR ME?
UH ...
ちら
GLANCE
PLEASE DO.
YOU DON'T HAVE MUCH OF A CHOICE
WHAT'S HE GONNA DO?
EXCITED
わくわく
SFF
サッ
I CAN TRY MAKING ONE, I GUESS
BUT I DON'T KNOW IF YOU'RE GONNA LIKE IT.
I'M NOT A SCULPTOR, YOU KNOW.
OH, THAT'S TOTALLY FINE.
THANK YOU SO MUCH.
ALL RIGHT THEN. I'LL GET TO IT.

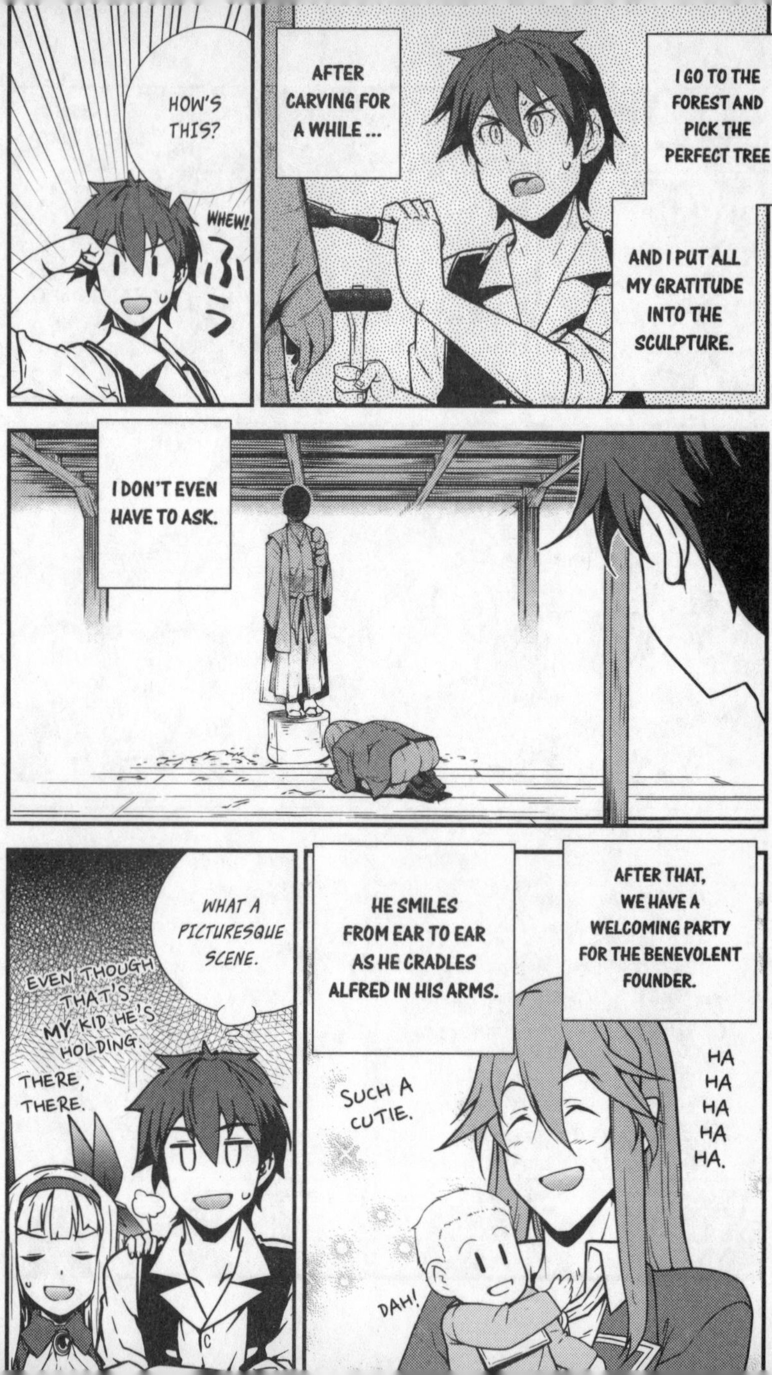
I GO TO THE FOREST AND PICK THE PERFECT TREE
AND I PUT ALL MY GRATITUDE INTO THE SCULPTURE.
AFTER CARVING FOR A WHILE ...
HOW'S THIS?
WHEW!
ふぅ
I DON'T EVEN HAVE TO ASK.
AFTER THAT, WE HAVE A WELCOMING PARTY FOR THE BENEVOLENT FOUNDER.
HE SMILES FROM EAR TO EAR AS HE CRADLES ALFRED IN HIS ARMS.
HA HA HA HA HA.
SUCH A CUTIE.
DAH!
WHAT A PICTURESQUE SCENE.
EVEN THOUGH THAT'S MY KID HE'S HOLDING.
THERE, THERE.

THE HOUSE

RESPONSIBLE FOR EVERYTHING IN THE VILLAGE CHIEF'S HOUSE, EXCEPT FOR COOKING AND CLEANING.
THIS ROLE IS THE TOUGHEST JOB OF THEM ALL.
I HAVE TO SEND OUT TWO GUARDS TO PROTECT HIM AT NIGHT.

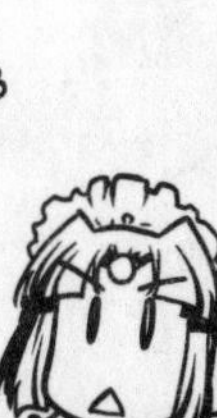

③

Farming life in another world.

CHAPTER 62: THE CHURCH AND THE PIANO

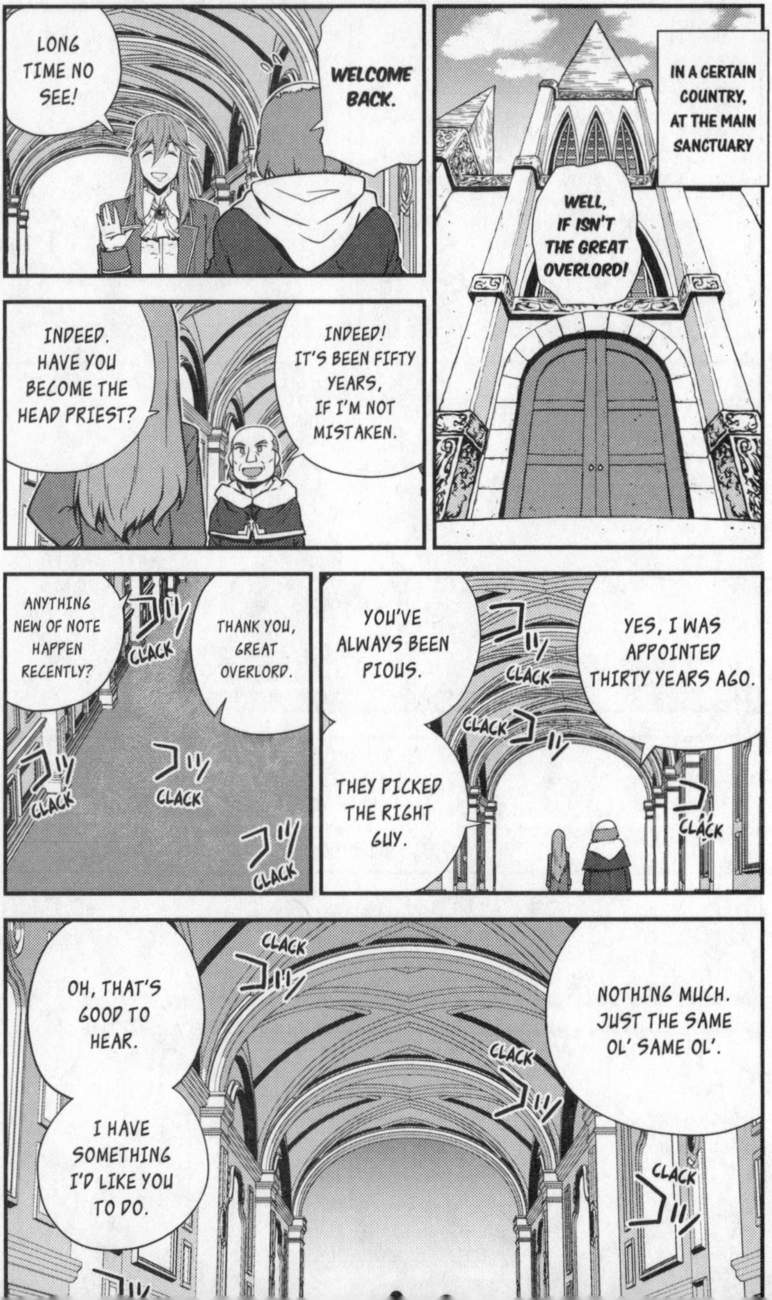

IN A CERTAIN COUNTRY, AT THE MAIN SANCTUARY
WELL, IF ISN'T THE GREAT OVERLORD!
WELCOME BACK.
LONG TIME NO SEE!
INDEED! IT'S BEEN FIFTY YEARS, IF I'M NOT MISTAKEN.
INDEED. HAVE YOU BECOME THE HEAD PRIEST?
YES, I WAS APPOINTED THIRTY YEARS AGO.
CLACK
CLACK
CLACK
YOU'VE ALWAYS BEEN PIOUS.
THEY PICKED THE RIGHT GUY.
THANK YOU, GREAT OVERLORD.
CLACK
ANYTHING NEW OF NOTE HAPPEN RECENTLY?
CLACK
CLACK
CLACK
NOTHING MUCH. JUST THE SAME OL' SAME OL'.
CLACK
CLACK
CLACK
OH, THAT'S GOOD TO HEAR.
I HAVE SOMETHING I'D LIKE YOU TO DO.

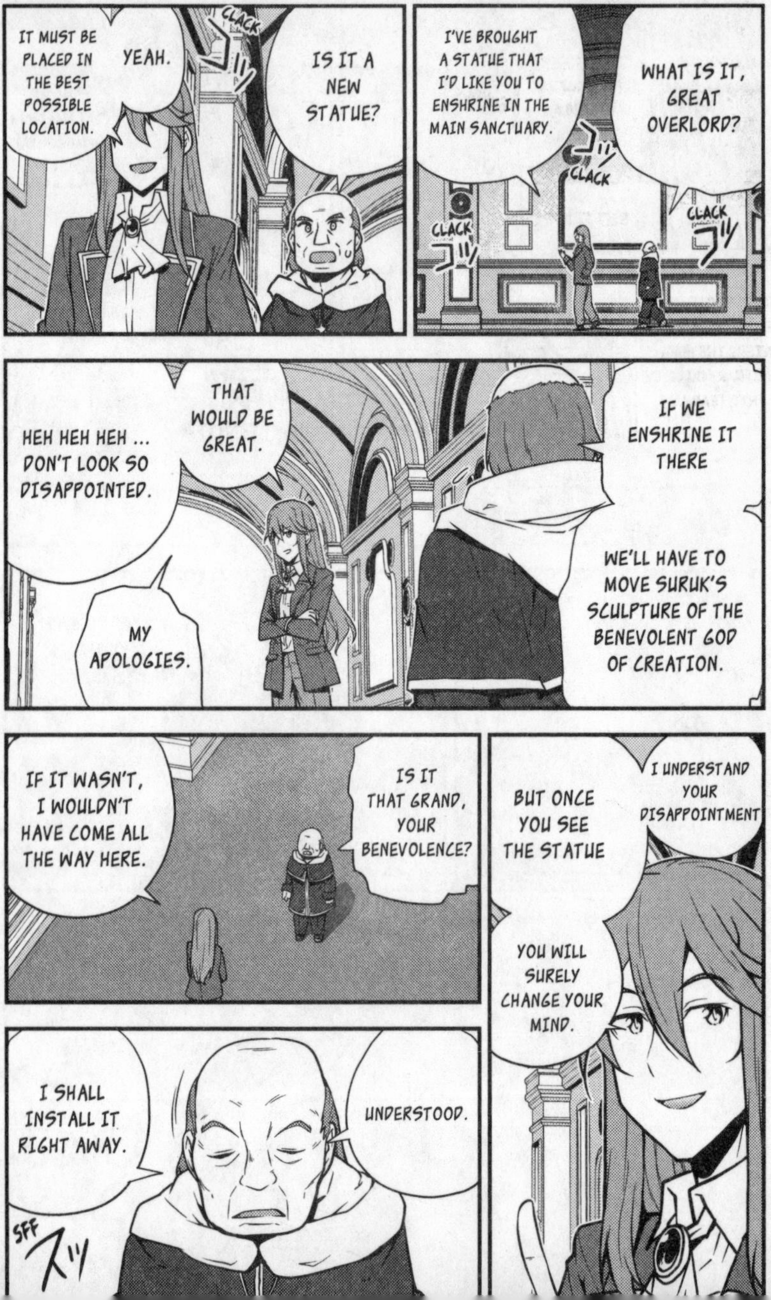
WHAT IS IT, GREAT OVERLORD?
CLACK
CLACK
I'VE BROUGHT A STATUE THAT I'D LIKE YOU TO ENSHRINE IN THE MAIN SANCTUARY.
CLACK
CLACK
IS IT A NEW STATUE?
YEAH.
IT MUST BE PLACED IN THE BEST POSSIBLE LOCATION.
IF WE ENSHRINE IT THERE
WE'LL HAVE TO MOVE SURUK'S SCULPTURE OF THE BENEVOLENT GOD OF CREATION.
THAT WOULD BE GREAT.
HEH HEH HEH ... DON'T LOOK SO DISAPPOINTED.
MY APOLOGIES.
I UNDERSTAND YOUR DISAPPOINTMENT
BUT ONCE YOU SEE THE STATUE
YOU WILL SURELY CHANGE YOUR MIND.
IS IT THAT GRAND, YOUR BENEVOLENCE?
IF IT WASN'T, I WOULDN'T HAVE COME ALL THE WAY HERE.
UNDERSTOOD.
I SHALL INSTALL IT RIGHT AWAY.
SFF

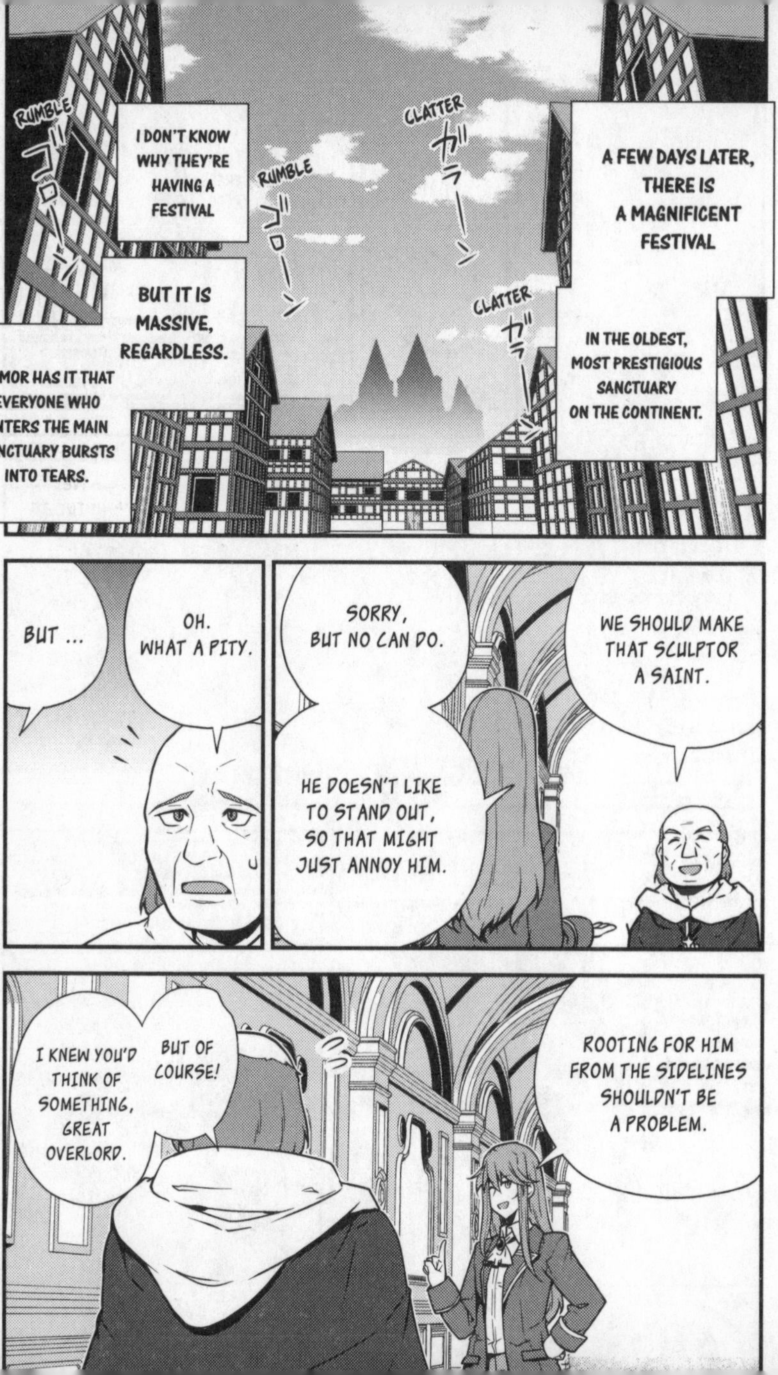
A FEW DAYS LATER, THERE IS A MAGNIFICENT FESTIVAL
CLATTER
IN THE OLDEST, MOST PRESTIGIOUS SANCTUARY ON THE CONTINENT.
CLATTER
RUMBLE
I DON'T KNOW WHY THEY'RE HAVING A FESTIVAL
RUMBLE
BUT IT IS MASSIVE, REGARDLESS.
RUMOR HAS IT THAT EVERYONE WHO ENTERS THE MAIN SANCTUARY BURSTS INTO TEARS.
WE SHOULD MAKE THAT SCULPTOR A SAINT.
SORRY, BUT NO CAN DO.
HE DOESN'T LIKE TO STAND OUT, SO THAT MIGHT JUST ANNOY HIM.
OH. WHAT A PITY.
BUT ...
ROOTING FOR HIM FROM THE SIDELINES SHOULDN'T BE A PROBLEM.
BUT OF COURSE!
I KNEW YOU'D THINK OF SOMETHING, GREAT OVERLORD.

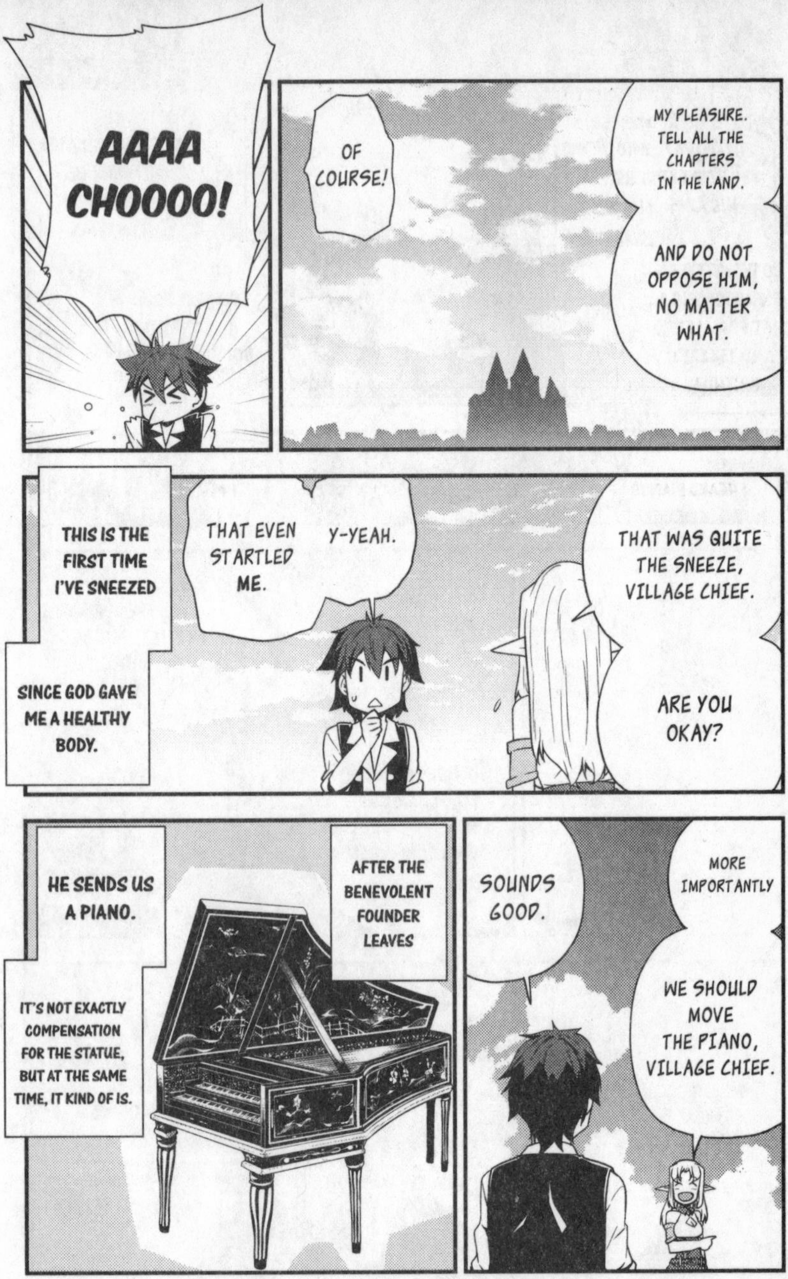
MY PLEASURE. TELL ALL THE CHAPTERS IN THE LAND.
AND DO NOT OPPOSE HIM, NO MATTER WHAT.
OF COURSE!
AAAA CHOOOO!
THAT WAS QUITE THE SNEEZE, VILLAGE CHIEF.
ARE YOU OKAY?
Y-YEAH.
THAT EVEN STARTLED ME.
THIS IS THE FIRST TIME I'VE SNEEZED
SINCE GOD GAVE ME A HEALTHY BODY.
MORE IMPORTANTLY
WE SHOULD MOVE THE PIANO, VILLAGE CHIEF.
SOUNDS GOOD.
AFTER THE BENEVOLENT FOUNDER LEAVES
HE SENDS US A PIANO.
IT'S NOT EXACTLY COMPENSATION FOR THE STATUE, BUT AT THE SAME TIME, IT KIND OF IS.

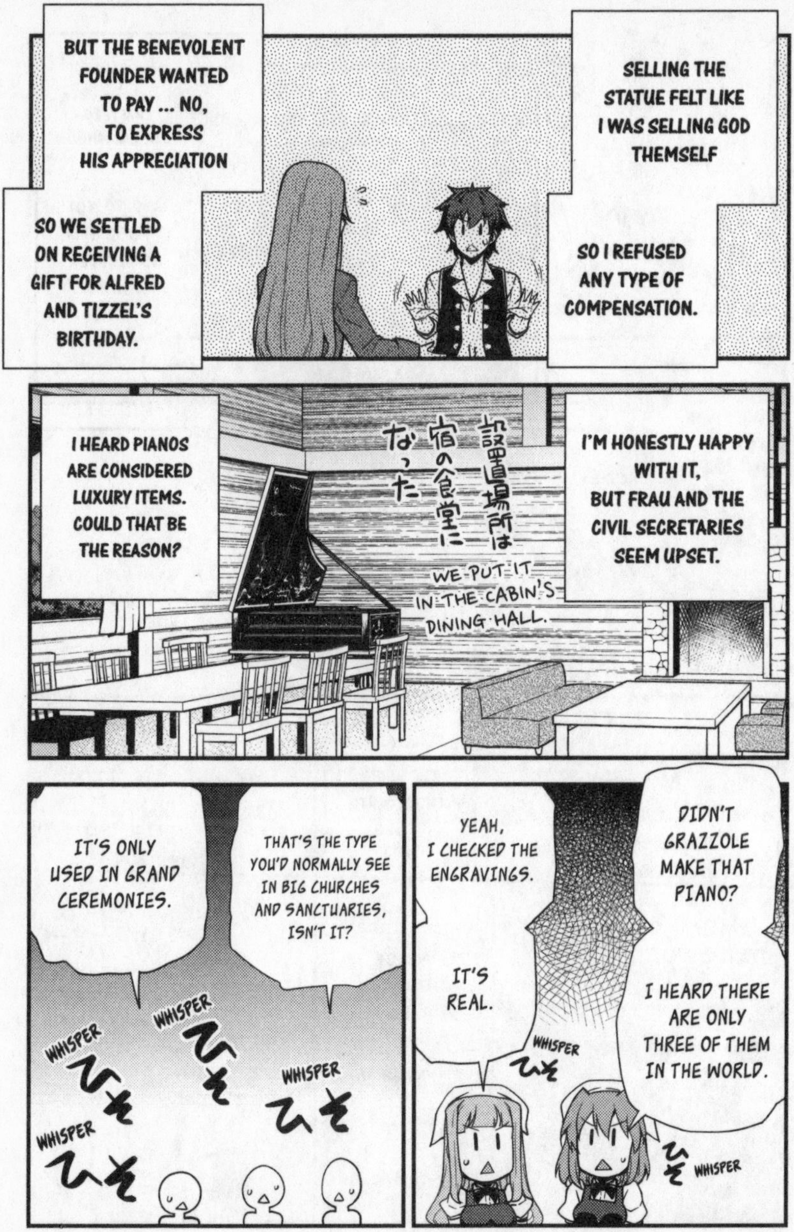
SELLING THE STATUE FELT LIKE I WAS SELLING GOD THEMSELF
SO I REFUSED ANY TYPE OF COMPENSATION.
BUT THE BENEVOLENT FOUNDER WANTED TO PAY ... NO, TO EXPRESS HIS APPRECIATION
SO WE SETTLED ON RECEIVING A GIFT FOR ALFRED AND TIZZEL'S BIRTHDAY.
I'M HONESTLY HAPPY WITH IT, BUT FRAU AND THE CIVIL SECRETARIES SEEM UPSET.
設置場所は宿の食堂になった
WE PUT IT IN THE CABIN'S DINING HALL.
I HEARD PIANOS ARE CONSIDERED LUXURY ITEMS. COULD THAT BE THE REASON?
DIDN'T GRAZZOLE MAKE THAT PIANO?
YEAH, I CHECKED THE ENGRAVINGS.
I HEARD THERE ARE ONLY THREE OF THEM IN THE WORLD.
IT'S REAL.
ひそ WHISPER
WHISPER ひそ
THAT'S THE TYPE YOU'D NORMALLY SEE IN BIG CHURCHES AND SANCTUARIES, ISN'T IT?
IT'S ONLY USED IN GRAND CEREMONIES.
WHISPER ひそ
WHISPER ひそ
WHISPER ひそ
WHISPER ひそ

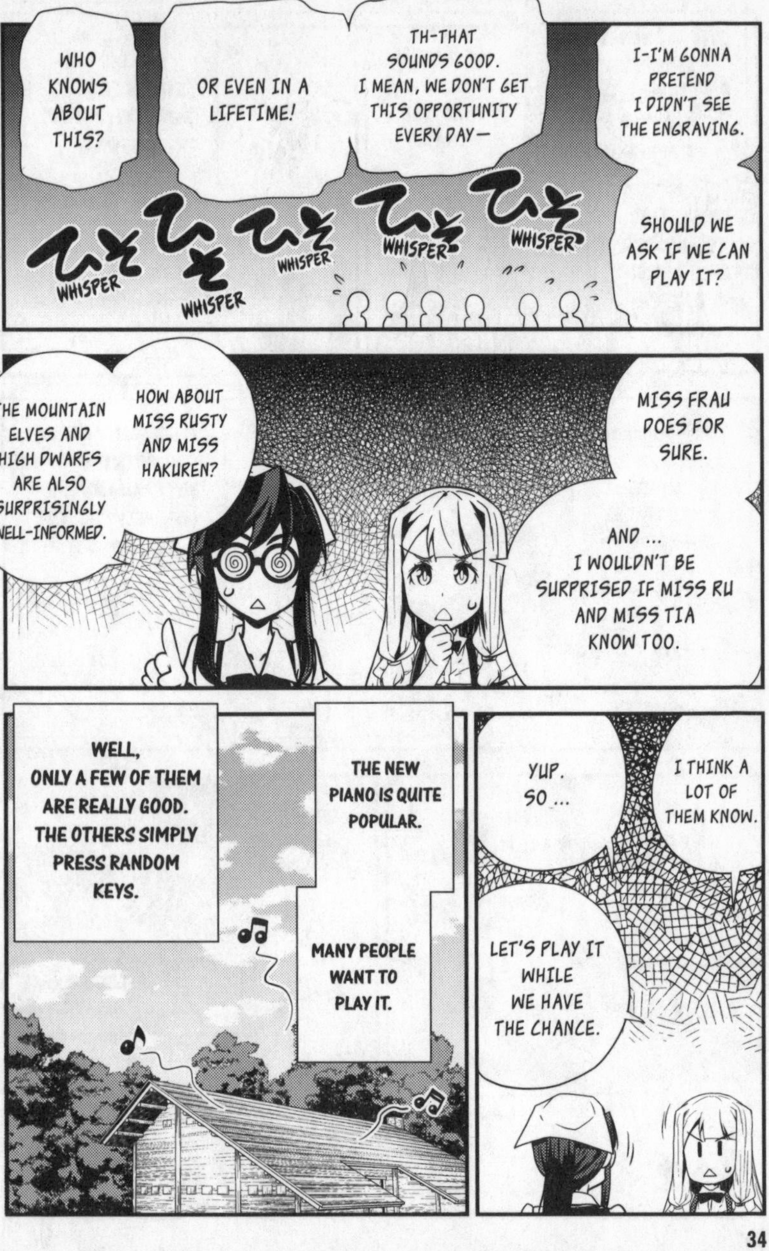
I-I'M GONNA PRETEND I DIDN'T SEE THE ENGRAVING.
SHOULD WE ASK IF WE CAN PLAY IT?
TH-THAT SOUNDS GOOD. I MEAN, WE DON'T GET THIS OPPORTUNITY EVERY DAY—
OR EVEN IN A LIFETIME!
WHO KNOWS ABOUT THIS?
ひそ WHISPER
ひそ WHISPER
ひそ WHISPER
ひそ WHISPER
ひそ WHISPER
MISS FRAU DOES FOR SURE.
AND ... I WOULDN'T BE SURPRISED IF MISS RU AND MISS TIA KNOW TOO.
HOW ABOUT MISS RUSTY AND MISS HAKUREN?
THE MOUNTAIN ELVES AND HIGH DWARFS ARE ALSO SURPRISINGLY WELL-INFORMED.
I THINK A LOT OF THEM KNOW.
YUP. SO ...
LET'S PLAY IT WHILE WE HAVE THE CHANCE.
THE NEW PIANO IS QUITE POPULAR.
MANY PEOPLE WANT TO PLAY IT.
WELL, ONLY A FEW OF THEM ARE REALLY GOOD. THE OTHERS SIMPLY PRESS RANDOM KEYS.

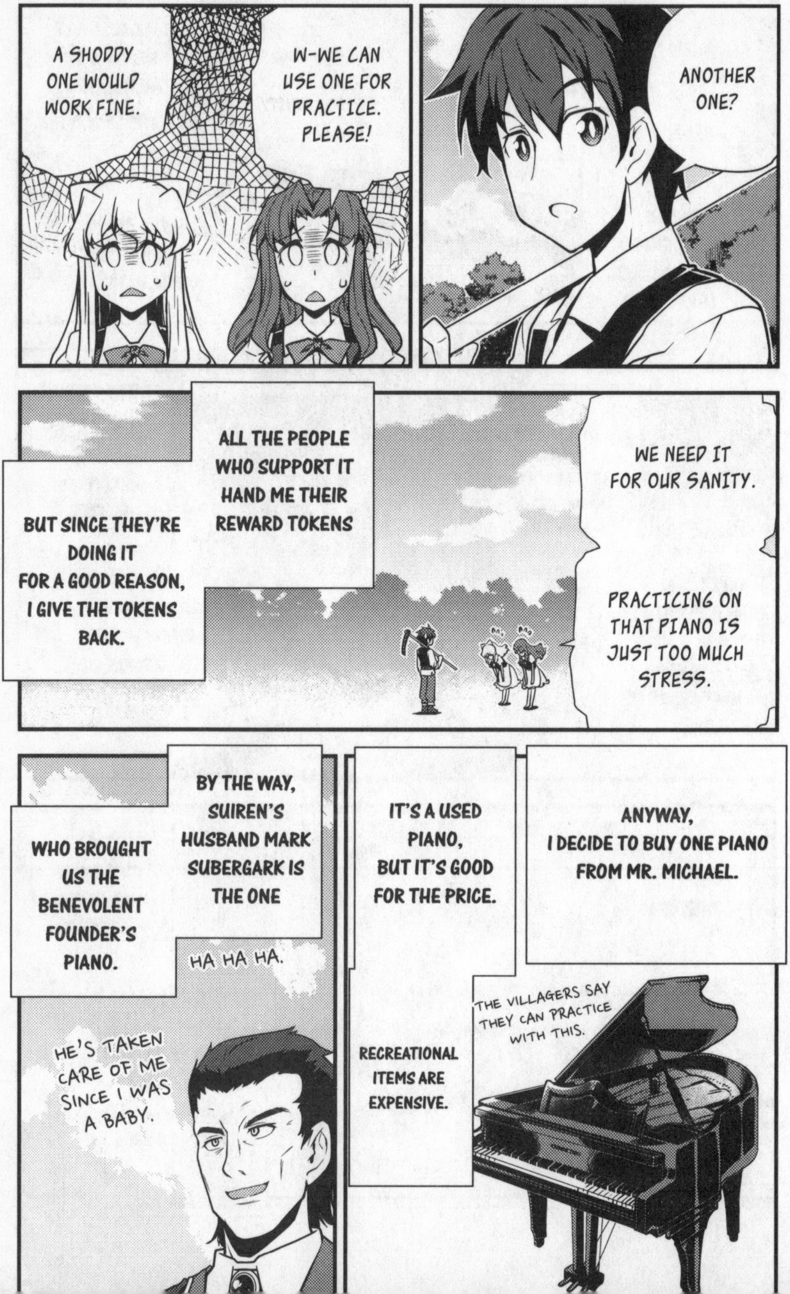
ANOTHER ONE?
W-WE CAN USE ONE FOR PRACTICE. PLEASE!
A SHODDY ONE WOULD WORK FINE.
WE NEED IT FOR OUR SANITY.
PRACTICING ON THAT PIANO IS JUST TOO MUCH STRESS.
ALL THE PEOPLE WHO SUPPORT IT HAND ME THEIR REWARD TOKENS
BUT SINCE THEY'RE DOING IT FOR A GOOD REASON, I GIVE THE TOKENS BACK.
ANYWAY, I DECIDE TO BUY ONE PIANO FROM MR. MICHAEL.
IT'S A USED PIANO, BUT IT'S GOOD FOR THE PRICE.
THE VILLAGERS SAY THEY CAN PRACTICE WITH THIS.
RECREATIONAL ITEMS ARE EXPENSIVE.
BY THE WAY, SUIREN'S HUSBAND MARK SUBERGARK IS THE ONE
WHO BROUGHT US THE BENEVOLENT FOUNDER'S PIANO.
HA HA HA.
HE'S TAKEN CARE OF ME SINCE I WAS A BABY.

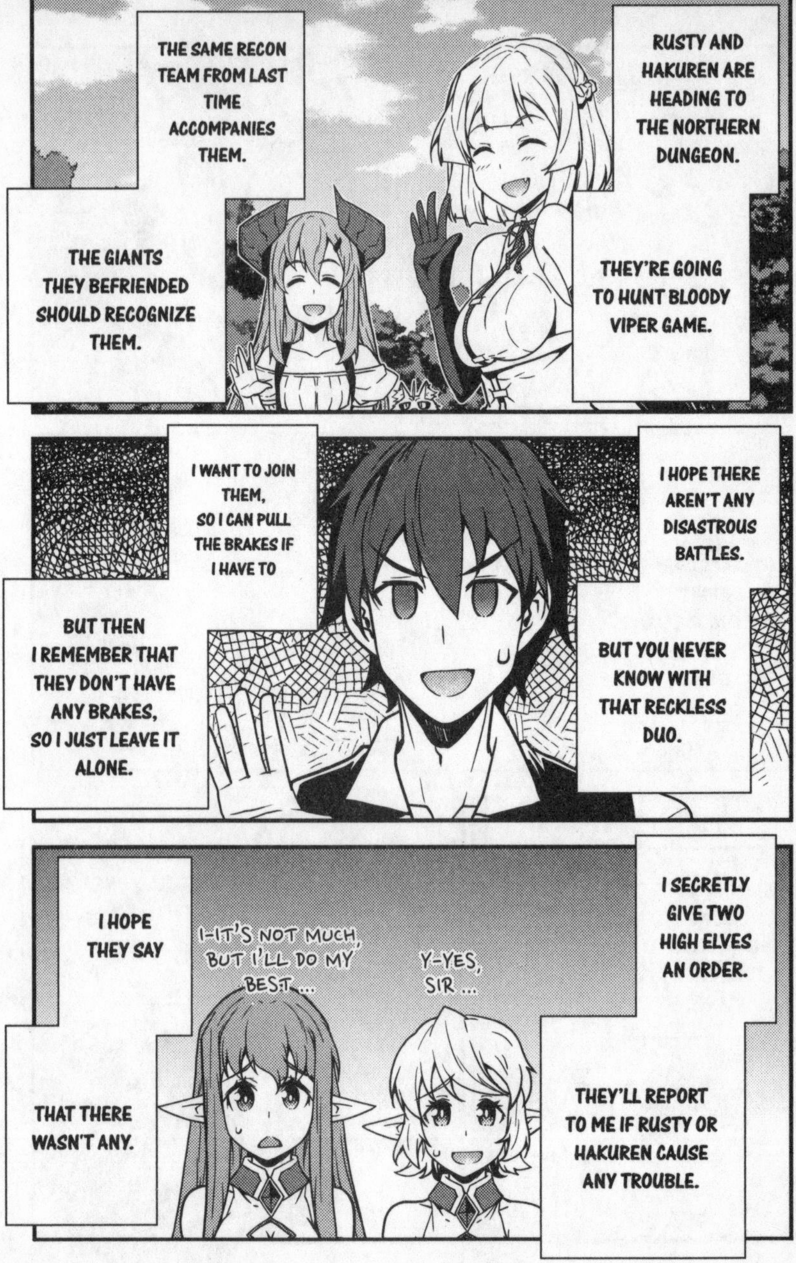
RUSTY AND HAKUREN ARE HEADING TO THE NORTHERN DUNGEON.
THEY'RE GOING TO HUNT BLOODY VIPER GAME.
THE SAME RECON TEAM FROM LAST TIME ACCOMPANIES THEM.
THE GIANTS THEY BEFRIENDED SHOULD RECOGNIZE THEM.
I HOPE THERE AREN'T ANY DISASTROUS BATTLES.
BUT YOU NEVER KNOW WITH THAT RECKLESS DUO.
I WANT TO JOIN THEM, SO I CAN PULL THE BRAKES IF I HAVE TO
BUT THEN I REMEMBER THAT THEY DON'T HAVE ANY BRAKES, SO I JUST LEAVE IT ALONE.
I SECRETLY GIVE TWO HIGH ELVES AN ORDER.
THEY'LL REPORT TO ME IF RUSTY OR HAKUREN CAUSE ANY TROUBLE.
Y-YES, SIR ...
I-IT'S NOT MUCH, BUT I'LL DO MY BEST ...
I HOPE THEY SAY
THAT THERE WASN'T ANY.

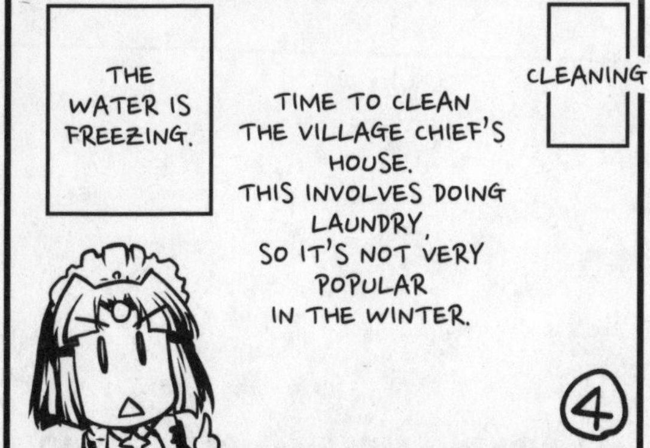

CLEANING
TIME TO CLEAN THE VILLAGE CHIEF'S HOUSE. THIS INVOLVES DOING LAUNDRY, SO IT'S NOT VERY POPULAR IN THE WINTER.
THE WATER IS FREEZING.
4

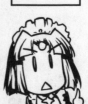

CHAPTER 63: BUILDING A NEW VILLAGE

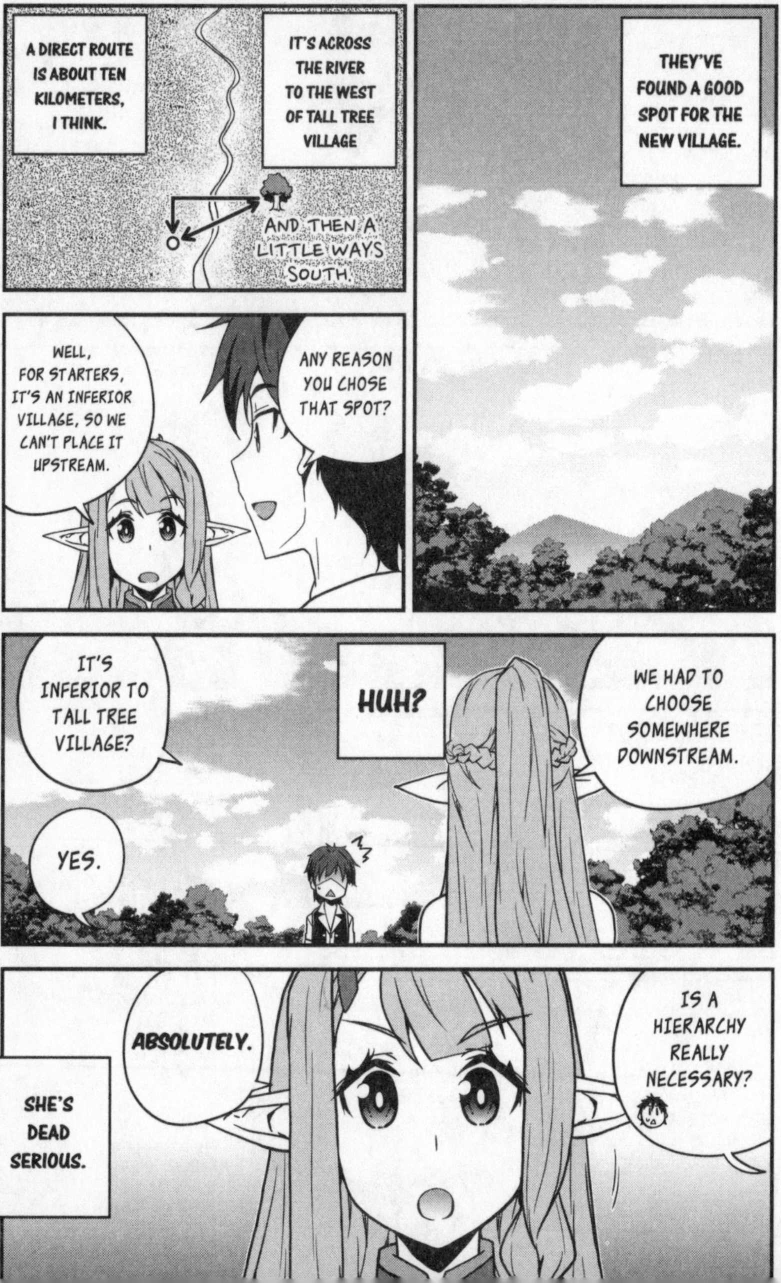

THEY'VE FOUND A GOOD SPOT FOR THE NEW VILLAGE.
IT'S ACROSS THE RIVER TO THE WEST OF TALL TREE VILLAGE
AND THEN A LITTLE WAYS SOUTH.
A DIRECT ROUTE IS ABOUT TEN KILOMETERS, I THINK.
ANY REASON YOU CHOSE THAT SPOT?
WELL, FOR STARTERS, IT'S AN INFERIOR VILLAGE, SO WE CAN'T PLACE IT UPSTREAM.
WE HAD TO CHOOSE SOMEWHERE DOWNSTREAM.
HUH?
IT'S INFERIOR TO TALL TREE VILLAGE?
YES.
IS A HIERARCHY REALLY NECESSARY?
ABSOLUTELY.
SHE'S DEAD SERIOUS.

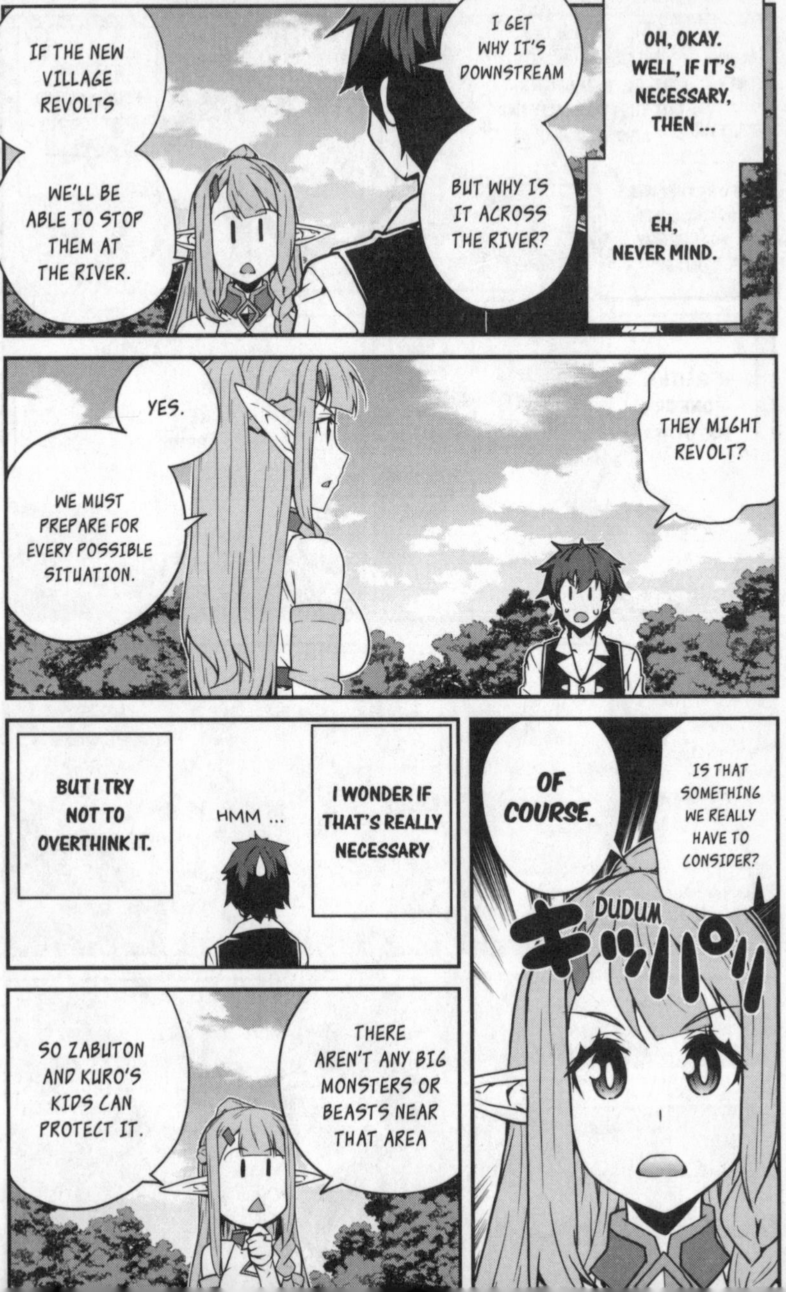
OH, OKAY. WELL, IF IT'S NECESSARY, THEN ...
EH, NEVER MIND.
I GET WHY IT'S DOWNSTREAM
BUT WHY IS IT ACROSS THE RIVER?
IF THE NEW VILLAGE REVOLTS
WE'LL BE ABLE TO STOP THEM AT THE RIVER.
THEY MIGHT REVOLT?
YES.
WE MUST PREPARE FOR EVERY POSSIBLE SITUATION.
IS THAT SOMETHING WE REALLY HAVE TO CONSIDER?
OF COURSE.
DUDUM
キッパリ
I WONDER IF THAT'S REALLY NECESSARY
HMM ...
BUT I TRY NOT TO OVERTHINK IT.
THERE AREN'T ANY BIG MONSTERS OR BEASTS NEAR THAT AREA
SO ZABUTON AND KURO'S KIDS CAN PROTECT IT.

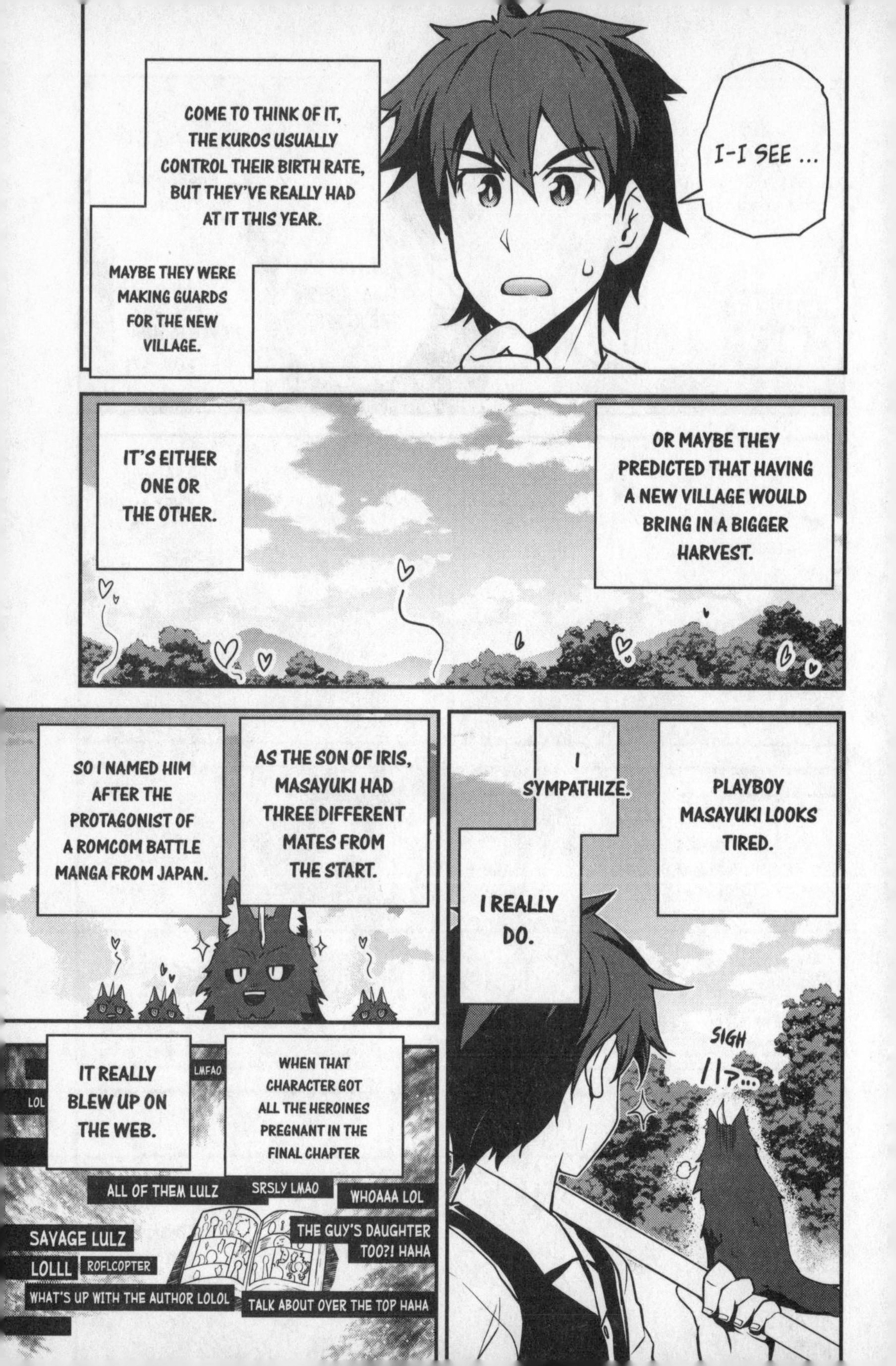
COME TO THINK OF IT, THE KUROS USUALLY CONTROL THEIR BIRTH RATE, BUT THEY'VE REALLY HAD AT IT THIS YEAR.
MAYBE THEY WERE MAKING GUARDS FOR THE NEW VILLAGE.
I-I SEE ...
OR MAYBE THEY PREDICTED THAT HAVING A NEW VILLAGE WOULD BRING IN A BIGGER HARVEST.
IT'S EITHER ONE OR THE OTHER.
PLAYBOY MASAYUKI LOOKS TIRED.
I SYMPATHIZE.
I REALLY DO.
SIGH
AS THE SON OF IRIS, MASAYUKI HAD THREE DIFFERENT MATES FROM THE START.
SO I NAMED HIM AFTER THE PROTAGONIST OF A ROMCOM BATTLE MANGA FROM JAPAN.
WHEN THAT CHARACTER GOT ALL THE HEROINES PREGNANT IN THE FINAL CHAPTER
IT REALLY BLEW UP ON THE WEB.
LMFAO
LOL
ALL OF THEM LULZ
SRSLY LMAO
WHOAAA LOL
THE GUY'S DAUGHTER TOO?! HAHA
SAVAGE LULZ
LOLLL
ROFLCOPTER
WHAT'S UP WITH THE AUTHOR LOLOL
TALK ABOUT OVER THE TOP HAHA

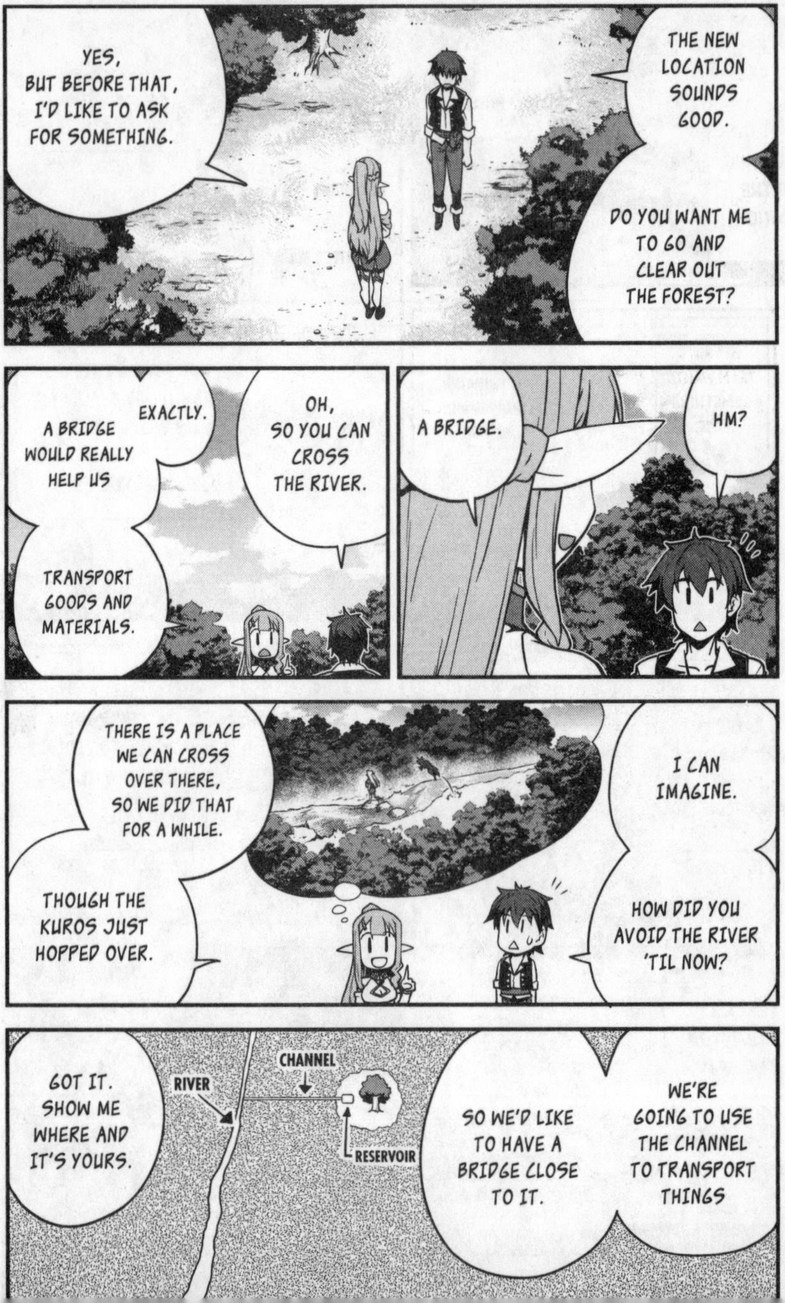
THE NEW LOCATION SOUNDS GOOD.
DO YOU WANT ME TO GO AND CLEAR OUT THE FOREST?
YES, BUT BEFORE THAT, I'D LIKE TO ASK FOR SOMETHING.
HM?
A BRIDGE.
OH, SO YOU CAN CROSS THE RIVER.
EXACTLY.
A BRIDGE WOULD REALLY HELP US
TRANSPORT GOODS AND MATERIALS.
HOW DID YOU AVOID THE RIVER 'TIL NOW?
THERE IS A PLACE WE CAN CROSS OVER THERE, SO WE DID THAT FOR A WHILE.
THOUGH THE KUROS JUST HOPPED OVER.
I CAN IMAGINE.
WE'RE GOING TO USE THE CHANNEL TO TRANSPORT THINGS
SO WE'D LIKE TO HAVE A BRIDGE CLOSE TO IT.
CHANNEL
RIVER
RESERVOIR
GOT IT. SHOW ME WHERE AND IT'S YOURS.

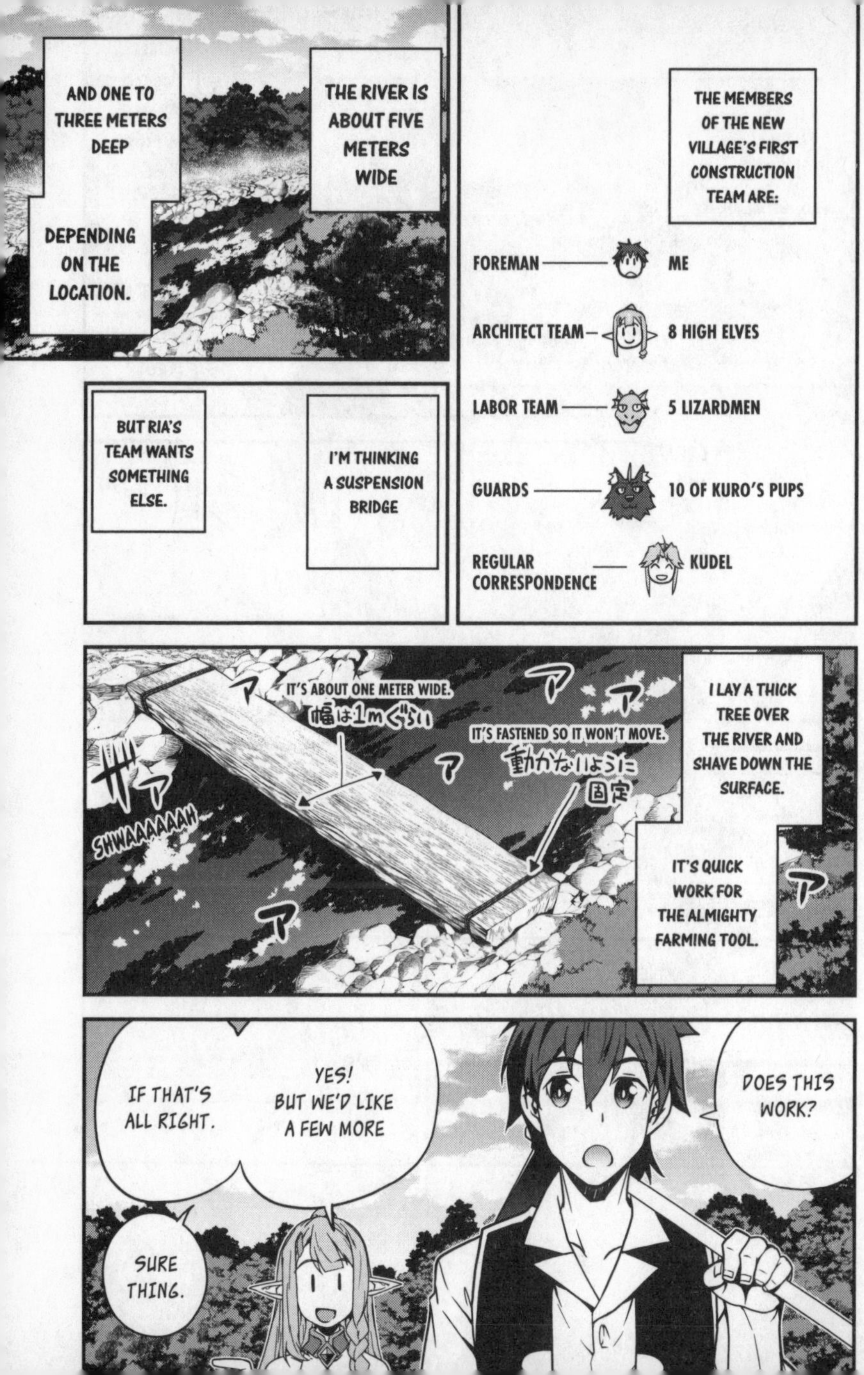
THE MEMBERS OF THE NEW VILLAGE'S FIRST CONSTRUCTION TEAM ARE:
FOREMAN — ME
ARCHITECT TEAM — 8 HIGH ELVES
LABOR TEAM — 5 LIZARDMEN
GUARDS — 10 OF KURO'S PUPS
REGULAR CORRESPONDENCE — KUDEL
THE RIVER IS ABOUT FIVE METERS WIDE
AND ONE TO THREE METERS DEEP
DEPENDING ON THE LOCATION.
I'M THINKING A SUSPENSION BRIDGE
BUT RIA'S TEAM WANTS SOMETHING ELSE.
I LAY A THICK TREE OVER THE RIVER AND SHAVE DOWN THE SURFACE.
IT'S QUICK WORK FOR THE ALMIGHTY FARMING TOOL.
IT'S FASTENED SO IT WON'T MOVE.
動かないように固定
IT'S ABOUT ONE METER WIDE.
幅は1mぐらい
ザァ
SHWAAAAAAH
DOES THIS WORK?
YES! BUT WE'D LIKE A FEW MORE
IF THAT'S ALL RIGHT.
SURE THING.

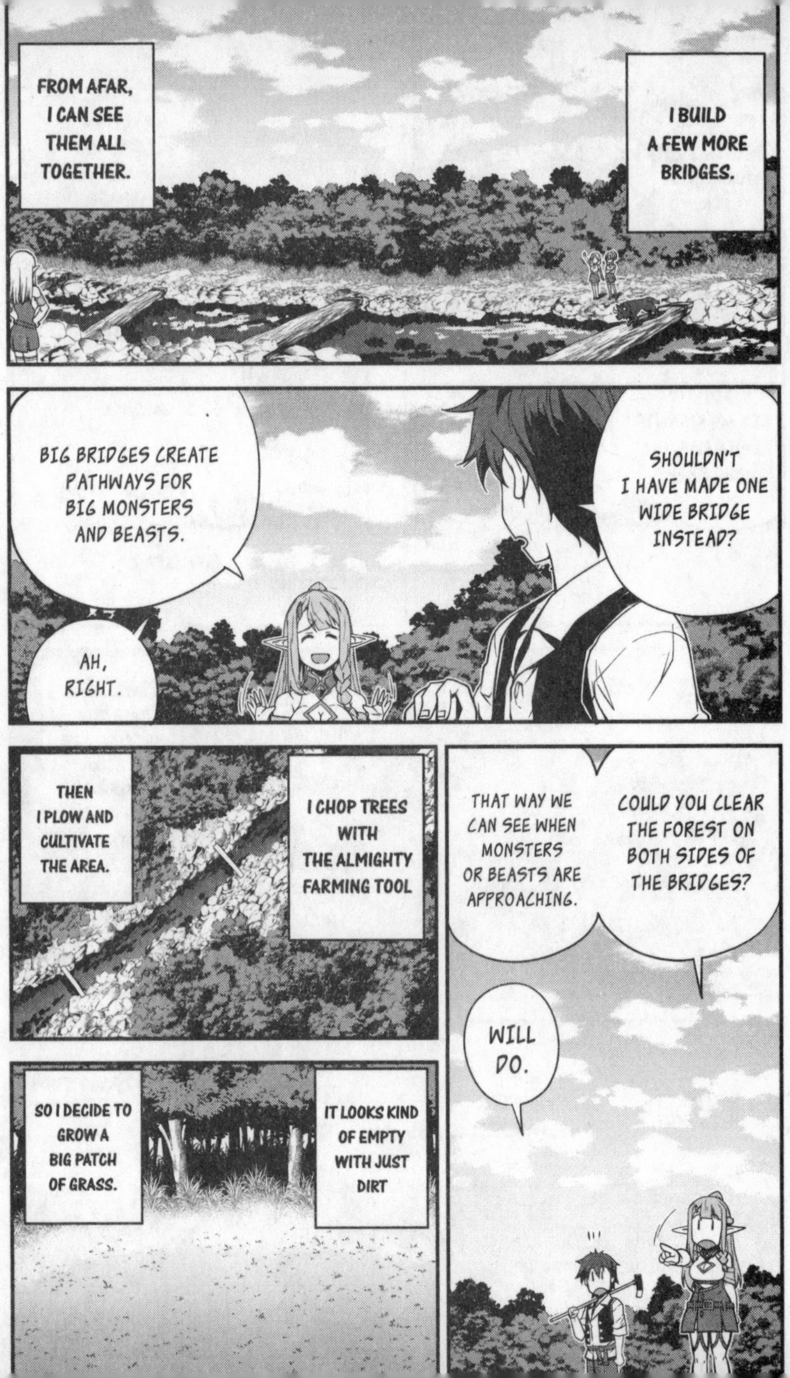
I BUILD A FEW MORE BRIDGES.
FROM AFAR, I CAN SEE THEM ALL TOGETHER.
SHOULDN'T I HAVE MADE ONE WIDE BRIDGE INSTEAD?
BIG BRIDGES CREATE PATHWAYS FOR BIG MONSTERS AND BEASTS.
AH, RIGHT.
COULD YOU CLEAR THE FOREST ON BOTH SIDES OF THE BRIDGES?
THAT WAY WE CAN SEE WHEN MONSTERS OR BEASTS ARE APPROACHING.
WILL DO.
I CHOP TREES WITH THE ALMIGHTY FARMING TOOL
THEN I PLOW AND CULTIVATE THE AREA.
IT LOOKS KIND OF EMPTY WITH JUST DIRT
SO I DECIDE TO GROW A BIG PATCH OF GRASS.

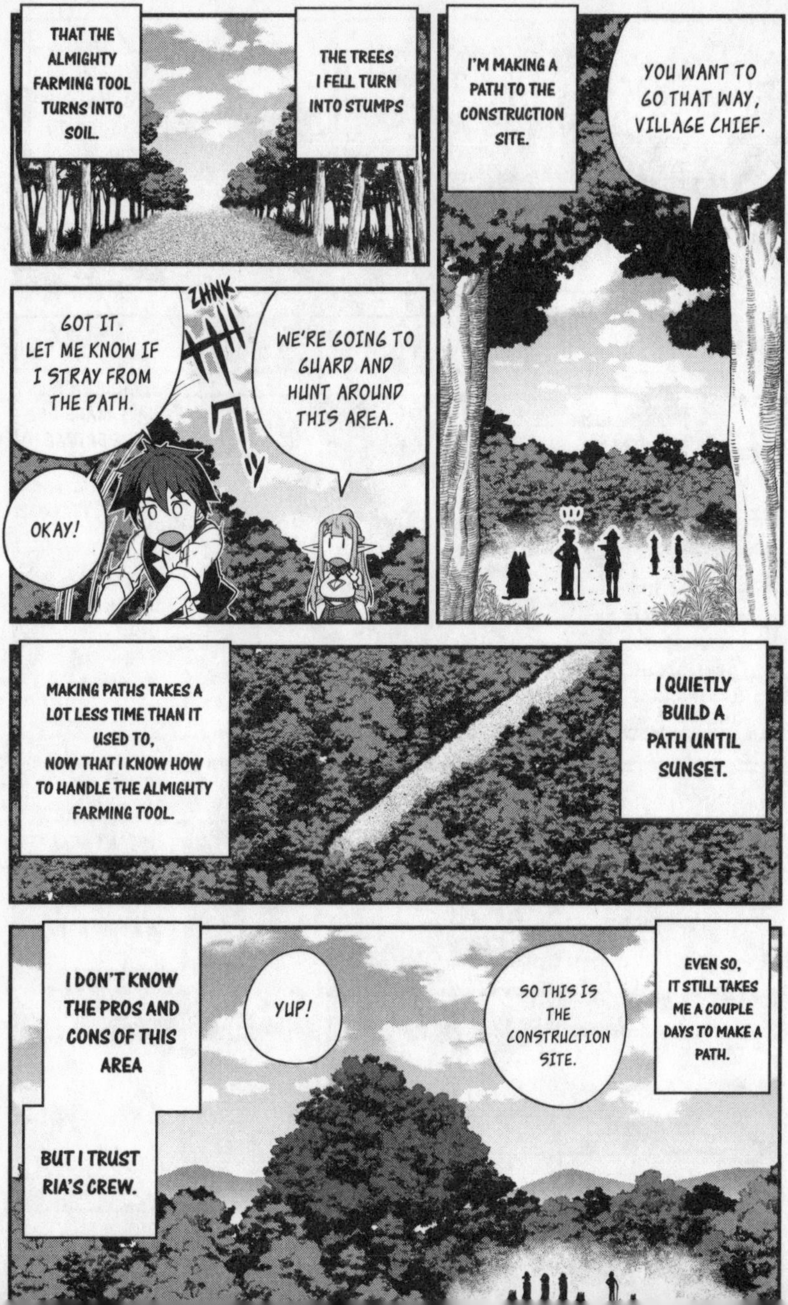
YOU WANT TO GO THAT WAY, VILLAGE CHIEF.
I'M MAKING A PATH TO THE CONSTRUCTION SITE.
THE TREES I FELL TURN INTO STUMPS
THAT THE ALMIGHTY FARMING TOOL TURNS INTO SOIL.
WE'RE GOING TO GUARD AND HUNT AROUND THIS AREA.
ZHNK
GOT IT. LET ME KNOW IF I STRAY FROM THE PATH.
OKAY!
I QUIETLY BUILD A PATH UNTIL SUNSET.
MAKING PATHS TAKES A LOT LESS TIME THAN IT USED TO, NOW THAT I KNOW HOW TO HANDLE THE ALMIGHTY FARMING TOOL.
EVEN SO, IT STILL TAKES ME A COUPLE DAYS TO MAKE A PATH.
SO THIS IS THE CONSTRUCTION SITE.
YUP!
I DON'T KNOW THE PROS AND CONS OF THIS AREA
BUT I TRUST RIA'S CREW.

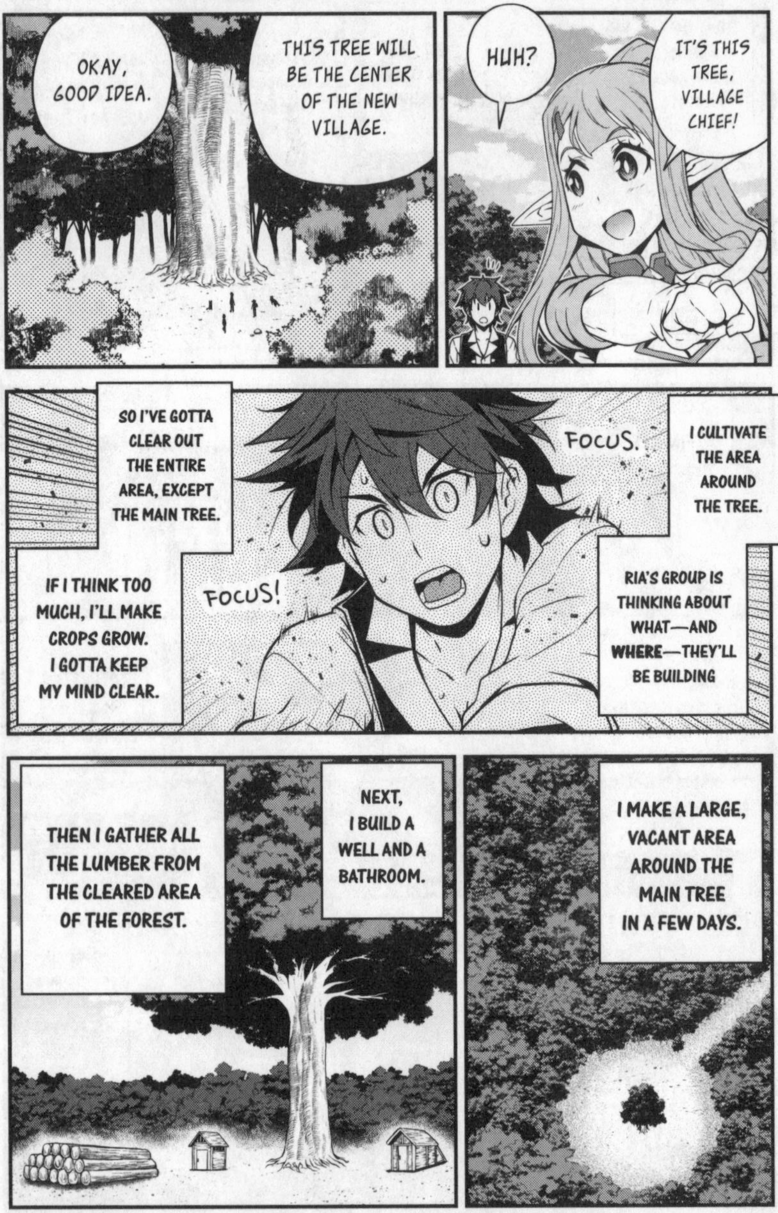
IT'S THIS TREE, VILLAGE CHIEF!
HUH?
THIS TREE WILL BE THE CENTER OF THE NEW VILLAGE.
OKAY, GOOD IDEA.
I CULTIVATE THE AREA AROUND THE TREE.
FOCUS.
RIA'S GROUP IS THINKING ABOUT WHAT—AND WHERE—THEY'LL BE BUILDING
SO I'VE GOTTA CLEAR OUT THE ENTIRE AREA, EXCEPT THE MAIN TREE.
FOCUS!
IF I THINK TOO MUCH, I'LL MAKE CROPS GROW. I GOTTA KEEP MY MIND CLEAR.
I MAKE A LARGE, VACANT AREA AROUND THE MAIN TREE IN A FEW DAYS.
NEXT, I BUILD A WELL AND A BATHROOM.
THEN I GATHER ALL THE LUMBER FROM THE CLEARED AREA OF THE FOREST.

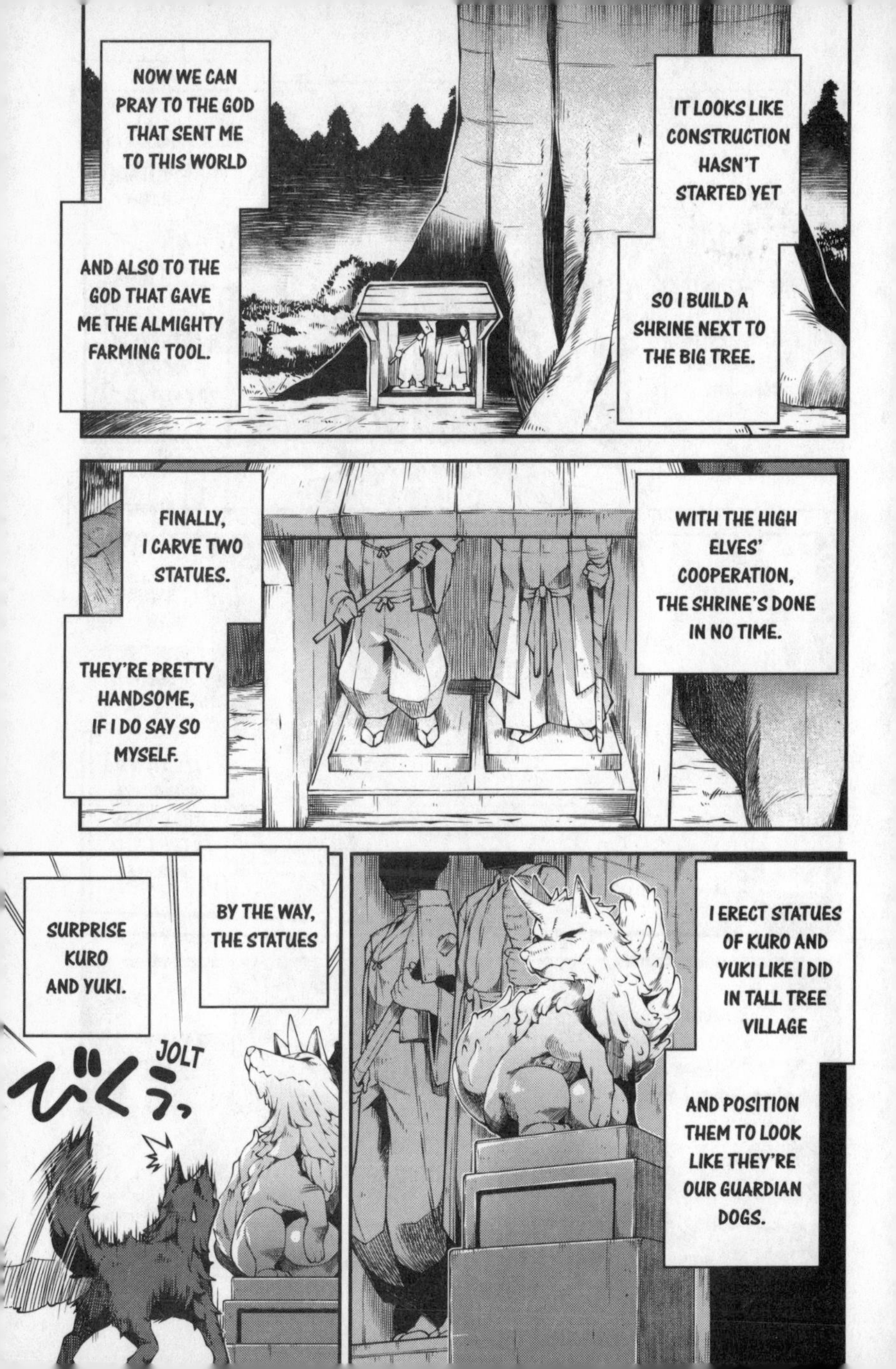
IT LOOKS LIKE CONSTRUCTION HASN'T STARTED YET
SO I BUILD A SHRINE NEXT TO THE BIG TREE.
NOW WE CAN PRAY TO THE GOD THAT SENT ME TO THIS WORLD
AND ALSO TO THE GOD THAT GAVE ME THE ALMIGHTY FARMING TOOL.
WITH THE HIGH ELVES' COOPERATION, THE SHRINE'S DONE IN NO TIME.
FINALLY, I CARVE TWO STATUES.
THEY'RE PRETTY HANDSOME, IF I DO SAY SO MYSELF.
I ERECT STATUES OF KURO AND YUKI LIKE I DID IN TALL TREE VILLAGE
AND POSITION THEM TO LOOK LIKE THEY'RE OUR GUARDIAN DOGS.
BY THE WAY, THE STATUES
SURPRISE KURO AND YUKI.
JOLT

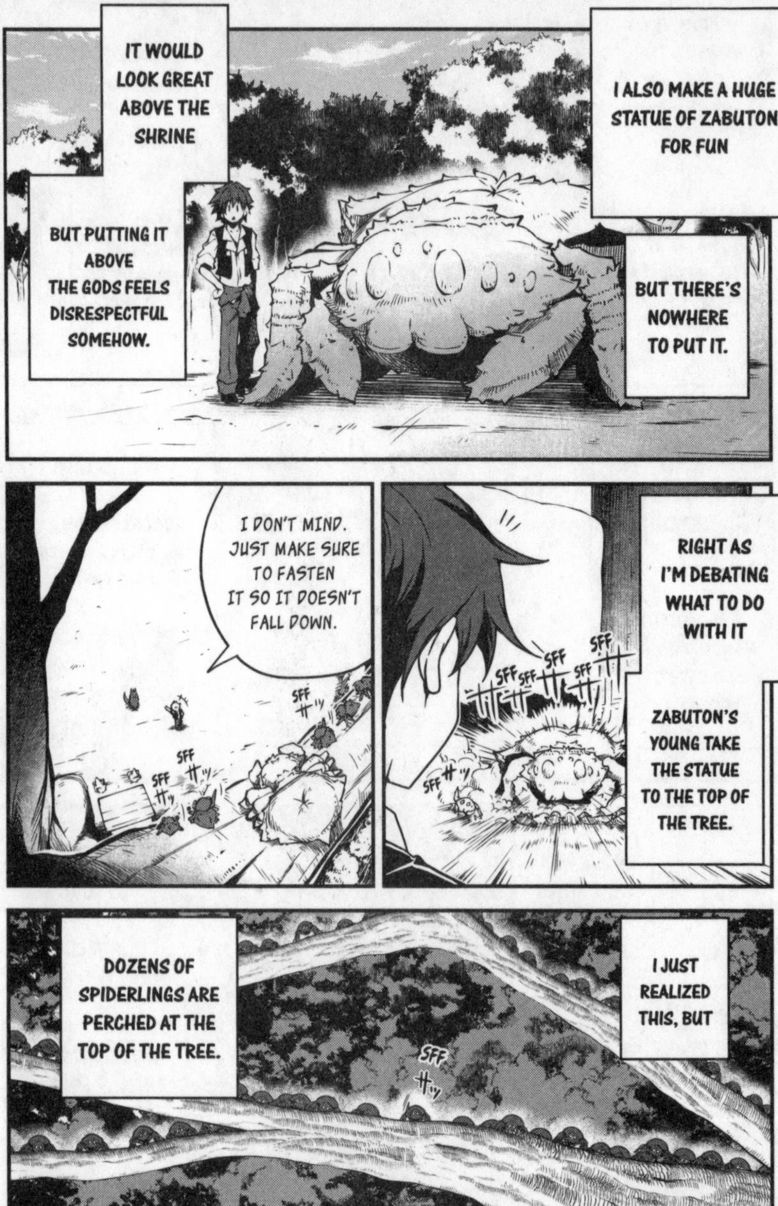
I ALSO MAKE A HUGE STATUE OF ZABUTON FOR FUN
BUT THERE'S NOWHERE TO PUT IT.
IT WOULD LOOK GREAT ABOVE THE SHRINE
BUT PUTTING IT ABOVE THE GODS FEELS DISRESPECTFUL SOMEHOW.
RIGHT AS I'M DEBATING WHAT TO DO WITH IT
SFF SFF SFF SFF SFF
ZABUTON'S YOUNG TAKE THE STATUE TO THE TOP OF THE TREE.
I DON'T MIND. JUST MAKE SURE TO FASTEN IT SO IT DOESN'T FALL DOWN.
SFF
SFF
SFF
I JUST REALIZED THIS, BUT
DOZENS OF SPIDERLINGS ARE PERCHED AT THE TOP OF THE TREE.
SFF

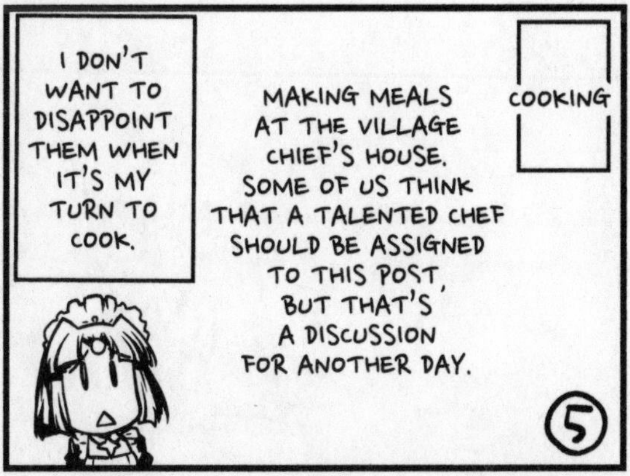
COOKING
MAKING MEALS AT THE VILLAGE CHIEF'S HOUSE. SOME OF US THINK THAT A TALENTED CHEF SHOULD BE ASSIGNED TO THIS POST, BUT THAT'S A DISCUSSION FOR ANOTHER DAY.
I DON'T WANT TO DISAPPOINT THEM WHEN IT'S MY TURN TO COOK.
5

Farming life in another world.

CHAPTER 64: BUILDING A NEW VILLAGE, THE RECON TEAM RETURNS

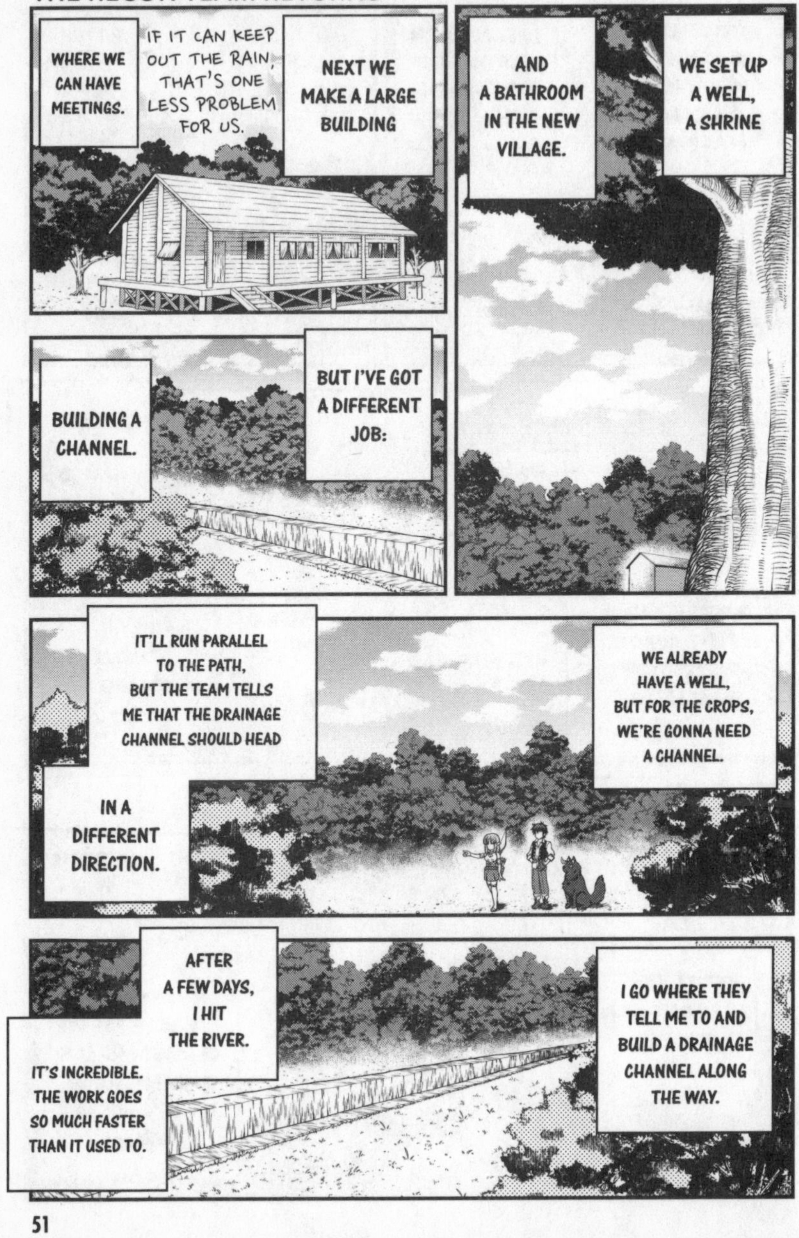
WE SET UP A WELL, A SHRINE
AND A BATHROOM IN THE NEW VILLAGE.
NEXT WE MAKE A LARGE BUILDING
IF IT CAN KEEP OUT THE RAIN, THAT'S ONE LESS PROBLEM FOR US.
WHERE WE CAN HAVE MEETINGS.
BUT I'VE GOT A DIFFERENT JOB:
BUILDING A CHANNEL.
WE ALREADY HAVE A WELL, BUT FOR THE CROPS, WE'RE GONNA NEED A CHANNEL.
IT'LL RUN PARALLEL TO THE PATH, BUT THE TEAM TELLS ME THAT THE DRAINAGE CHANNEL SHOULD HEAD
IN A DIFFERENT DIRECTION.
I GO WHERE THEY TELL ME TO AND BUILD A DRAINAGE CHANNEL ALONG THE WAY.
AFTER A FEW DAYS, I HIT THE RIVER.
IT'S INCREDIBLE. THE WORK GOES SO MUCH FASTER THAN IT USED TO.

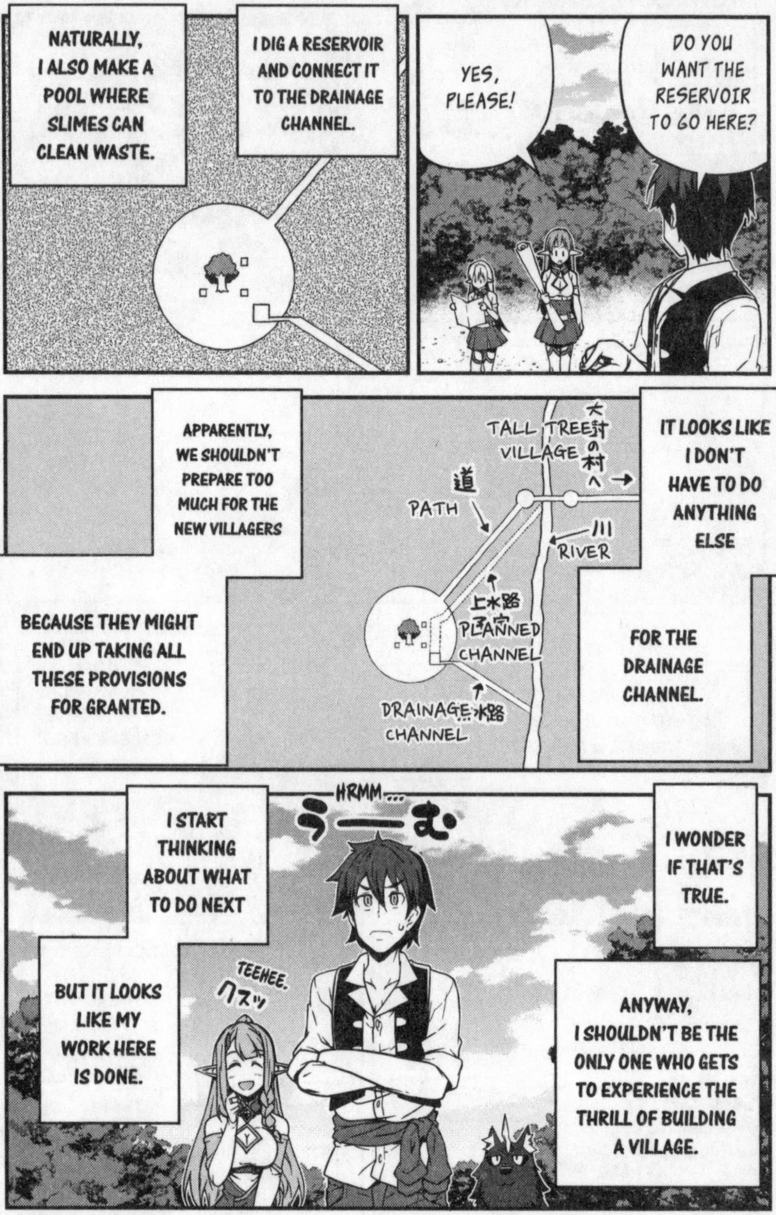

DO YOU WANT THE RESERVOIR TO GO HERE?
YES, PLEASE!
I DIG A RESERVOIR AND CONNECT IT TO THE DRAINAGE CHANNEL.
NATURALLY, I ALSO MAKE A POOL WHERE SLIMES CAN CLEAN WASTE.
IT LOOKS LIKE I DON'T HAVE TO DO ANYTHING ELSE
FOR THE DRAINAGE CHANNEL.
TALL TREE VILLAGE
道
PATH
川
RIVER
PLANNED CHANNEL
DRAINAGE CHANNEL
APPARENTLY, WE SHOULDN'T PREPARE TOO MUCH FOR THE NEW VILLAGERS
BECAUSE THEY MIGHT END UP TAKING ALL THESE PROVISIONS FOR GRANTED.
I WONDER IF THAT'S TRUE.
HRMM...
うーむ
I START THINKING ABOUT WHAT TO DO NEXT
ANYWAY, I SHOULDN'T BE THE ONLY ONE WHO GETS TO EXPERIENCE THE THRILL OF BUILDING A VILLAGE.
TEEHEE.
クスッ
BUT IT LOOKS LIKE MY WORK HERE IS DONE.

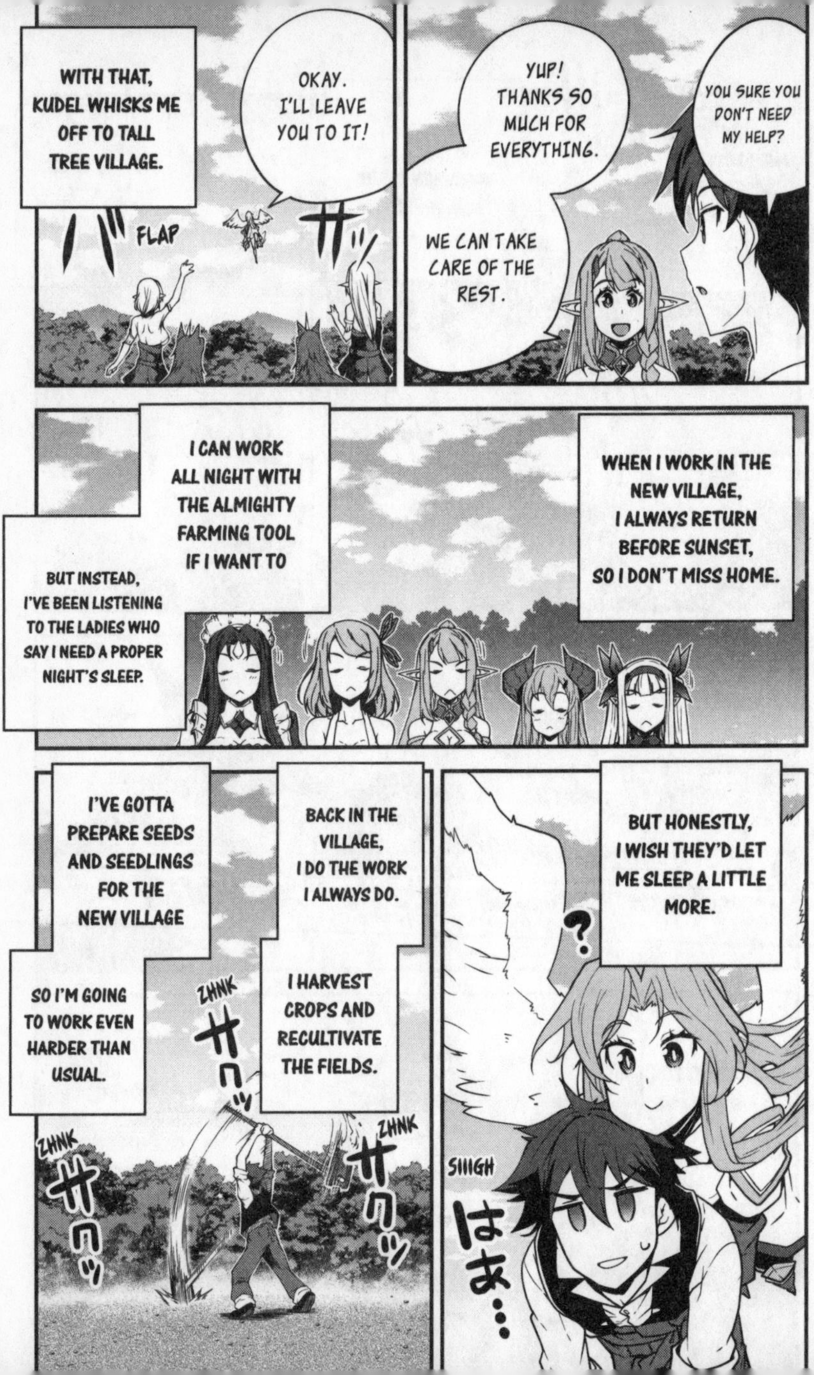
YOU SURE YOU DON'T NEED MY HELP?
YUP! THANKS SO MUCH FOR EVERYTHING.
WE CAN TAKE CARE OF THE REST.
OKAY. I'LL LEAVE YOU TO IT!
WITH THAT, KUDEL WHISKS ME OFF TO TALL TREE VILLAGE.
FLAP
WHEN I WORK IN THE NEW VILLAGE, I ALWAYS RETURN BEFORE SUNSET, SO I DON'T MISS HOME.
I CAN WORK ALL NIGHT WITH THE ALMIGHTY FARMING TOOL IF I WANT TO
BUT INSTEAD, I'VE BEEN LISTENING TO THE LADIES WHO SAY I NEED A PROPER NIGHT'S SLEEP.
BUT HONESTLY, I WISH THEY'D LET ME SLEEP A LITTLE MORE.
?
SIIIGH
はあ…
BACK IN THE VILLAGE, I DO THE WORK I ALWAYS DO.
I HARVEST CROPS AND RECULTIVATE THE FIELDS.
I'VE GOTTA PREPARE SEEDS AND SEEDLINGS FOR THE NEW VILLAGE
SO I'M GOING TO WORK EVEN HARDER THAN USUAL.
ZHNK
サクッ
ZHNK
サクッ
ZHNK
サクッ

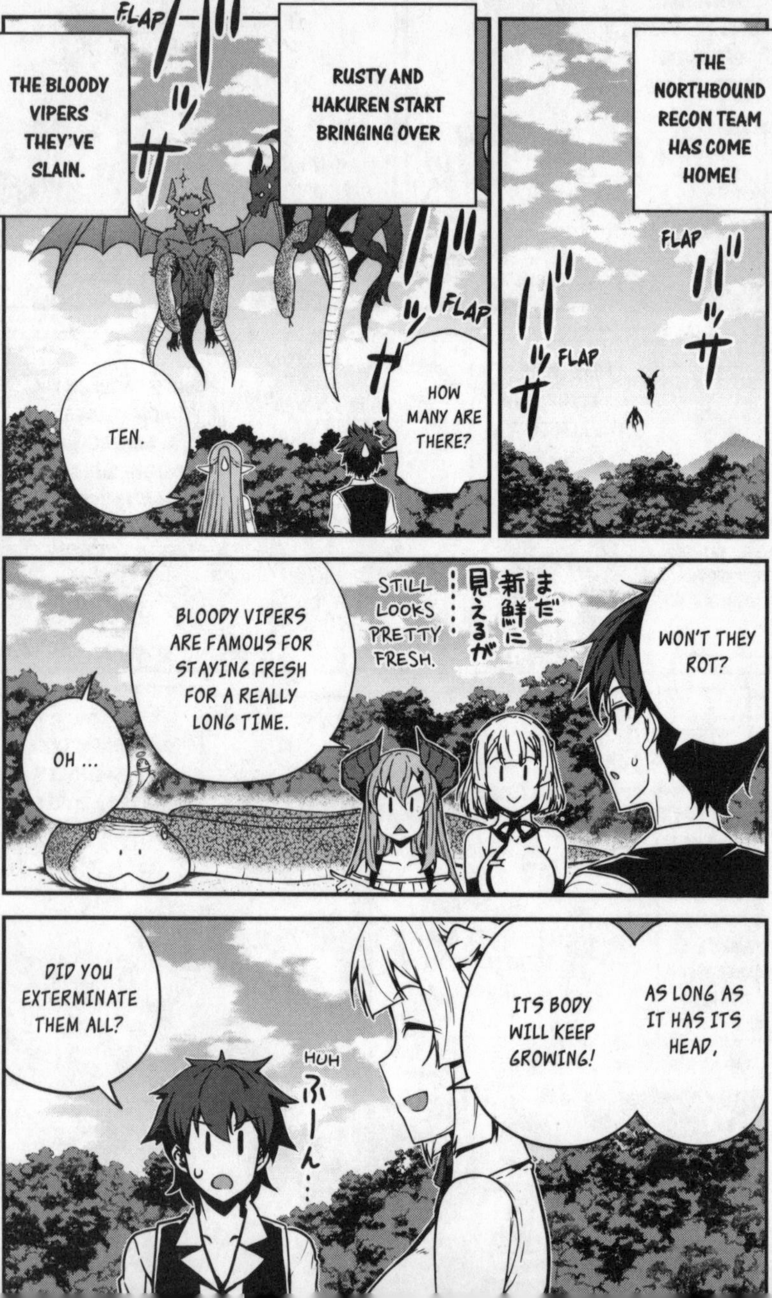
THE NORTHBOUND RECON TEAM HAS COME HOME!
FLAP
FLAP
RUSTY AND HAKUREN START BRINGING OVER
FLAP
THE BLOODY VIPERS THEY'VE SLAIN.
FLAP
HOW MANY ARE THERE?
TEN.
WON'T THEY ROT?
まだ新鮮に見えるが……
STILL LOOKS PRETTY FRESH.
BLOODY VIPERS ARE FAMOUS FOR STAYING FRESH FOR A REALLY LONG TIME.
OH ...
AS LONG AS IT HAS ITS HEAD,
ITS BODY WILL KEEP GROWING!
HUH
ふーん…
DID YOU EXTERMINATE THEM ALL?

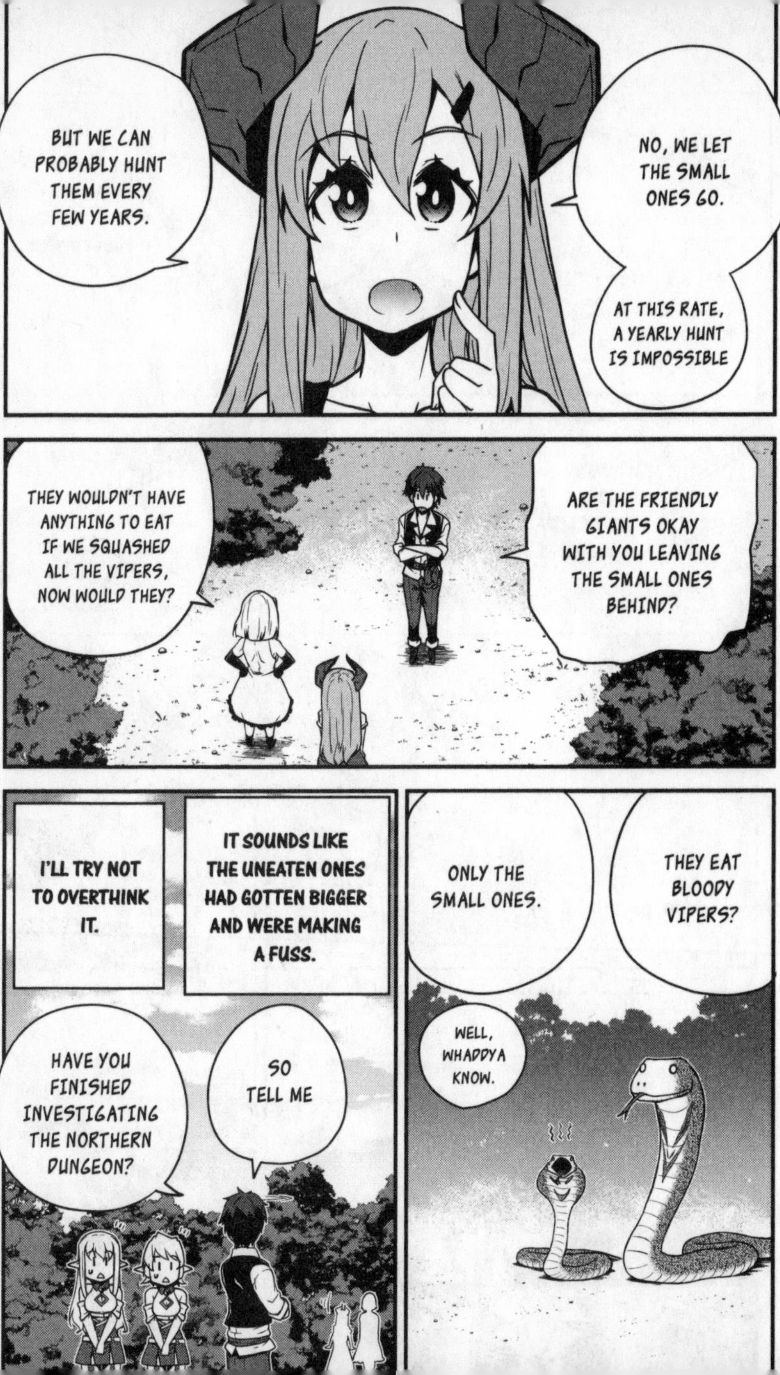
NO, WE LET THE SMALL ONES GO.
AT THIS RATE, A YEARLY HUNT IS IMPOSSIBLE
BUT WE CAN PROBABLY HUNT THEM EVERY FEW YEARS.
ARE THE FRIENDLY GIANTS OKAY WITH YOU LEAVING THE SMALL ONES BEHIND?
THEY WOULDN'T HAVE ANYTHING TO EAT IF WE SQUASHED ALL THE VIPERS, NOW WOULD THEY?
THEY EAT BLOODY VIPERS?
ONLY THE SMALL ONES.
WELL, WHADDYA KNOW.
IT SOUNDS LIKE THE UNEATEN ONES HAD GOTTEN BIGGER AND WERE MAKING A FUSS.
I'LL TRY NOT TO OVERTHINK IT.
SO TELL ME
HAVE YOU FINISHED INVESTIGATING THE NORTHERN DUNGEON?

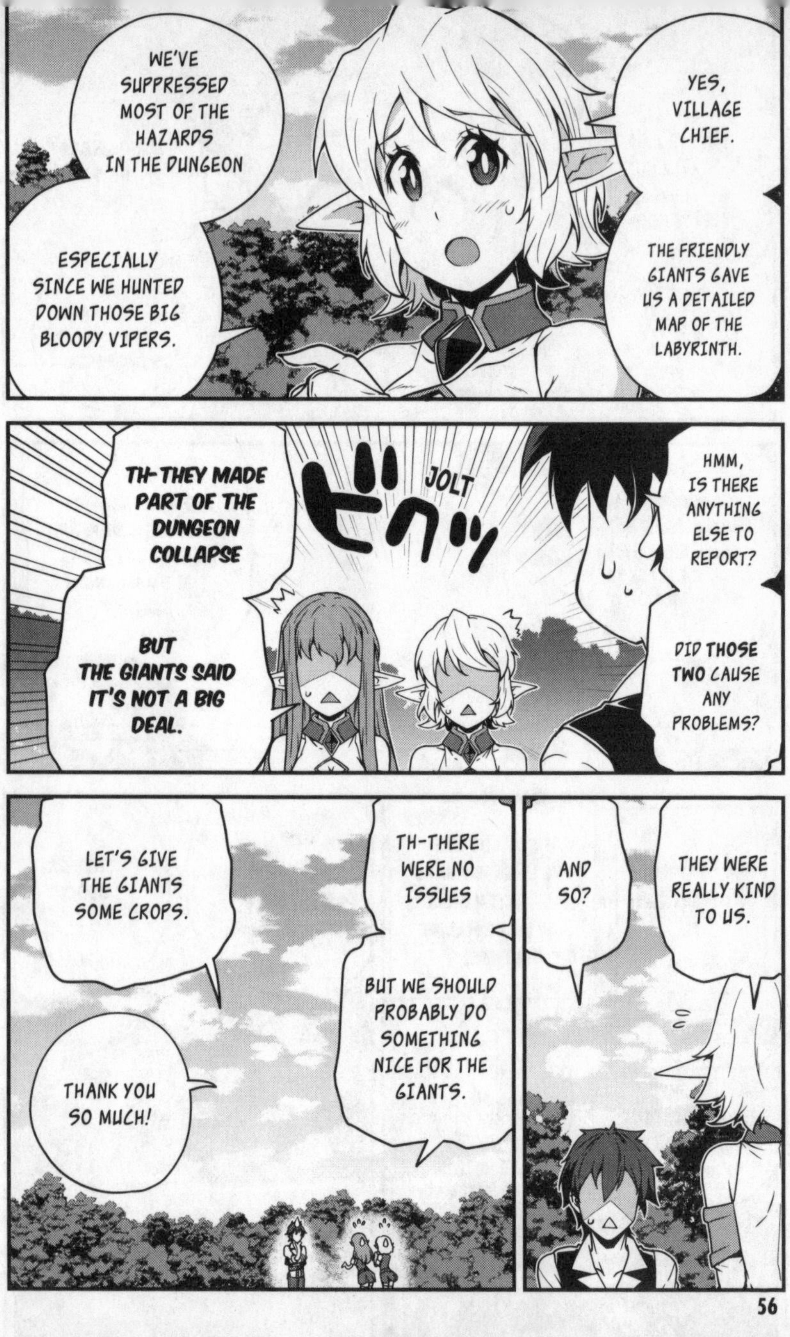
YES, VILLAGE CHIEF.
THE FRIENDLY GIANTS GAVE US A DETAILED MAP OF THE LABYRINTH.
WE'VE SUPPRESSED MOST OF THE HAZARDS IN THE DUNGEON
ESPECIALLY SINCE WE HUNTED DOWN THOSE BIG BLOODY VIPERS.
HMM, IS THERE ANYTHING ELSE TO REPORT?
DID THOSE TWO CAUSE ANY PROBLEMS?
JOLT
TH-THEY MADE PART OF THE DUNGEON COLLAPSE
BUT THE GIANTS SAID IT'S NOT A BIG DEAL.
THEY WERE REALLY KIND TO US.
AND SO?
TH-THERE WERE NO ISSUES
BUT WE SHOULD PROBABLY DO SOMETHING NICE FOR THE GIANTS.
LET'S GIVE THE GIANTS SOME CROPS.
THANK YOU SO MUCH!

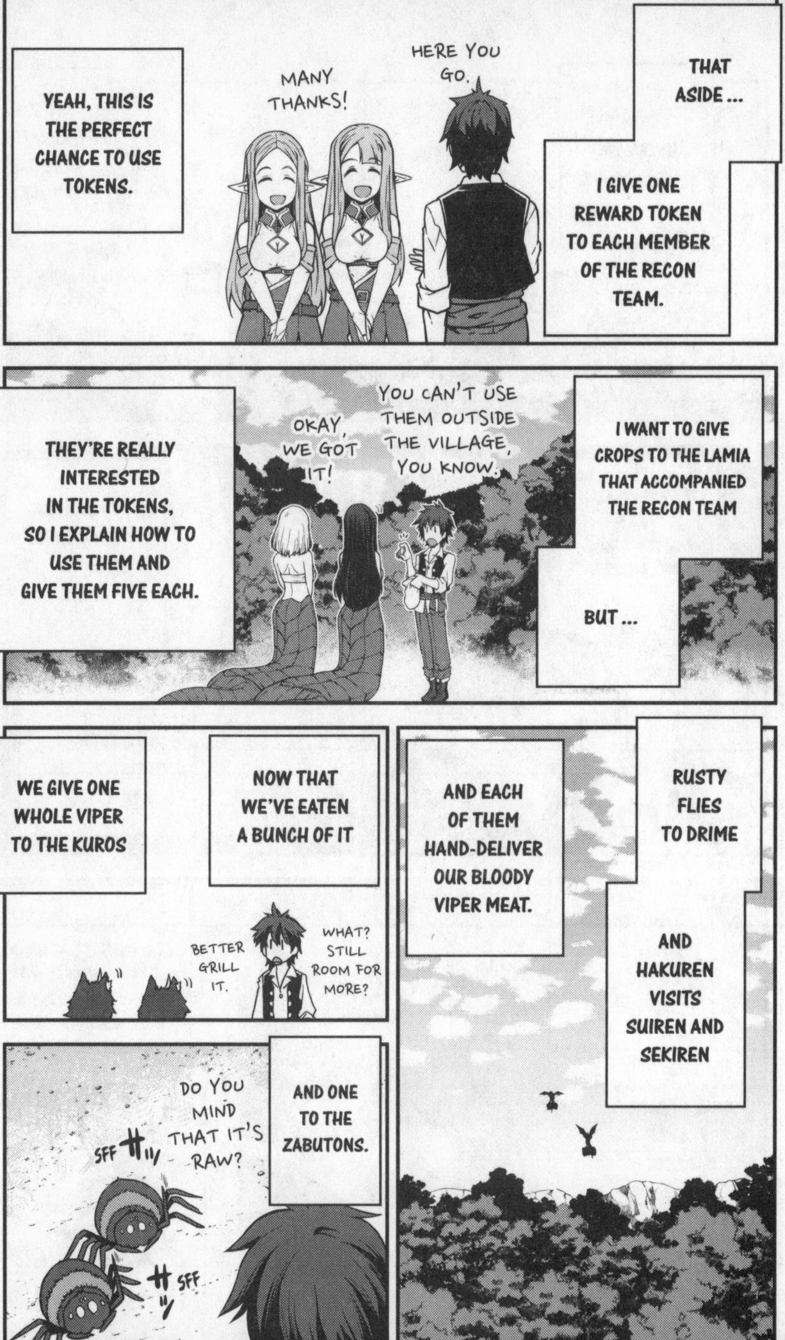
THAT ASIDE ...
I GIVE ONE REWARD TOKEN TO EACH MEMBER OF THE RECON TEAM.
HERE YOU GO.
MANY THANKS!
YEAH, THIS IS THE PERFECT CHANCE TO USE TOKENS.
I WANT TO GIVE CROPS TO THE LAMIA THAT ACCOMPANIED THE RECON TEAM
BUT ...
YOU CAN'T USE THEM OUTSIDE THE VILLAGE, YOU KNOW.
OKAY, WE GOT IT!
THEY'RE REALLY INTERESTED IN THE TOKENS, SO I EXPLAIN HOW TO USE THEM AND GIVE THEM FIVE EACH.
RUSTY FLIES TO DRIME
AND HAKUREN VISITS SUIREN AND SEKIREN
AND EACH OF THEM HAND-DELIVER OUR BLOODY VIPER MEAT.
NOW THAT WE'VE EATEN A BUNCH OF IT
WE GIVE ONE WHOLE VIPER TO THE KUROS
WHAT? STILL ROOM FOR MORE?
BETTER GRILL IT.
AND ONE TO THE ZABUTONS.
DO YOU MIND THAT IT'S RAW?
SFF
SFF

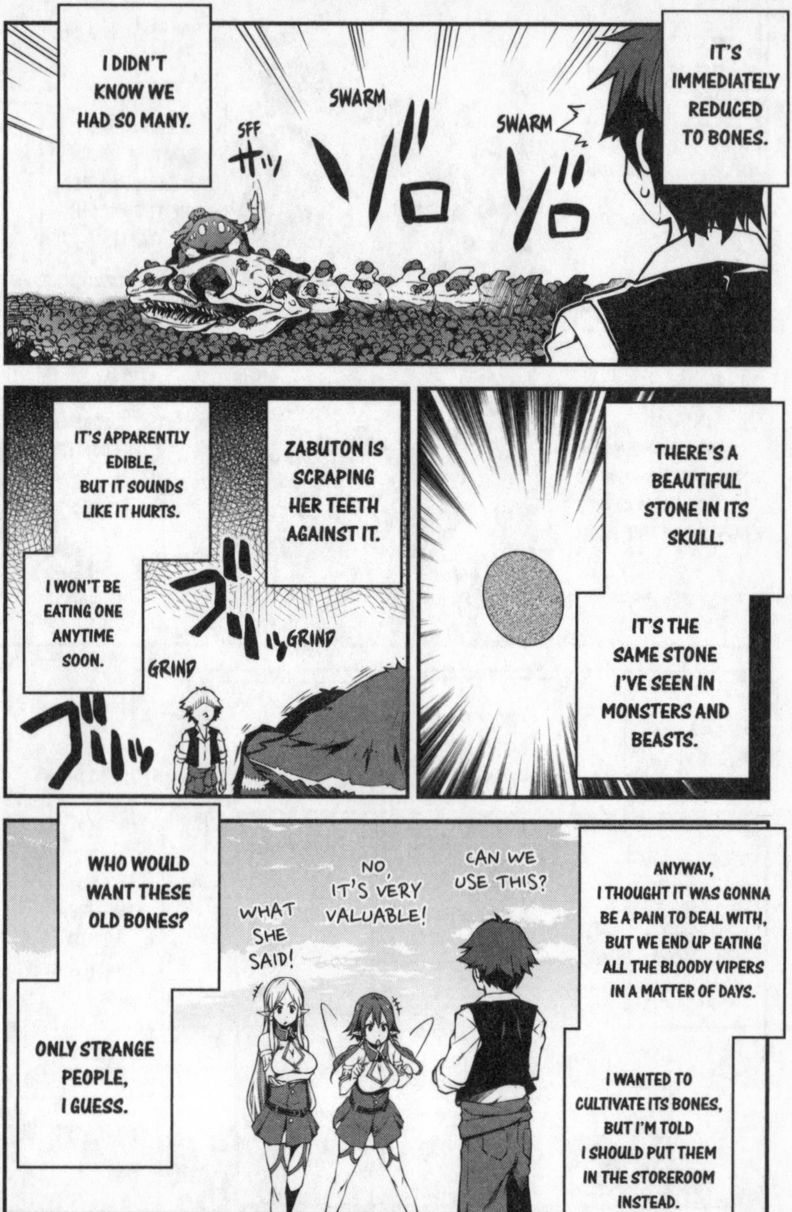
IT'S IMMEDIATELY REDUCED TO BONES.
SWARM
ゾロ
SWARM
ゾロ
SFF
ザッ
I DIDN'T KNOW WE HAD SO MANY.
THERE'S A BEAUTIFUL STONE IN ITS SKULL.
IT'S THE SAME STONE I'VE SEEN IN MONSTERS AND BEASTS.
ZABUTON IS SCRAPING HER TEETH AGAINST IT.
IT'S APPARENTLY EDIBLE, BUT IT SOUNDS LIKE IT HURTS.
I WON'T BE EATING ONE ANYTIME SOON.
GRIND
GRIND
ANYWAY, I THOUGHT IT WAS GONNA BE A PAIN TO DEAL WITH, BUT WE END UP EATING ALL THE BLOODY VIPERS IN A MATTER OF DAYS.
I WANTED TO CULTIVATE ITS BONES, BUT I'M TOLD I SHOULD PUT THEM IN THE STOREROOM INSTEAD.
CAN WE USE THIS?
NO, IT'S VERY VALUABLE!
WHAT SHE SAID!
WHO WOULD WANT THESE OLD BONES?
ONLY STRANGE PEOPLE, I GUESS.

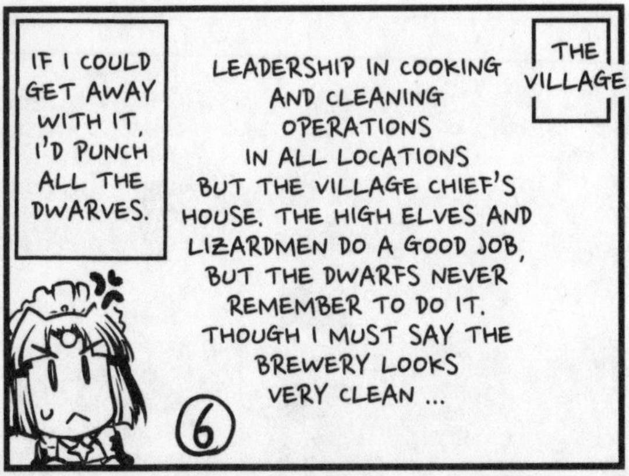
THE VILLAGE
LEADERSHIP IN COOKING AND CLEANING OPERATIONS IN ALL LOCATIONS BUT THE VILLAGE CHIEF'S HOUSE. THE HIGH ELVES AND LIZARDMEN DO A GOOD JOB, BUT THE DWARFS NEVER REMEMBER TO DO IT. THOUGH I MUST SAY THE BREWERY LOOKS VERY CLEAN ...
IF I COULD GET AWAY WITH IT, I'D PUNCH ALL THE DWARVES.
6

Farming life in another world.

CHAPTER 65: ONE MOUNTAIN ELF'S REBELLION

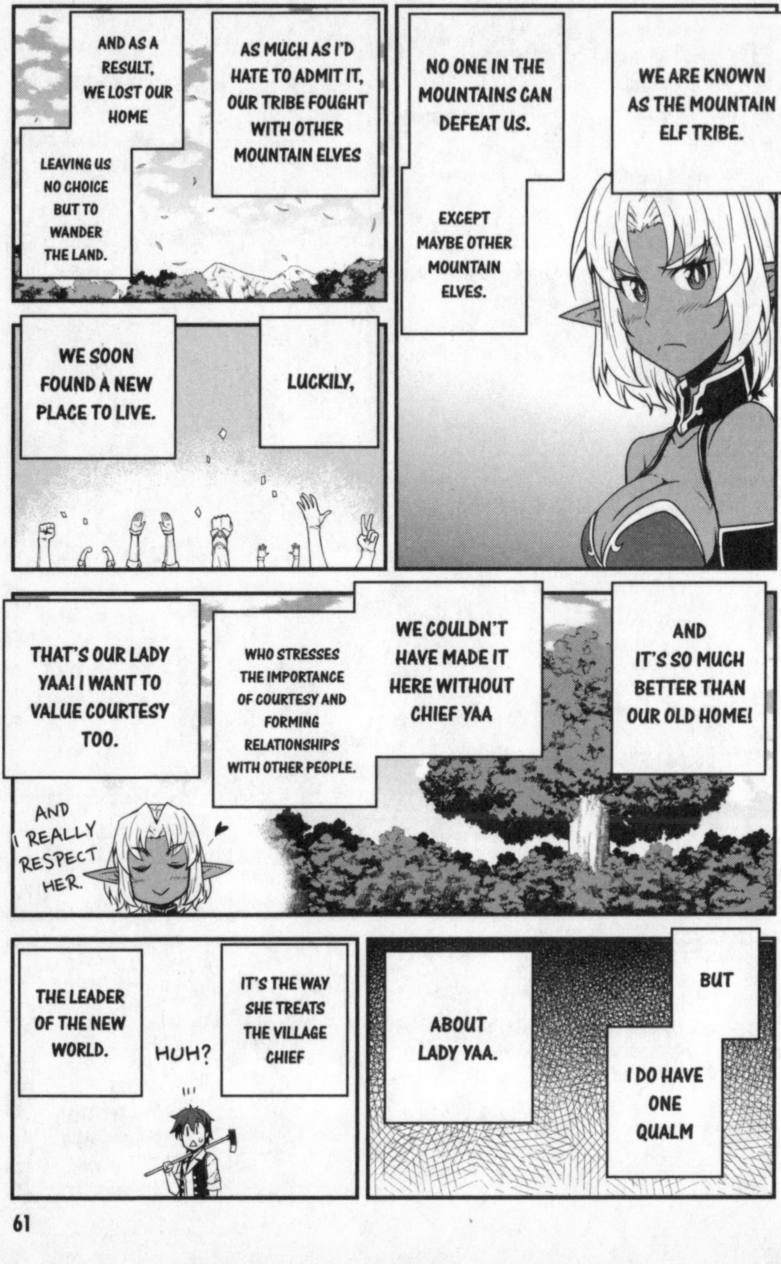

WE ARE KNOWN AS THE MOUNTAIN ELF TRIBE.
NO ONE IN THE MOUNTAINS CAN DEFEAT US.
EXCEPT MAYBE OTHER MOUNTAIN ELVES.
AS MUCH AS I'D HATE TO ADMIT IT, OUR TRIBE FOUGHT WITH OTHER MOUNTAIN ELVES
AND AS A RESULT, WE LOST OUR HOME
LEAVING US NO CHOICE BUT TO WANDER THE LAND.
LUCKILY,
WE SOON FOUND A NEW PLACE TO LIVE.
AND IT'S SO MUCH BETTER THAN OUR OLD HOME!
WE COULDN'T HAVE MADE IT HERE WITHOUT CHIEF YAA
WHO STRESSES THE IMPORTANCE OF COURTESY AND FORMING RELATIONSHIPS WITH OTHER PEOPLE.
THAT'S OUR LADY YAA! I WANT TO VALUE COURTESY TOO.
AND I REALLY RESPECT HER.
BUT
I DO HAVE ONE QUALM
ABOUT LADY YAA.
IT'S THE WAY SHE TREATS THE VILLAGE CHIEF
THE LEADER OF THE NEW WORLD.
HUH?

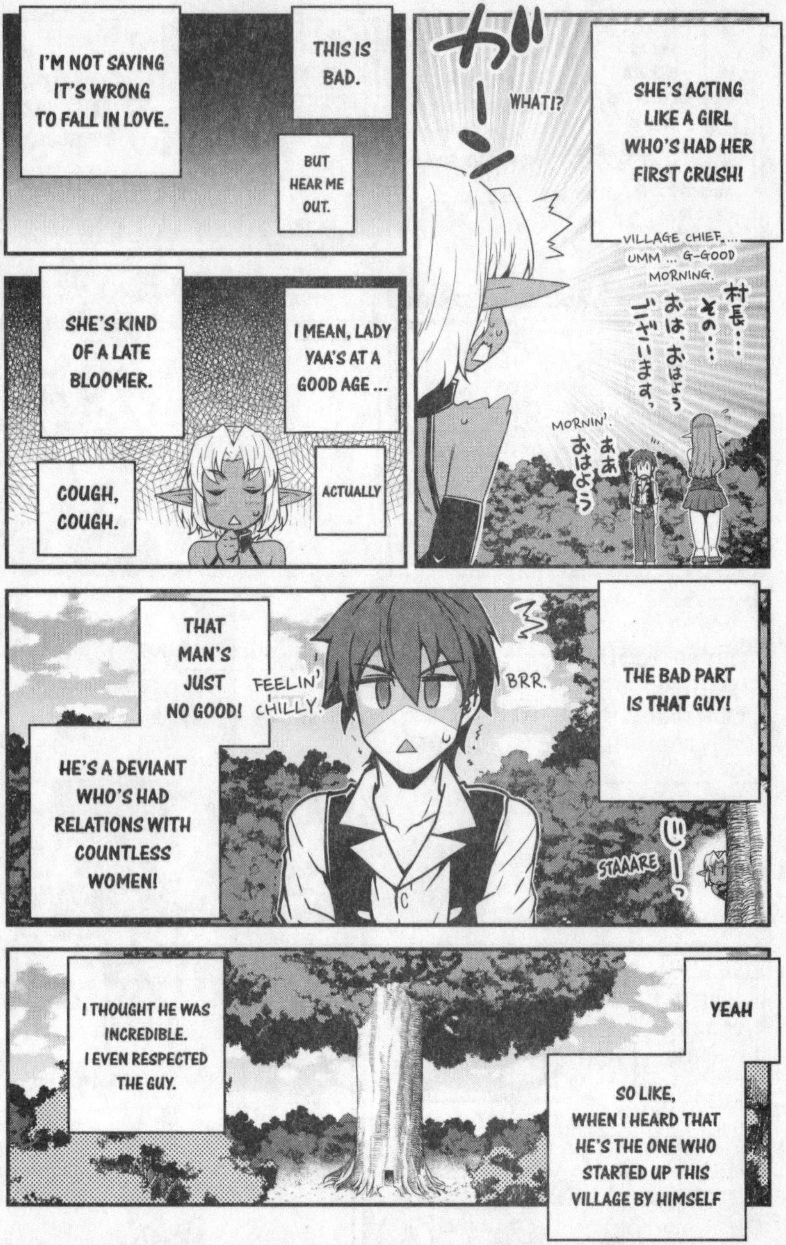
わ゛ーっ
WHAT!?
SHE'S ACTING LIKE A GIRL WHO'S HAD HER FIRST CRUSH!
VILLAGE CHIEF ... UMM ... G-GOOD MORNING.
村長・・・ その・・・ おは、おはようございます。
MORNIN'.
ああ おはよう
THIS IS BAD.
I'M NOT SAYING IT'S WRONG TO FALL IN LOVE.
BUT HEAR ME OUT.
I MEAN, LADY YAA'S AT A GOOD AGE ...
SHE'S KIND OF A LATE BLOOMER.
ACTUALLY
COUGH, COUGH.
THE BAD PART IS THAT GUY!
BRR.
STAAARE
じーっ
FEELIN' CHILLY.
THAT MAN'S JUST NO GOOD!
HE'S A DEVIANT WHO'S HAD RELATIONS WITH COUNTLESS WOMEN!
YEAH
SO LIKE, WHEN I HEARD THAT HE'S THE ONE WHO STARTED UP THIS VILLAGE BY HIMSELF
I THOUGHT HE WAS INCREDIBLE. I EVEN RESPECTED THE GUY.

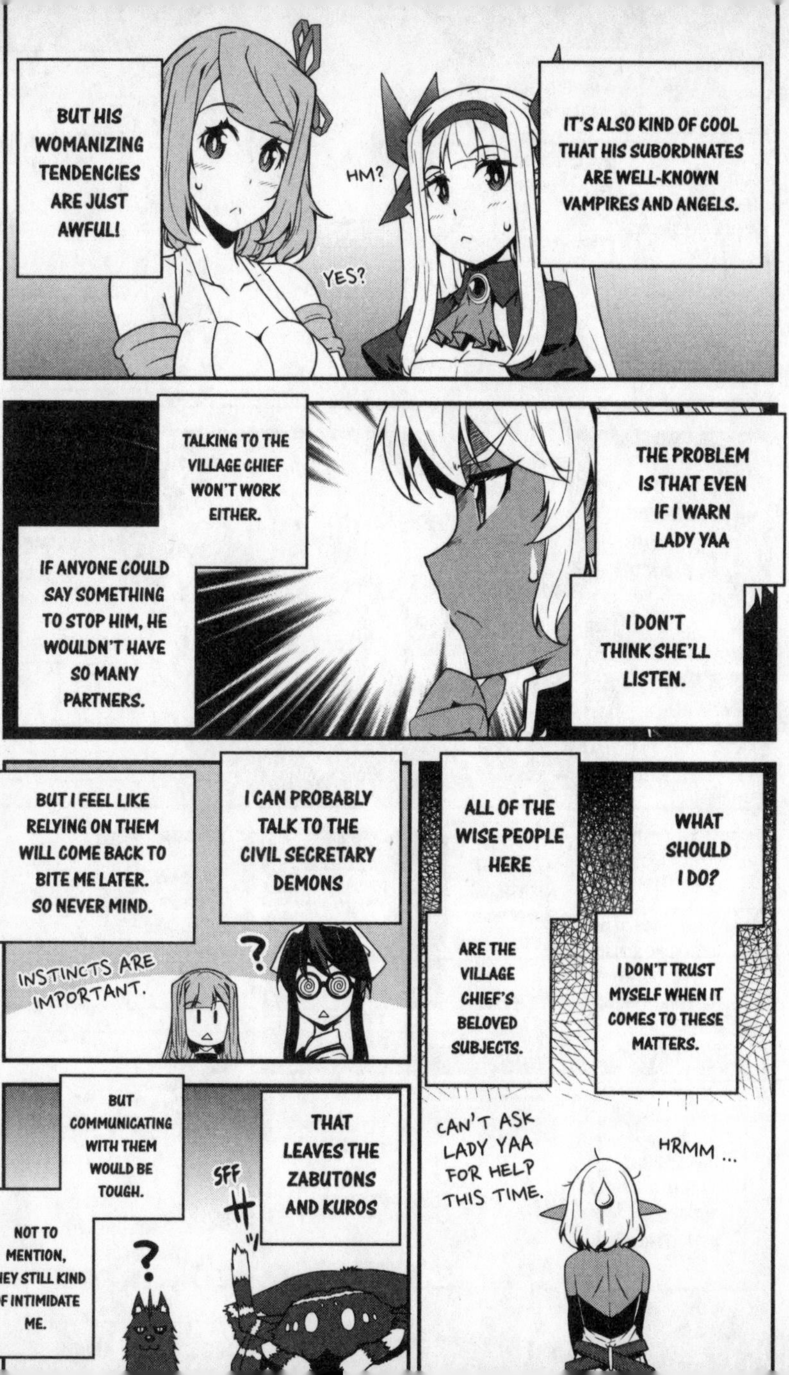
IT'S ALSO KIND OF COOL THAT HIS SUBORDINATES ARE WELL-KNOWN VAMPIRES AND ANGELS.
HM?
BUT HIS WOMANIZING TENDENCIES ARE JUST AWFUL!
YES?
THE PROBLEM IS THAT EVEN IF I WARN LADY YAA
I DON'T THINK SHE'LL LISTEN.
TALKING TO THE VILLAGE CHIEF WON'T WORK EITHER.
IF ANYONE COULD SAY SOMETHING TO STOP HIM, HE WOULDN'T HAVE SO MANY PARTNERS.
ALL OF THE WISE PEOPLE HERE
ARE THE VILLAGE CHIEF'S BELOVED SUBJECTS.
WHAT SHOULD I DO?
I DON'T TRUST MYSELF WHEN IT COMES TO THESE MATTERS.
HRMM ...
CAN'T ASK LADY YAA FOR HELP THIS TIME.
I CAN PROBABLY TALK TO THE CIVIL SECRETARY DEMONS
BUT I FEEL LIKE RELYING ON THEM WILL COME BACK TO BITE ME LATER. SO NEVER MIND.
?
INSTINCTS ARE IMPORTANT.
THAT LEAVES THE ZABUTONS AND KUROS
SFF
BUT COMMUNICATING WITH THEM WOULD BE TOUGH.
NOT TO MENTION, THEY STILL KIND OF INTIMIDATE ME.
?

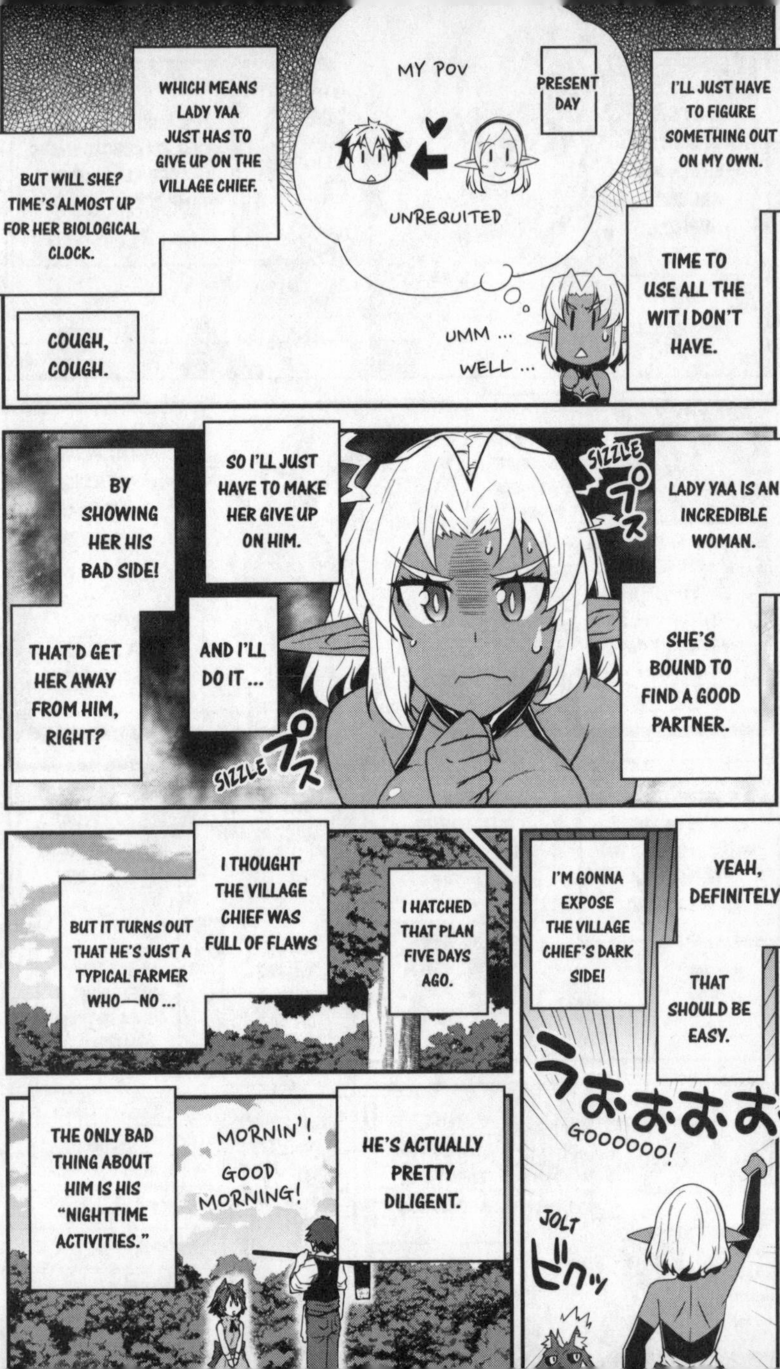
I'LL JUST HAVE TO FIGURE SOMETHING OUT ON MY OWN.
PRESENT DAY
MY POV
UNREQUITED
WHICH MEANS LADY YAA JUST HAS TO GIVE UP ON THE VILLAGE CHIEF.
BUT WILL SHE? TIME'S ALMOST UP FOR HER BIOLOGICAL CLOCK.
TIME TO USE ALL THE WIT I DON'T HAVE.
UMM ... WELL ...
COUGH, COUGH.
LADY YAA IS AN INCREDIBLE WOMAN.
SIZZLE プス
SO I'LL JUST HAVE TO MAKE HER GIVE UP ON HIM.
BY SHOWING HER HIS BAD SIDE!
SHE'S BOUND TO FIND A GOOD PARTNER.
AND I'LL DO IT ...
THAT'D GET HER AWAY FROM HIM, RIGHT?
SIZZLE プス
YEAH, DEFINITELY!
I'M GONNA EXPOSE THE VILLAGE CHIEF'S DARK SIDE!
THAT SHOULD BE EASY.
うおおおお GOOOOOO!
JOLT ビクッ
I HATCHED THAT PLAN FIVE DAYS AGO.
I THOUGHT THE VILLAGE CHIEF WAS FULL OF FLAWS
BUT IT TURNS OUT THAT HE'S JUST A TYPICAL FARMER WHO—NO ...
HE'S ACTUALLY PRETTY DILIGENT.
MORNIN'!
GOOD MORNING!
THE ONLY BAD THING ABOUT HIM IS HIS "NIGHTTIME ACTIVITIES."

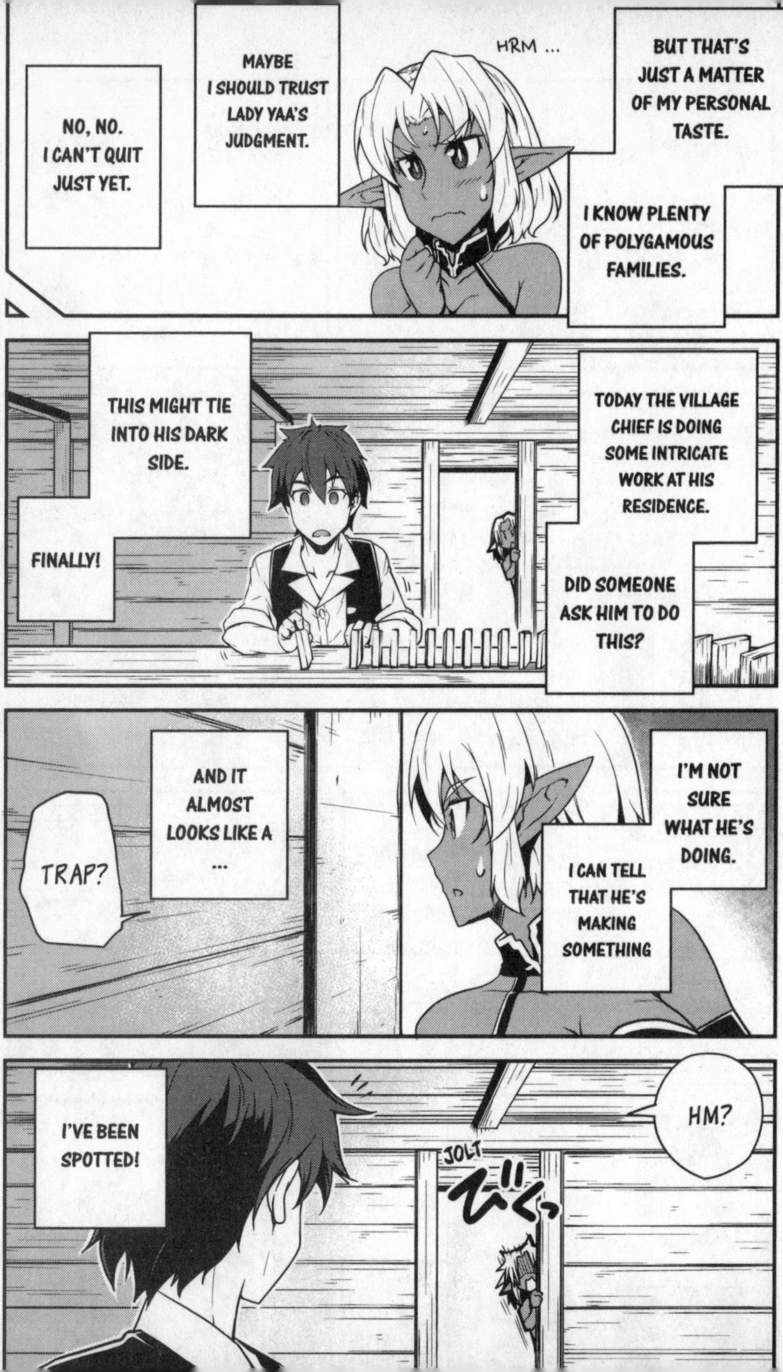
HRM ...
BUT THAT'S JUST A MATTER OF MY PERSONAL TASTE.
I KNOW PLENTY OF POLYGAMOUS FAMILIES.
MAYBE I SHOULD TRUST LADY YAA'S JUDGMENT.
NO, NO. I CAN'T QUIT JUST YET.
TODAY THE VILLAGE CHIEF IS DOING SOME INTRICATE WORK AT HIS RESIDENCE.
DID SOMEONE ASK HIM TO DO THIS?
THIS MIGHT TIE INTO HIS DARK SIDE.
FINALLY!
I'M NOT SURE WHAT HE'S DOING.
I CAN TELL THAT HE'S MAKING SOMETHING
AND IT ALMOST LOOKS LIKE A ...
TRAP?
HM?
JOLT
I'VE BEEN SPOTTED!

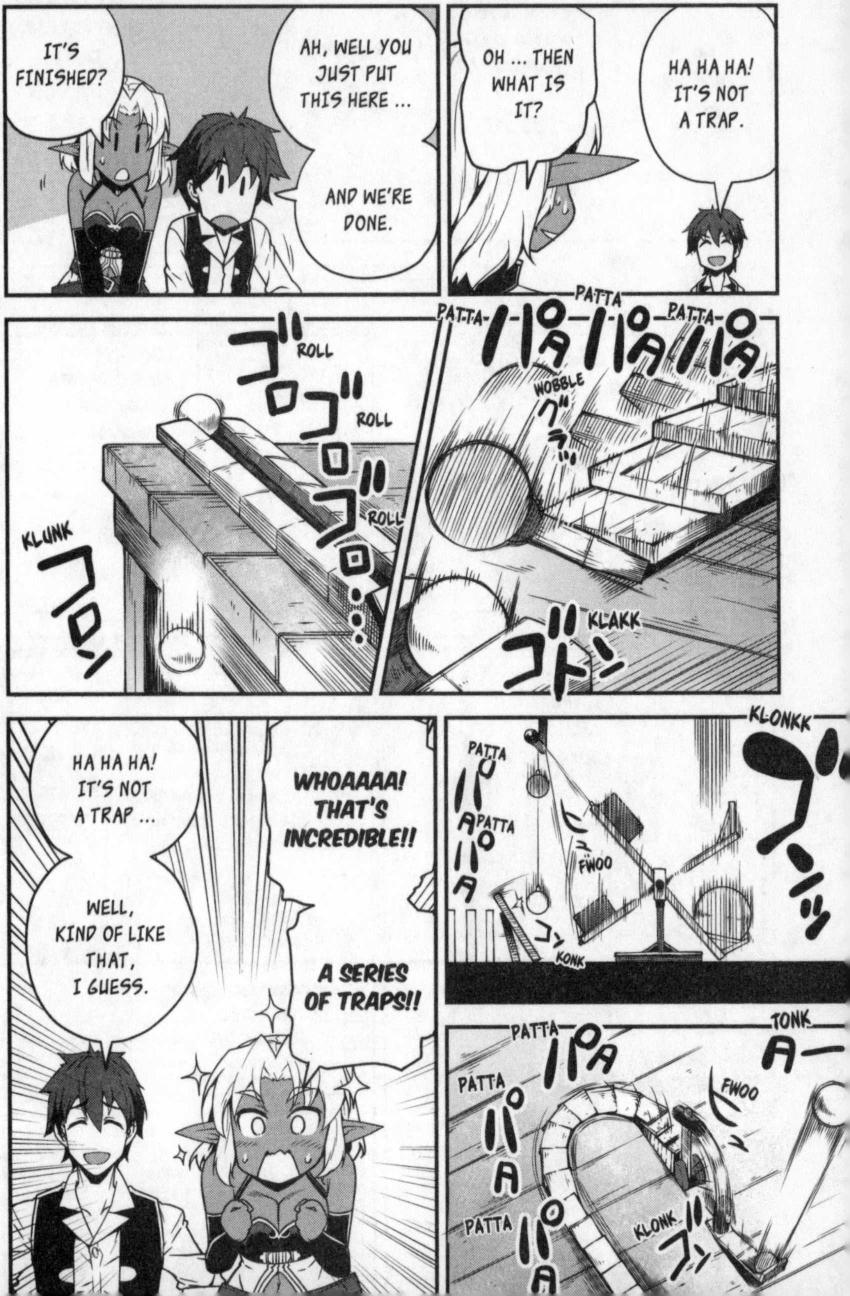
HA HA HA! IT'S NOT A TRAP.
OH ... THEN WHAT IS IT?
AH, WELL YOU JUST PUT THIS HERE ...
AND WE'RE DONE.
IT'S FINISHED?
PATTA
PATTA
PATTA
WOBBLE
KLAKK
ROLL
ROLL
ROLL
KLUNK
KLONKK
PATTA
PATTA
FWOO
KONK
TONK
PATTA
FWOO
PATTA
PATTA
KLONK
WHOAAAA! THAT'S INCREDIBLE!!
A SERIES OF TRAPS!!
HA HA HA! IT'S NOT A TRAP ...
WELL, KIND OF LIKE THAT, I GUESS.

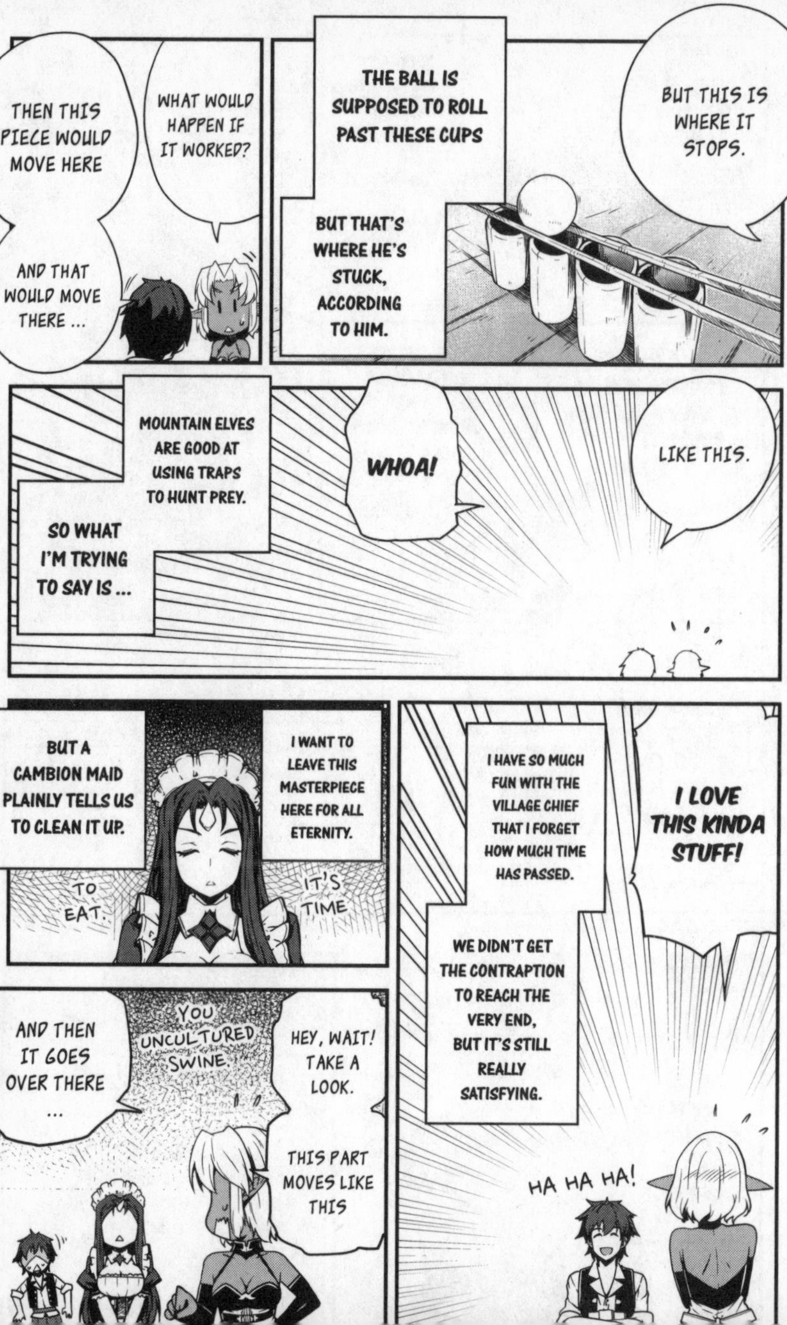
BUT THIS IS WHERE IT STOPS.
THE BALL IS SUPPOSED TO ROLL PAST THESE CUPS
BUT THAT'S WHERE HE'S STUCK, ACCORDING TO HIM.
WHAT WOULD HAPPEN IF IT WORKED?
THEN THIS PIECE WOULD MOVE HERE
AND THAT WOULD MOVE THERE ...
LIKE THIS.
WHOA!
MOUNTAIN ELVES ARE GOOD AT USING TRAPS TO HUNT PREY.
SO WHAT I'M TRYING TO SAY IS ...
I LOVE THIS KINDA STUFF!
I HAVE SO MUCH FUN WITH THE VILLAGE CHIEF THAT I FORGET HOW MUCH TIME HAS PASSED.
WE DIDN'T GET THE CONTRAPTION TO REACH THE VERY END, BUT IT'S STILL REALLY SATISFYING.
HA HA HA!
I WANT TO LEAVE THIS MASTERPIECE HERE FOR ALL ETERNITY.
BUT A CAMBION MAID PLAINLY TELLS US TO CLEAN IT UP.
IT'S TIME
TO EAT.
HEY, WAIT! TAKE A LOOK.
THIS PART MOVES LIKE THIS
YOU UNCULTURED SWINE.
AND THEN IT GOES OVER THERE ...

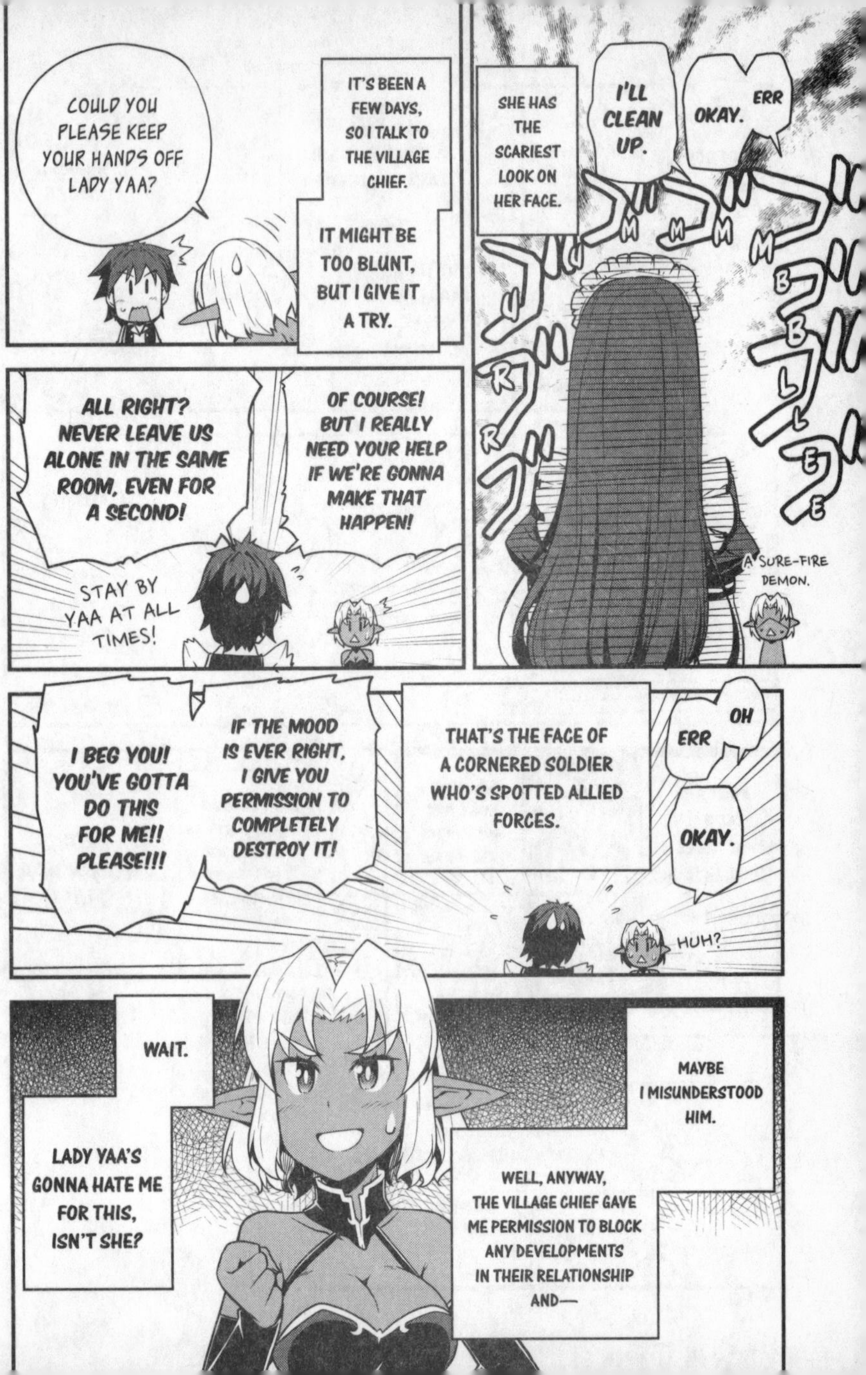
ERR
OKAY.
I'LL CLEAN UP.
SHE HAS THE SCARIEST LOOK ON HER FACE.
RRUUMMMMBBLLEE
A SURE-FIRE DEMON.
IT'S BEEN A FEW DAYS, SO I TALK TO THE VILLAGE CHIEF.
IT MIGHT BE TOO BLUNT, BUT I GIVE IT A TRY.
COULD YOU PLEASE KEEP YOUR HANDS OFF LADY YAA?
OF COURSE! BUT I REALLY NEED YOUR HELP IF WE'RE GONNA MAKE THAT HAPPEN!
ALL RIGHT? NEVER LEAVE US ALONE IN THE SAME ROOM, EVEN FOR A SECOND!
STAY BY YAA AT ALL TIMES!
OH
ERR
OKAY.
THAT'S THE FACE OF A CORNERED SOLDIER WHO'S SPOTTED ALLIED FORCES.
IF THE MOOD IS EVER RIGHT, I GIVE YOU PERMISSION TO COMPLETELY DESTROY IT!
I BEG YOU! YOU'VE GOTTA DO THIS FOR ME!! PLEASE!!!
HUH?
MAYBE I MISUNDERSTOOD HIM.
WELL, ANYWAY, THE VILLAGE CHIEF GAVE ME PERMISSION TO BLOCK ANY DEVELOPMENTS IN THEIR RELATIONSHIP AND—
WAIT.
LADY YAA'S GONNA HATE ME FOR THIS, ISN'T SHE?

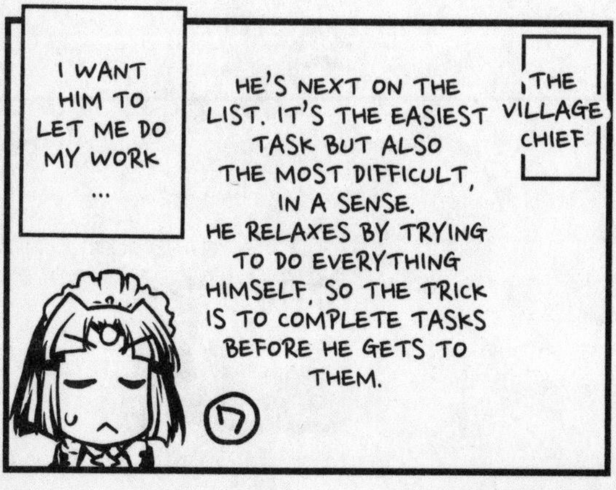
THE VILLAGE CHIEF
HE'S NEXT ON THE LIST. IT'S THE EASIEST TASK BUT ALSO THE MOST DIFFICULT, IN A SENSE. HE RELAXES BY TRYING TO DO EVERYTHING HIMSELF, SO THE TRICK IS TO COMPLETE TASKS BEFORE HE GETS TO THEM.
I WANT HIM TO LET ME DO MY WORK ...
17

うおおおお
GOOOOOO!

JOLT
ビクッ

Farming life in another world.

CHAPTER 66: A DAY IN THE LIFE OF THE VILLAGE CHIEF: MORNING

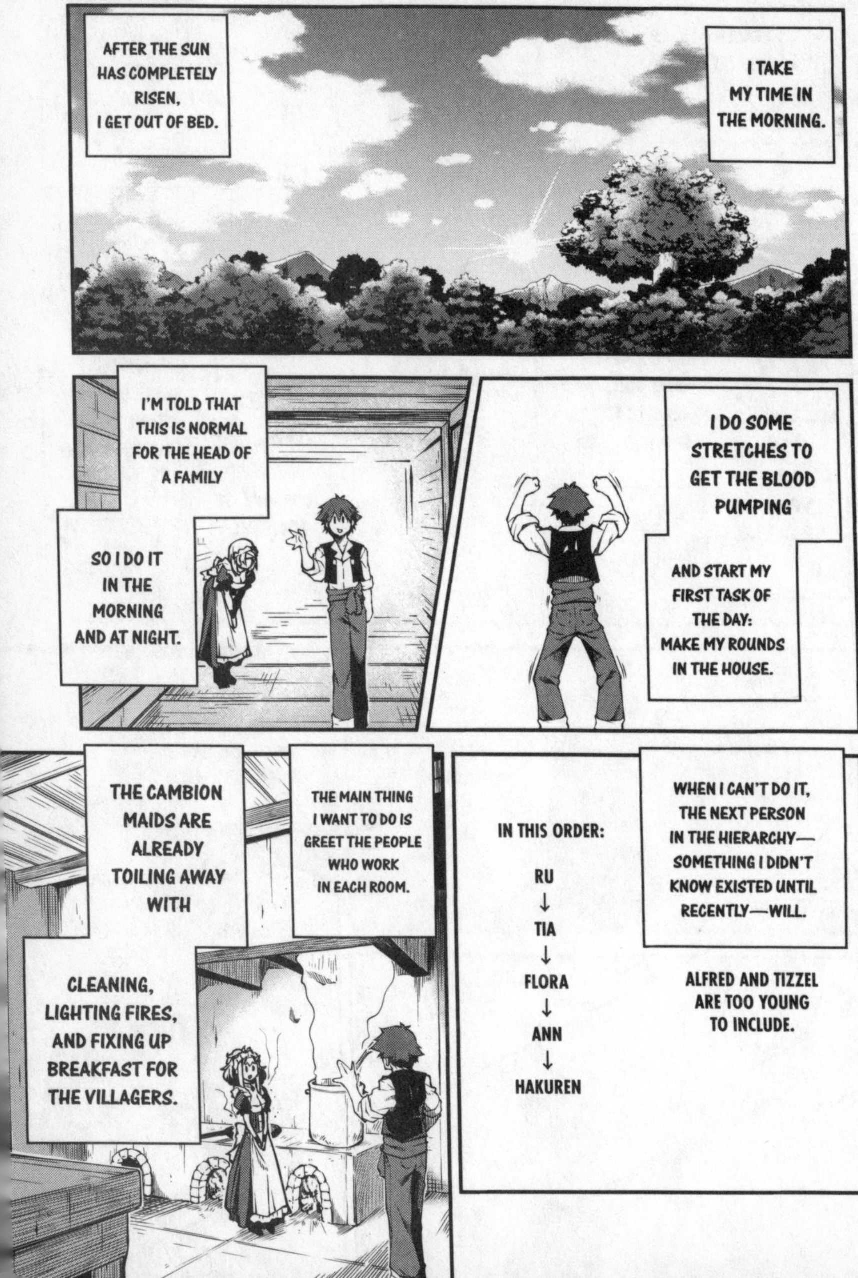
I TAKE MY TIME IN THE MORNING.
AFTER THE SUN HAS COMPLETELY RISEN, I GET OUT OF BED.
I DO SOME STRETCHES TO GET THE BLOOD PUMPING
AND START MY FIRST TASK OF THE DAY: MAKE MY ROUNDS IN THE HOUSE.
I'M TOLD THAT THIS IS NORMAL FOR THE HEAD OF A FAMILY
SO I DO IT IN THE MORNING AND AT NIGHT.
WHEN I CAN'T DO IT, THE NEXT PERSON IN THE HIERARCHY—SOMETHING I DIDN'T KNOW EXISTED UNTIL RECENTLY—WILL.
IN THIS ORDER:
RU ↓ TIA ↓ FLORA ↓ ANN ↓ HAKUREN
ALFRED AND TIZZEL ARE TOO YOUNG TO INCLUDE.
THE MAIN THING I WANT TO DO IS GREET THE PEOPLE WHO WORK IN EACH ROOM.
THE CAMBION MAIDS ARE ALREADY TOILING AWAY WITH
CLEANING, LIGHTING FIRES, AND FIXING UP BREAKFAST FOR THE VILLAGERS.

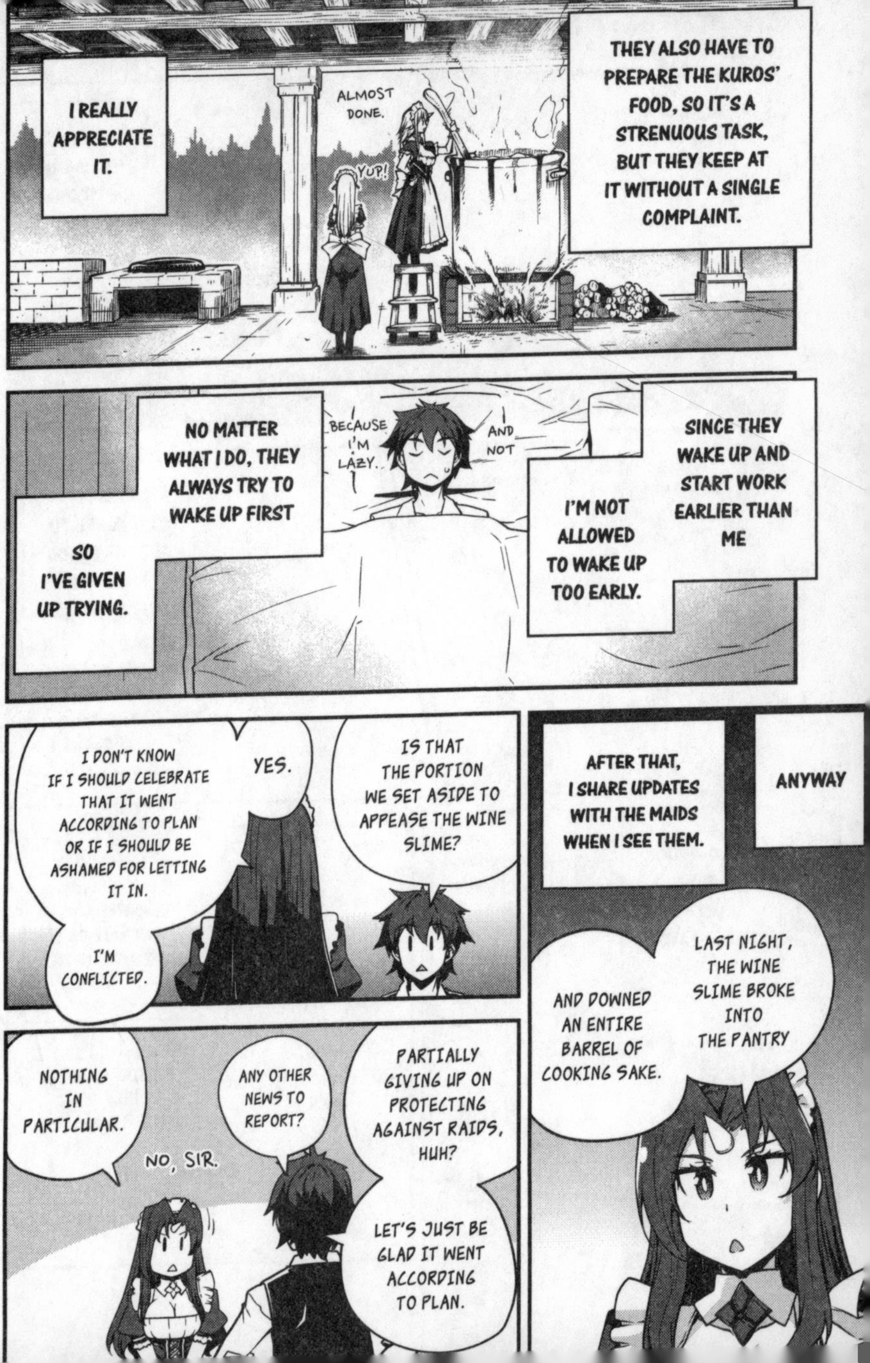
THEY ALSO HAVE TO PREPARE THE KUROS' FOOD, SO IT'S A STRENUOUS TASK, BUT THEY KEEP AT IT WITHOUT A SINGLE COMPLAINT.
ALMOST DONE.
YUP!
I REALLY APPRECIATE IT.
SINCE THEY WAKE UP AND START WORK EARLIER THAN ME
I'M NOT ALLOWED TO WAKE UP TOO EARLY.
AND NOT
BECAUSE I'M LAZY..
NO MATTER WHAT I DO, THEY ALWAYS TRY TO WAKE UP FIRST
SO I'VE GIVEN UP TRYING.
ANYWAY
AFTER THAT, I SHARE UPDATES WITH THE MAIDS WHEN I SEE THEM.
LAST NIGHT, THE WINE SLIME BROKE INTO THE PANTRY
AND DOWNED AN ENTIRE BARREL OF COOKING SAKE.
IS THAT THE PORTION WE SET ASIDE TO APPEASE THE WINE SLIME?
YES.
I DON'T KNOW IF I SHOULD CELEBRATE THAT IT WENT ACCORDING TO PLAN OR IF I SHOULD BE ASHAMED FOR LETTING IT IN.
I'M CONFLICTED.
PARTIALLY GIVING UP ON PROTECTING AGAINST RAIDS, HUH?
LET'S JUST BE GLAD IT WENT ACCORDING TO PLAN.
ANY OTHER NEWS TO REPORT?
NOTHING IN PARTICULAR.
NO, SIR.

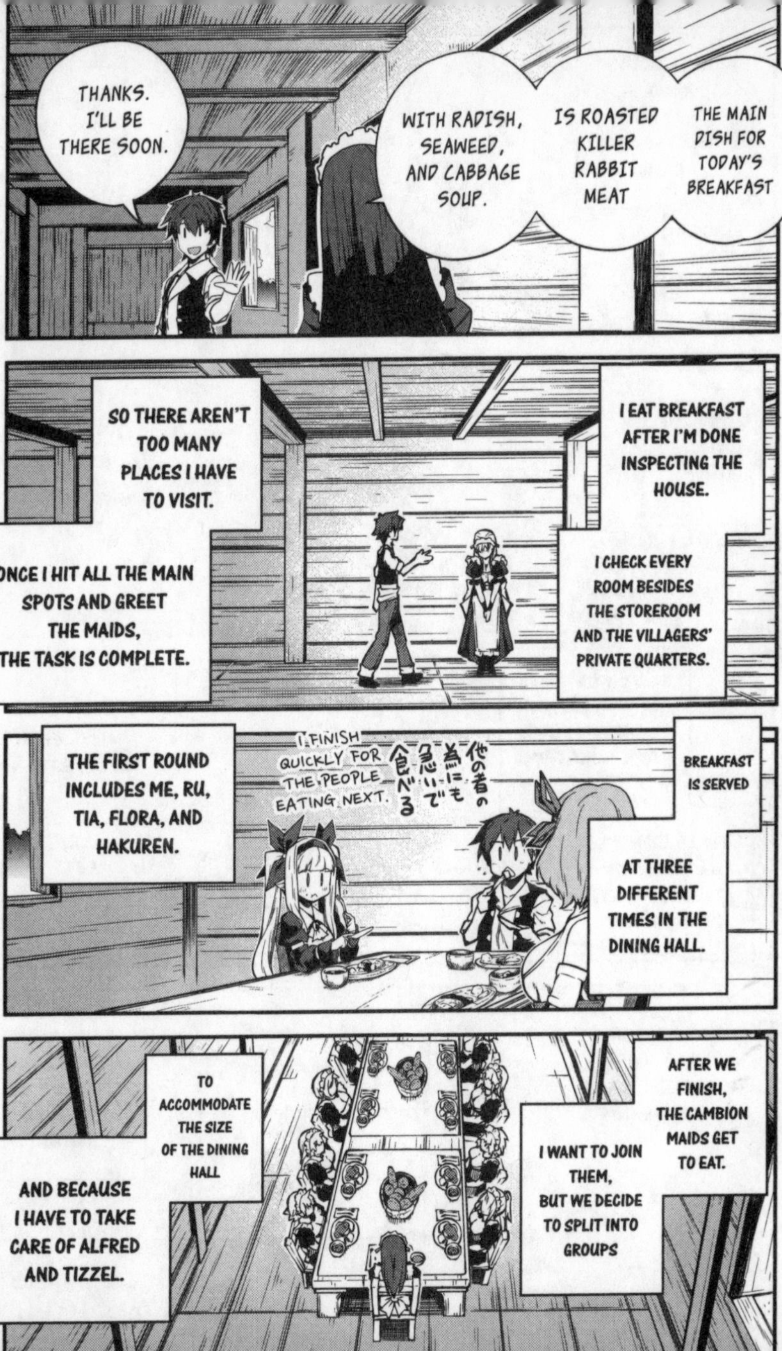
THE MAIN DISH FOR TODAY'S BREAKFAST
IS ROASTED KILLER RABBIT MEAT
WITH RADISH, SEAWEED, AND CABBAGE SOUP.
THANKS. I'LL BE THERE SOON.
I EAT BREAKFAST AFTER I'M DONE INSPECTING THE HOUSE.
I CHECK EVERY ROOM BESIDES THE STOREROOM AND THE VILLAGERS' PRIVATE QUARTERS.
SO THERE AREN'T TOO MANY PLACES I HAVE TO VISIT.
ONCE I HIT ALL THE MAIN SPOTS AND GREET THE MAIDS, THE TASK IS COMPLETE.
BREAKFAST IS SERVED
AT THREE DIFFERENT TIMES IN THE DINING HALL.
他の者の為にも急いで食べる
I FINISH QUICKLY FOR THE PEOPLE EATING NEXT.
THE FIRST ROUND INCLUDES ME, RU, TIA, FLORA, AND HAKUREN.
AFTER WE FINISH, THE CAMBION MAIDS GET TO EAT.
I WANT TO JOIN THEM, BUT WE DECIDE TO SPLIT INTO GROUPS
TO ACCOMMODATE THE SIZE OF THE DINING HALL
AND BECAUSE I HAVE TO TAKE CARE OF ALFRED AND TIZZEL.

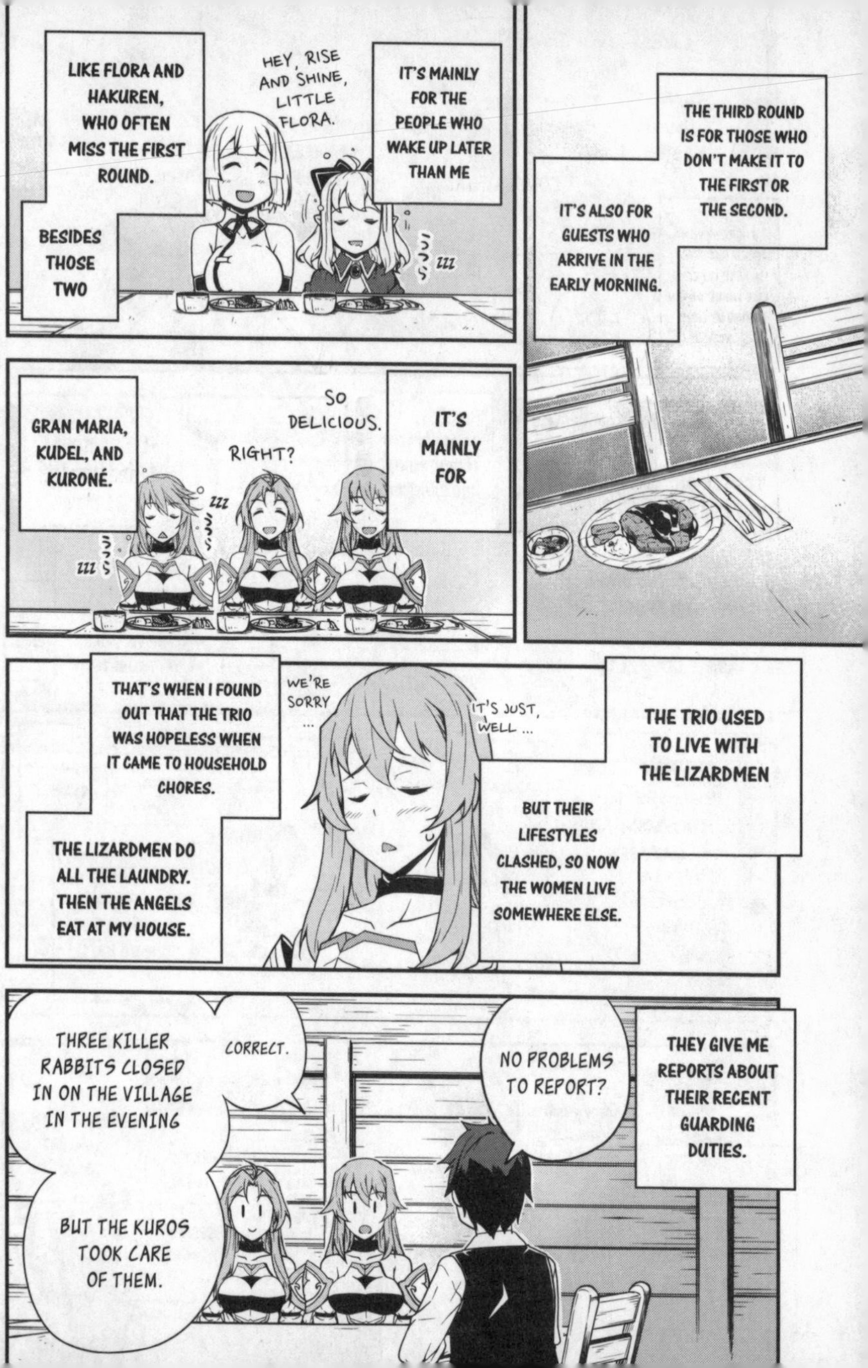
THE THIRD ROUND IS FOR THOSE WHO DON'T MAKE IT TO THE FIRST OR THE SECOND.
IT'S ALSO FOR GUESTS WHO ARRIVE IN THE EARLY MORNING.
IT'S MAINLY FOR THE PEOPLE WHO WAKE UP LATER THAN ME
HEY, RISE AND SHINE, LITTLE FLORA.
LIKE FLORA AND HAKUREN, WHO OFTEN MISS THE FIRST ROUND.
ZZZ
BESIDES THOSE TWO
IT'S MAINLY FOR
SO DELICIOUS.
RIGHT?
ZZZ
GRAN MARIA, KUDEL, AND KURONÉ.
ZZZ
THE TRIO USED TO LIVE WITH THE LIZARDMEN
IT'S JUST, WELL ...
WE'RE SORRY ...
THAT'S WHEN I FOUND OUT THAT THE TRIO WAS HOPELESS WHEN IT CAME TO HOUSEHOLD CHORES.
BUT THEIR LIFESTYLES CLASHED, SO NOW THE WOMEN LIVE SOMEWHERE ELSE.
THE LIZARDMEN DO ALL THE LAUNDRY. THEN THE ANGELS EAT AT MY HOUSE.
THEY GIVE ME REPORTS ABOUT THEIR RECENT GUARDING DUTIES.
NO PROBLEMS TO REPORT?
CORRECT.
THREE KILLER RABBITS CLOSED IN ON THE VILLAGE IN THE EVENING
BUT THE KUROS TOOK CARE OF THEM.

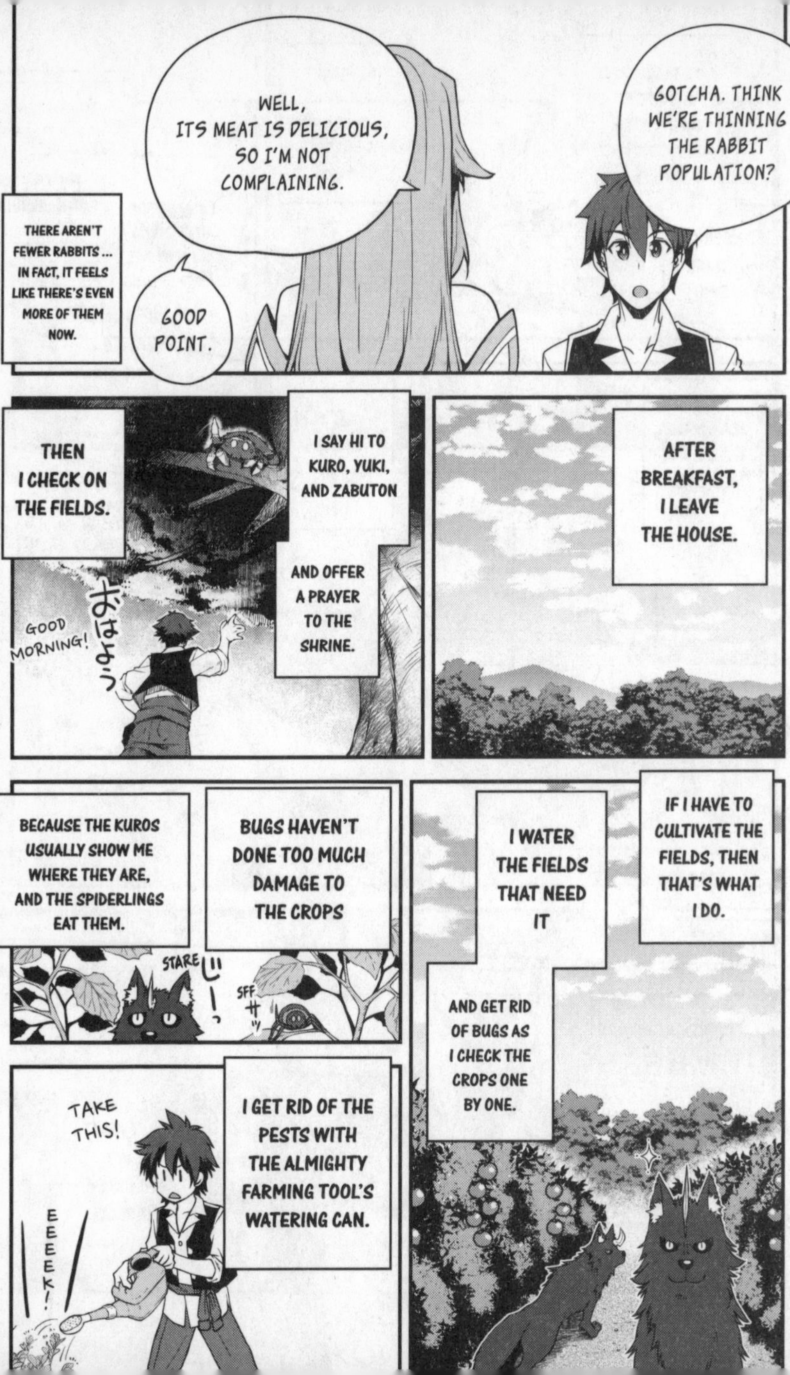
GOTCHA. THINK WE'RE THINNING THE RABBIT POPULATION?
WELL, ITS MEAT IS DELICIOUS, SO I'M NOT COMPLAINING.
GOOD POINT.
THERE AREN'T FEWER RABBITS ... IN FACT, IT FEELS LIKE THERE'S EVEN MORE OF THEM NOW.
AFTER BREAKFAST, I LEAVE THE HOUSE.
I SAY HI TO KURO, YUKI, AND ZABUTON
AND OFFER A PRAYER TO THE SHRINE.
GOOD MORNING!
THEN I CHECK ON THE FIELDS.
IF I HAVE TO CULTIVATE THE FIELDS, THEN THAT'S WHAT I DO.
I WATER THE FIELDS THAT NEED IT
AND GET RID OF BUGS AS I CHECK THE CROPS ONE BY ONE.
BUGS HAVEN'T DONE TOO MUCH DAMAGE TO THE CROPS
BECAUSE THE KUROS USUALLY SHOW ME WHERE THEY ARE, AND THE SPIDERLINGS EAT THEM.
STARE
SFF
I GET RID OF THE PESTS WITH THE ALMIGHTY FARMING TOOL'S WATERING CAN.
TAKE THIS!
EEEEK!

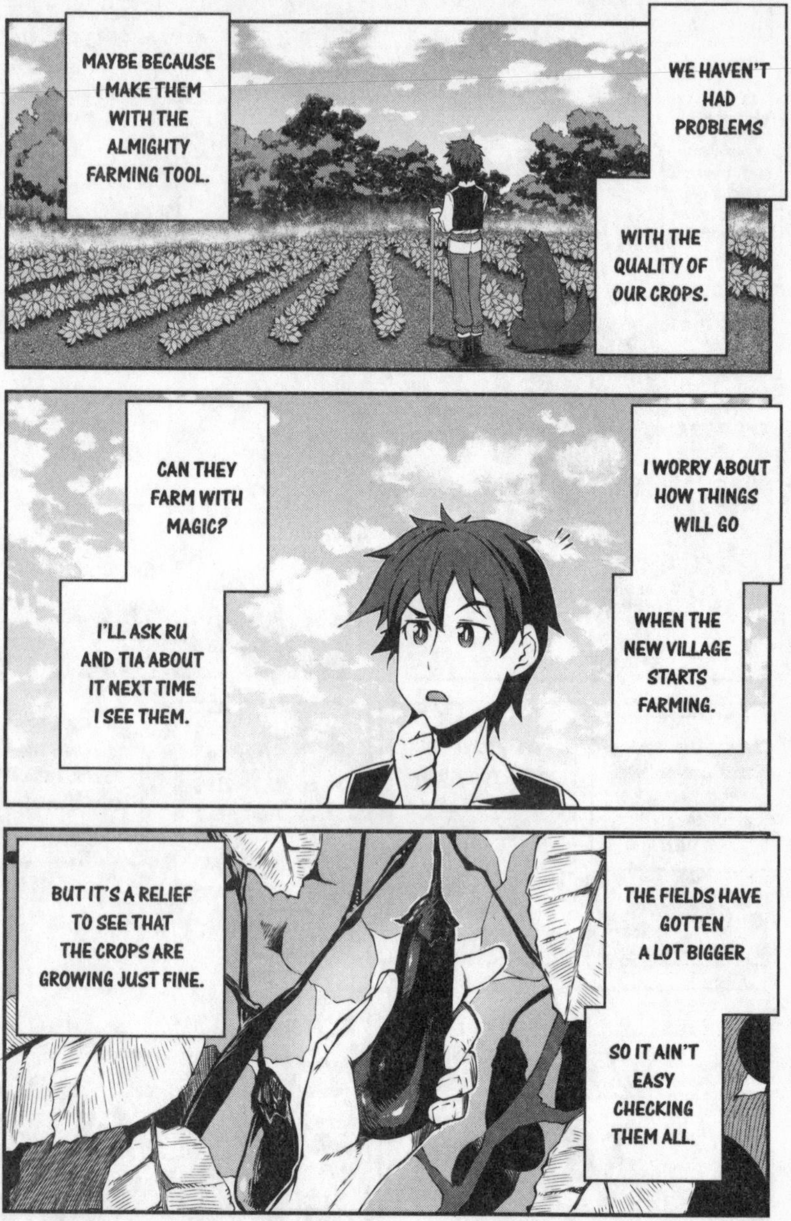
WE HAVEN'T HAD PROBLEMS
WITH THE QUALITY OF OUR CROPS.
MAYBE BECAUSE I MAKE THEM WITH THE ALMIGHTY FARMING TOOL.
I WORRY ABOUT HOW THINGS WILL GO
WHEN THE NEW VILLAGE STARTS FARMING.
CAN THEY FARM WITH MAGIC?
I'LL ASK RU AND TIA ABOUT IT NEXT TIME I SEE THEM.
THE FIELDS HAVE GOTTEN A LOT BIGGER
SO IT AIN'T EASY CHECKING THEM ALL.
BUT IT'S A RELIEF TO SEE THAT THE CROPS ARE GROWING JUST FINE.

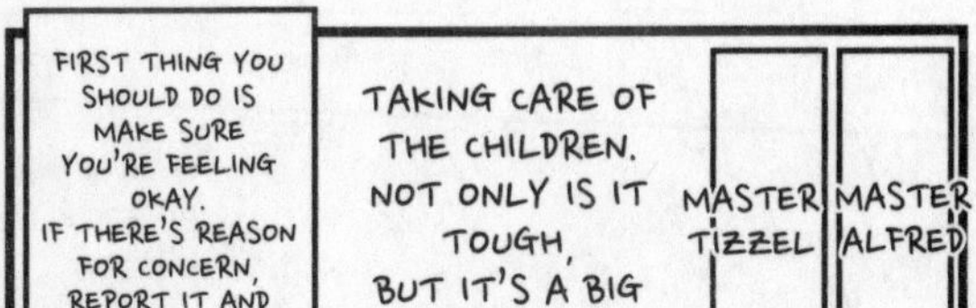

MASTER ALFRED
MASTER TIZZEL
TAKING CARE OF THE CHILDREN. NOT ONLY IS IT TOUGH, BUT IT'S A BIG RESPONSIBILITY. EVEN SO, IT'S A PRETTY POPULAR JOB SINCE THERE'S A CHANCE THAT ONE OF THE TOTS WILL REMEMBER OUR NAMES.
FIRST THING YOU SHOULD DO IS MAKE SURE YOU'RE FEELING OKAY. IF THERE'S REASON FOR CONCERN, REPORT IT AND HAVE SOMEONE REPLACE YOU.
8

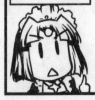

Farming life in another world.

CHAPTER 67: A DAY IN THE LIFE OF THE VILLAGE CHIEF: NOONTIME TO NIGHTTIME

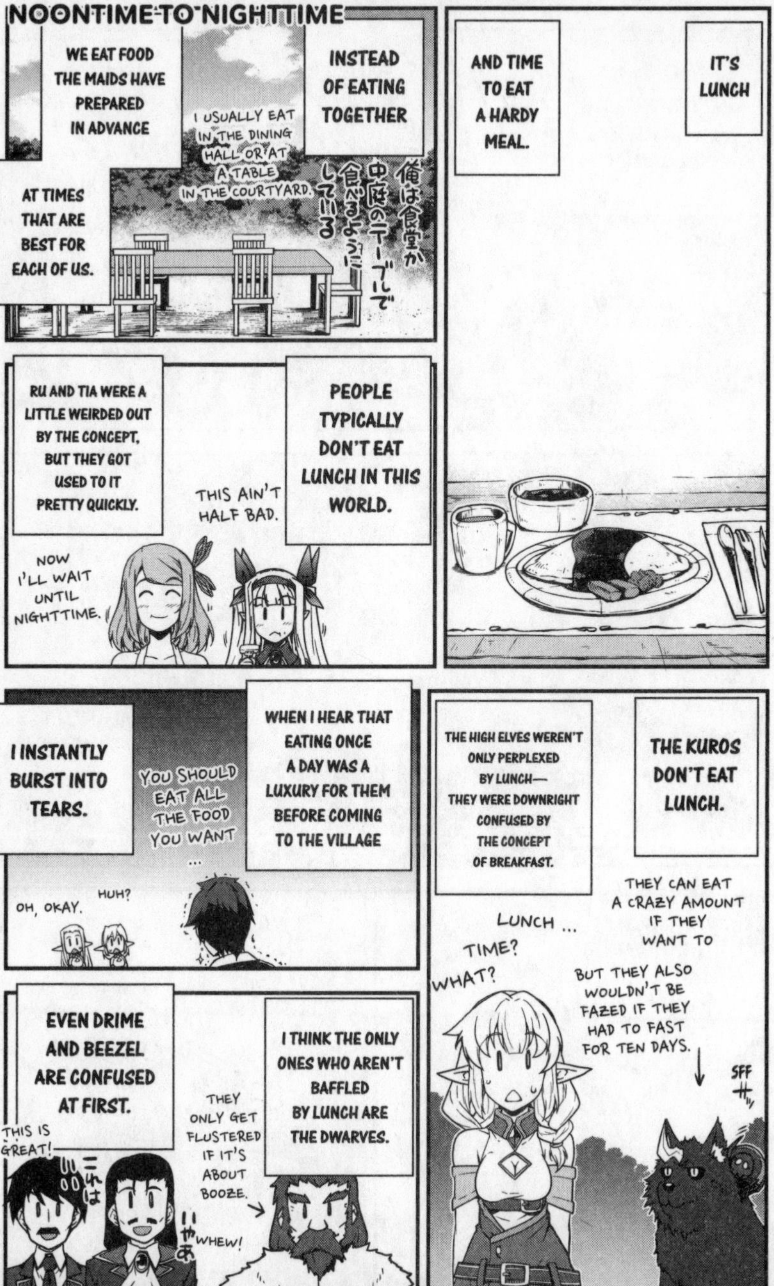
IT'S LUNCH
AND TIME TO EAT A HARDY MEAL.
INSTEAD OF EATING TOGETHER
WE EAT FOOD THE MAIDS HAVE PREPARED IN ADVANCE
AT TIMES THAT ARE BEST FOR EACH OF US.
俺は食堂か中庭のテーブルで食べるようにしている
I USUALLY EAT IN THE DINING HALL OR AT A TABLE IN THE COURTYARD.
PEOPLE TYPICALLY DON'T EAT LUNCH IN THIS WORLD.
RU AND TIA WERE A LITTLE WEIRDED OUT BY THE CONCEPT, BUT THEY GOT USED TO IT PRETTY QUICKLY.
THIS AIN'T HALF BAD.
NOW I'LL WAIT UNTIL NIGHTTIME.
THE KUROS DON'T EAT LUNCH.
THE HIGH ELVES WEREN'T ONLY PERPLEXED BY LUNCH— THEY WERE DOWNRIGHT CONFUSED BY THE CONCEPT OF BREAKFAST.
THEY CAN EAT A CRAZY AMOUNT IF THEY WANT TO
LUNCH ... TIME?
WHAT?
BUT THEY ALSO WOULDN'T BE FAZED IF THEY HAD TO FAST FOR TEN DAYS.
SFF
WHEN I HEAR THAT EATING ONCE A DAY WAS A LUXURY FOR THEM BEFORE COMING TO THE VILLAGE
I INSTANTLY BURST INTO TEARS.
YOU SHOULD EAT ALL THE FOOD YOU WANT ...
HUH?
OH, OKAY.
I THINK THE ONLY ONES WHO AREN'T BAFFLED BY LUNCH ARE THE DWARVES.
THEY ONLY GET FLUSTERED IF IT'S ABOUT BOOZE.
いやあ
WHEW!
EVEN DRIME AND BEEZEL ARE CONFUSED AT FIRST.
これは
THIS IS GREAT!

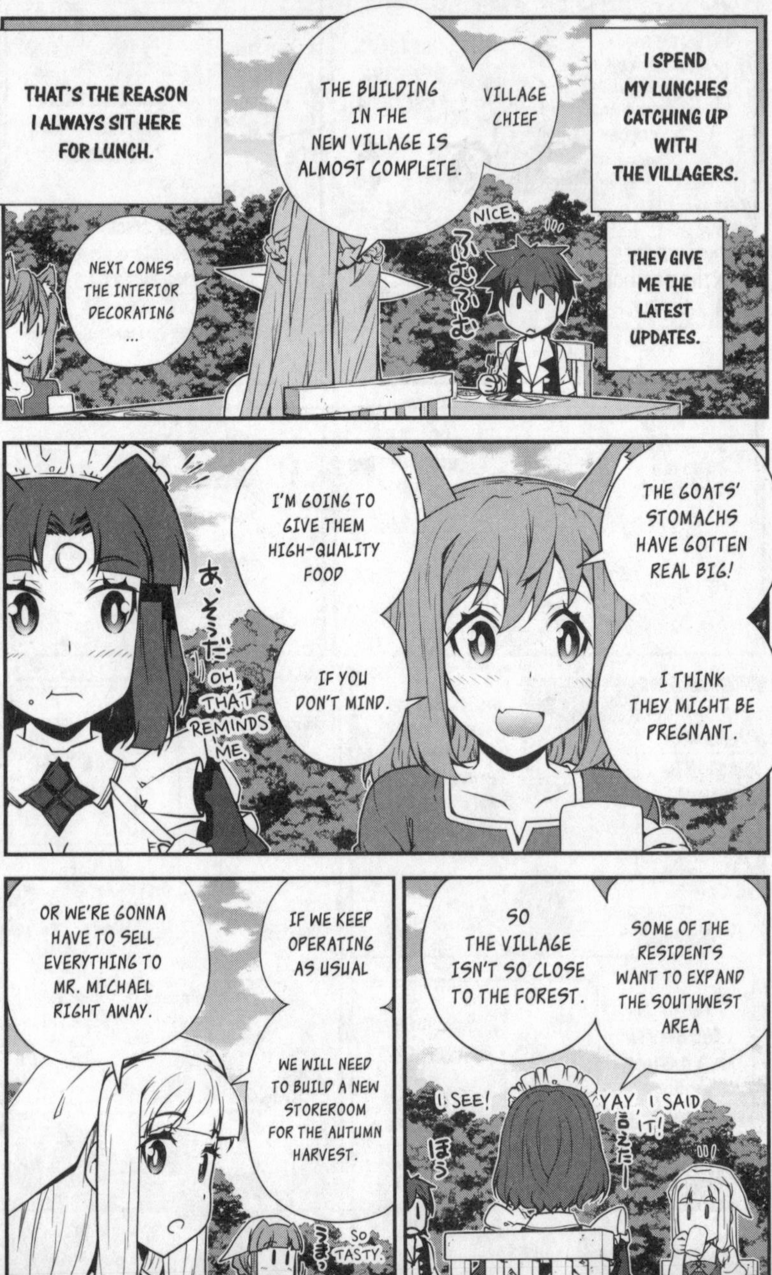
I SPEND MY LUNCHES CATCHING UP WITH THE VILLAGERS.
THEY GIVE ME THE LATEST UPDATES.
VILLAGE CHIEF
THE BUILDING IN THE NEW VILLAGE IS ALMOST COMPLETE.
NICE.
ふむふむ
NEXT COMES THE INTERIOR DECORATING ...
THAT'S THE REASON I ALWAYS SIT HERE FOR LUNCH.
THE GOATS' STOMACHS HAVE GOTTEN REAL BIG!
I THINK THEY MIGHT BE PREGNANT.
I'M GOING TO GIVE THEM HIGH-QUALITY FOOD
IF YOU DON'T MIND.
あ、そうだ
OH, THAT REMINDS ME.
SOME OF THE RESIDENTS WANT TO EXPAND THE SOUTHWEST AREA
SO THE VILLAGE ISN'T SO CLOSE TO THE FOREST.
YAY, I SAID IT!
言えたー
I SEE!
ほう
IF WE KEEP OPERATING AS USUAL
WE WILL NEED TO BUILD A NEW STOREROOM FOR THE AUTUMN HARVEST.
OR WE'RE GONNA HAVE TO SELL EVERYTHING TO MR. MICHAEL RIGHT AWAY.
うまっ
SO TASTY.

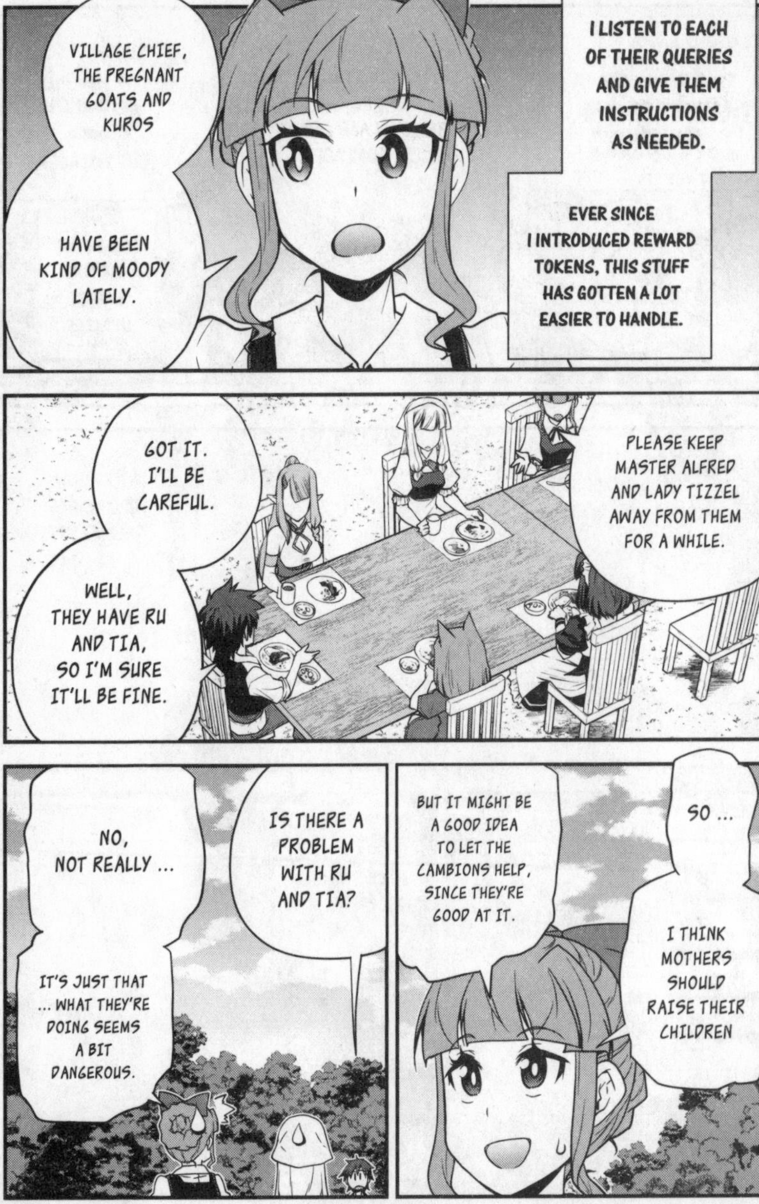
I LISTEN TO EACH OF THEIR QUERIES AND GIVE THEM INSTRUCTIONS AS NEEDED.
EVER SINCE I INTRODUCED REWARD TOKENS, THIS STUFF HAS GOTTEN A LOT EASIER TO HANDLE.
VILLAGE CHIEF, THE PREGNANT GOATS AND KUROS
HAVE BEEN KIND OF MOODY LATELY.
PLEASE KEEP MASTER ALFRED AND LADY TIZZEL AWAY FROM THEM FOR A WHILE.
GOT IT. I'LL BE CAREFUL.
WELL, THEY HAVE RU AND TIA, SO I'M SURE IT'LL BE FINE.
SO ...
I THINK MOTHERS SHOULD RAISE THEIR CHILDREN
BUT IT MIGHT BE A GOOD IDEA TO LET THE CAMBIONS HELP, SINCE THEY'RE GOOD AT IT.
IS THERE A PROBLEM WITH RU AND TIA?
NO, NOT REALLY ...
IT'S JUST THAT ... WHAT THEY'RE DOING SEEMS A BIT DANGEROUS.

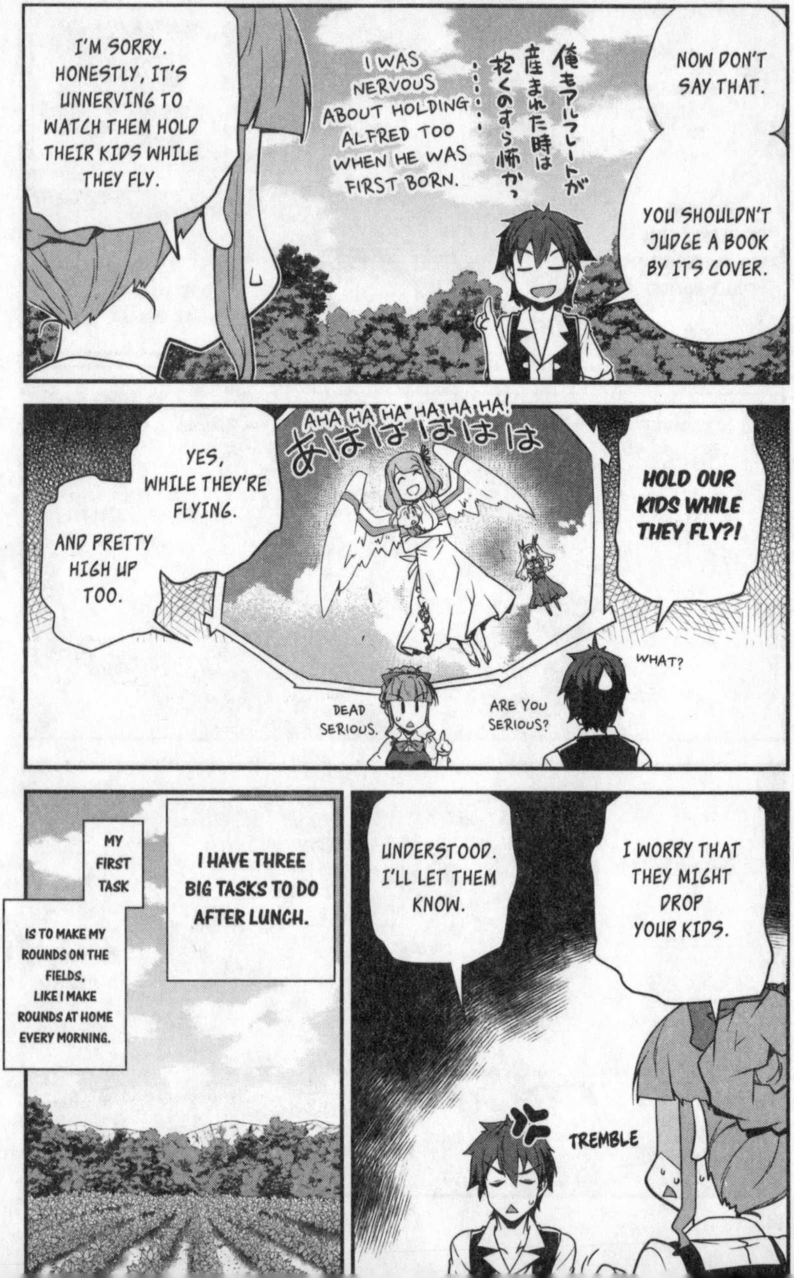
NOW DON'T SAY THAT.
YOU SHOULDN'T JUDGE A BOOK BY ITS COVER.
俺もアルフレートが産まれた時は抱くのすら怖かっ・・・・・
I WAS NERVOUS ABOUT HOLDING ALFRED TOO WHEN HE WAS FIRST BORN.
I'M SORRY. HONESTLY, IT'S UNNERVING TO WATCH THEM HOLD THEIR KIDS WHILE THEY FLY.
HOLD OUR KIDS WHILE THEY FLY?!
AHA HA HA HA HA HA!
あははははは
YES, WHILE THEY'RE FLYING.
AND PRETTY HIGH UP TOO.
WHAT?
ARE YOU SERIOUS?
DEAD SERIOUS.
I WORRY THAT THEY MIGHT DROP YOUR KIDS.
UNDERSTOOD. I'LL LET THEM KNOW.
TREMBLE
I HAVE THREE BIG TASKS TO DO AFTER LUNCH.
MY FIRST TASK
IS TO MAKE MY ROUNDS ON THE FIELDS, LIKE I MAKE ROUNDS AT HOME EVERY MORNING.

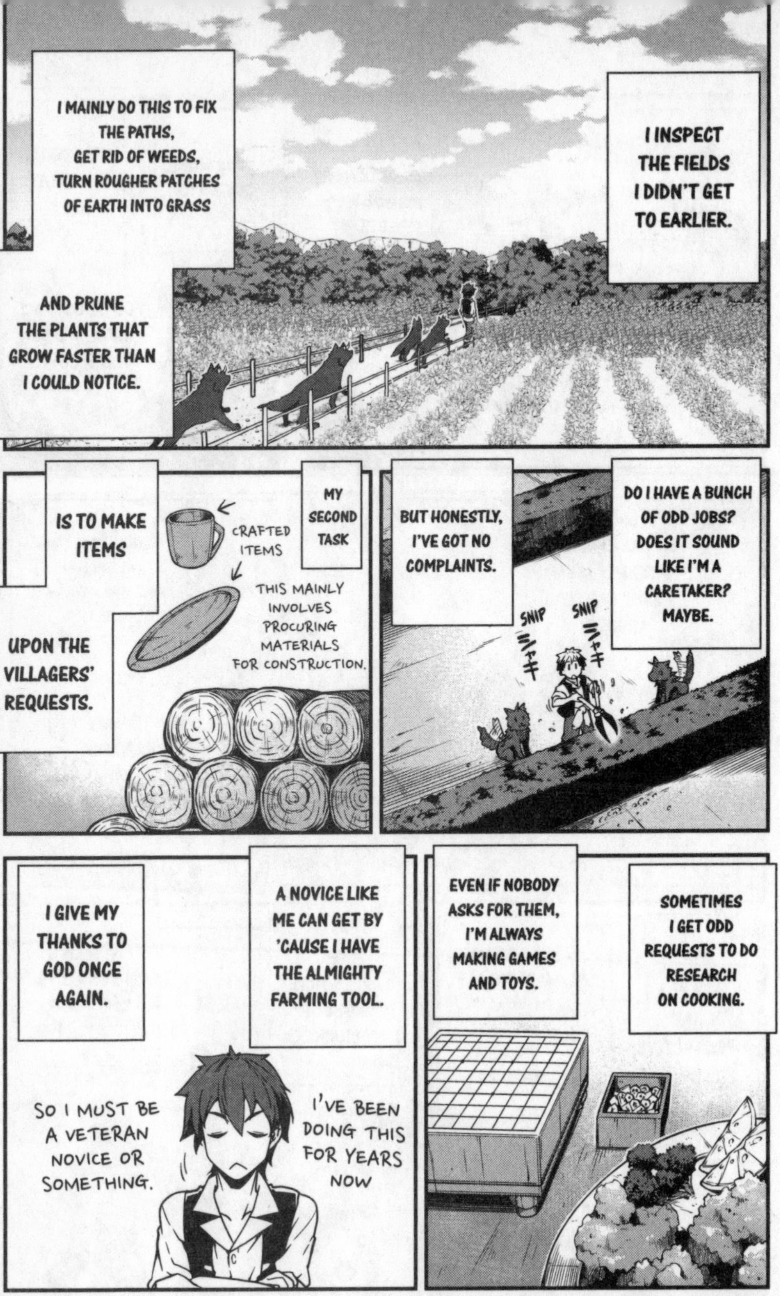
I INSPECT THE FIELDS I DIDN'T GET TO EARLIER.
I MAINLY DO THIS TO FIX THE PATHS, GET RID OF WEEDS, TURN ROUGHER PATCHES OF EARTH INTO GRASS
AND PRUNE THE PLANTS THAT GROW FASTER THAN I COULD NOTICE.
DO I HAVE A BUNCH OF ODD JOBS? DOES IT SOUND LIKE I'M A CARETAKER? MAYBE.
BUT HONESTLY, I'VE GOT NO COMPLAINTS.
SNIP シャキ
SNIP シャキ
MY SECOND TASK
IS TO MAKE ITEMS
CRAFTED ITEMS
THIS MAINLY INVOLVES PROCURING MATERIALS FOR CONSTRUCTION.
UPON THE VILLAGERS' REQUESTS.
SOMETIMES I GET ODD REQUESTS TO DO RESEARCH ON COOKING.
EVEN IF NOBODY ASKS FOR THEM, I'M ALWAYS MAKING GAMES AND TOYS.
A NOVICE LIKE ME CAN GET BY 'CAUSE I HAVE THE ALMIGHTY FARMING TOOL.
I GIVE MY THANKS TO GOD ONCE AGAIN.
I'VE BEEN DOING THIS FOR YEARS NOW
SO I MUST BE A VETERAN NOVICE OR SOMETHING.

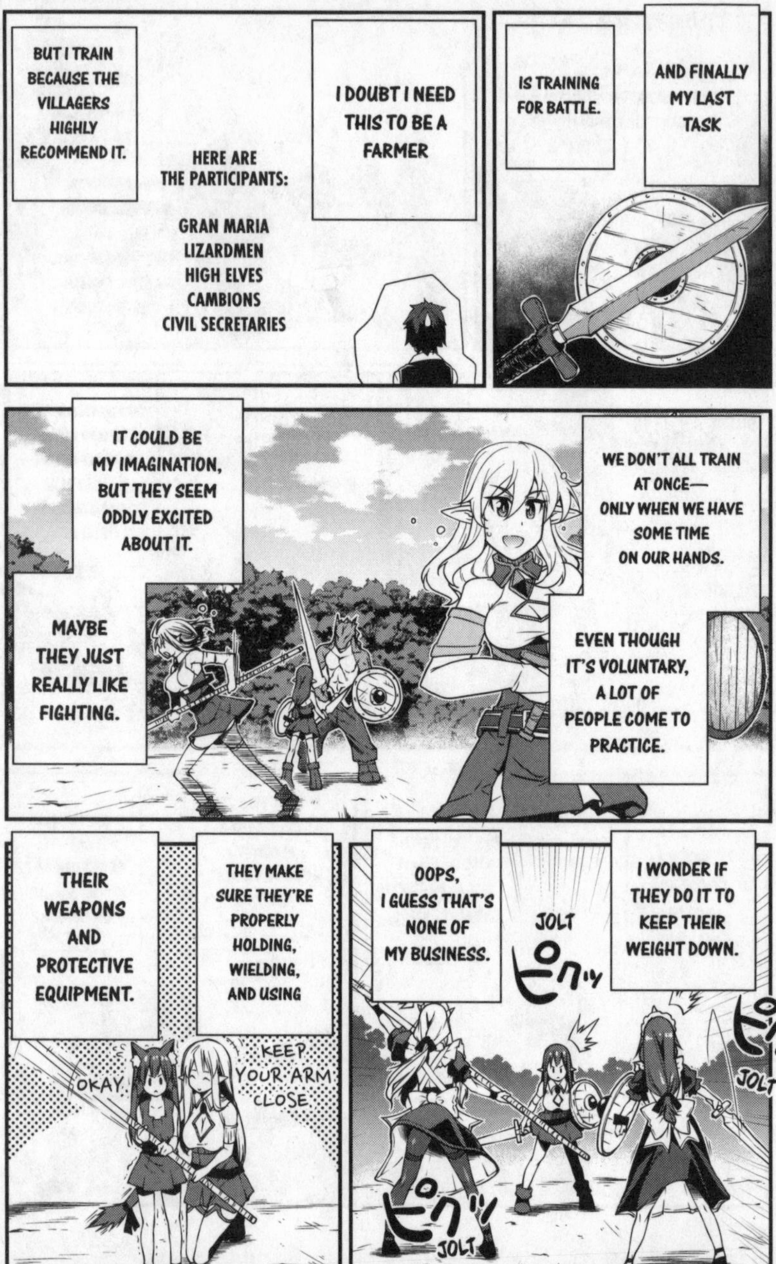
AND FINALLY MY LAST TASK
IS TRAINING FOR BATTLE.
I DOUBT I NEED THIS TO BE A FARMER
BUT I TRAIN BECAUSE THE VILLAGERS HIGHLY RECOMMEND IT.
HERE ARE THE PARTICIPANTS:
GRAN MARIA
LIZARDMEN
HIGH ELVES
CAMBIONS
CIVIL SECRETARIES
WE DON'T ALL TRAIN AT ONCE— ONLY WHEN WE HAVE SOME TIME ON OUR HANDS.
EVEN THOUGH IT'S VOLUNTARY, A LOT OF PEOPLE COME TO PRACTICE.
IT COULD BE MY IMAGINATION, BUT THEY SEEM ODDLY EXCITED ABOUT IT.
MAYBE THEY JUST REALLY LIKE FIGHTING.
I WONDER IF THEY DO IT TO KEEP THEIR WEIGHT DOWN.
OOPS, I GUESS THAT'S NONE OF MY BUSINESS.
JOLT
JOLT
JOLT
THEY MAKE SURE THEY'RE PROPERLY HOLDING, WIELDING, AND USING
THEIR WEAPONS AND PROTECTIVE EQUIPMENT.
KEEP YOUR ARM CLOSE
OKAY.

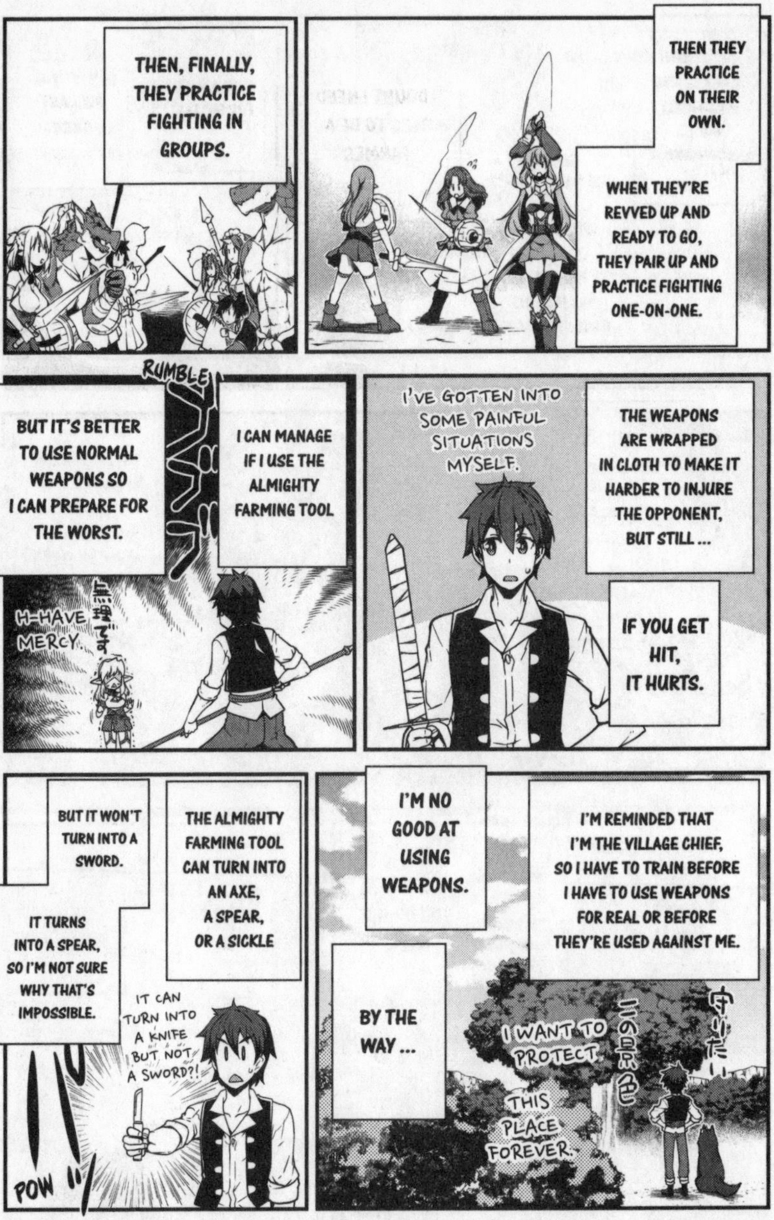
THEN THEY PRACTICE ON THEIR OWN.
WHEN THEY'RE REVVED UP AND READY TO GO, THEY PAIR UP AND PRACTICE FIGHTING ONE-ON-ONE.
THEN, FINALLY, THEY PRACTICE FIGHTING IN GROUPS.
THE WEAPONS ARE WRAPPED IN CLOTH TO MAKE IT HARDER TO INJURE THE OPPONENT, BUT STILL ...
IF YOU GET HIT, IT HURTS.
I'VE GOTTEN INTO SOME PAINFUL SITUATIONS MYSELF.
RUMBLE
I CAN MANAGE IF I USE THE ALMIGHTY FARMING TOOL
BUT IT'S BETTER TO USE NORMAL WEAPONS SO I CAN PREPARE FOR THE WORST.
無理です
H-HAVE MERCY.
I'M REMINDED THAT I'M THE VILLAGE CHIEF, SO I HAVE TO TRAIN BEFORE I HAVE TO USE WEAPONS FOR REAL OR BEFORE THEY'RE USED AGAINST ME.
I'M NO GOOD AT USING WEAPONS.
守りたい
この景色
I WANT TO PROTECT THIS PLACE FOREVER.
BY THE WAY ...
THE ALMIGHTY FARMING TOOL CAN TURN INTO AN AXE, A SPEAR, OR A SICKLE
BUT IT WON'T TURN INTO A SWORD.
IT TURNS INTO A SPEAR, SO I'M NOT SURE WHY THAT'S IMPOSSIBLE.
IT CAN TURN INTO A KNIFE BUT NOT A SWORD?!
POW

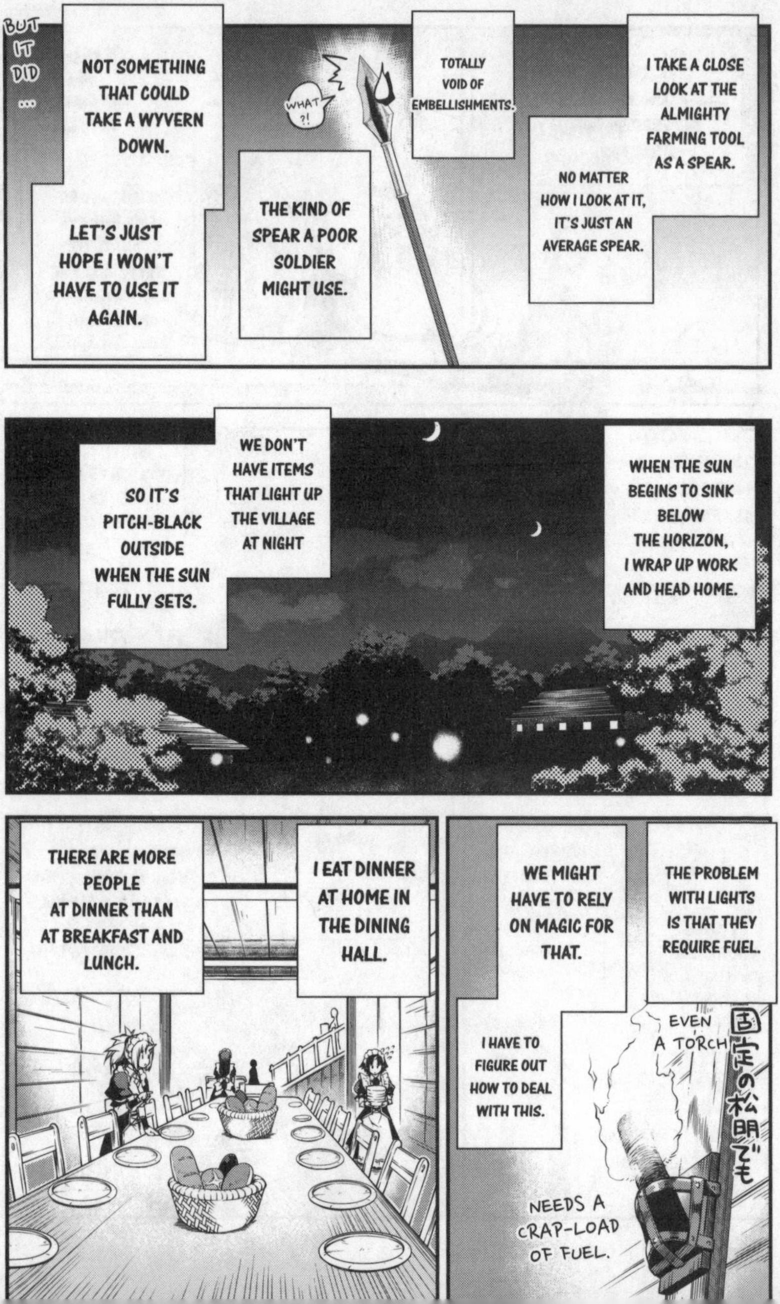
I TAKE A CLOSE LOOK AT THE ALMIGHTY FARMING TOOL AS A SPEAR.
NO MATTER HOW I LOOK AT IT, IT'S JUST AN AVERAGE SPEAR.
TOTALLY VOID OF EMBELLISHMENTS.
WHAT?!
THE KIND OF SPEAR A POOR SOLDIER MIGHT USE.
NOT SOMETHING THAT COULD TAKE A WYVERN DOWN.
LET'S JUST HOPE I WON'T HAVE TO USE IT AGAIN.
BUT IT DID ...
WHEN THE SUN BEGINS TO SINK BELOW THE HORIZON, I WRAP UP WORK AND HEAD HOME.
WE DON'T HAVE ITEMS THAT LIGHT UP THE VILLAGE AT NIGHT
SO IT'S PITCH-BLACK OUTSIDE WHEN THE SUN FULLY SETS.
THE PROBLEM WITH LIGHTS IS THAT THEY REQUIRE FUEL.
WE MIGHT HAVE TO RELY ON MAGIC FOR THAT.
I HAVE TO FIGURE OUT HOW TO DEAL WITH THIS.
固定の松明でも
EVEN A TORCH
NEEDS A CRAP-LOAD OF FUEL.
I EAT DINNER AT HOME IN THE DINING HALL.
THERE ARE MORE PEOPLE AT DINNER THAN AT BREAKFAST AND LUNCH.

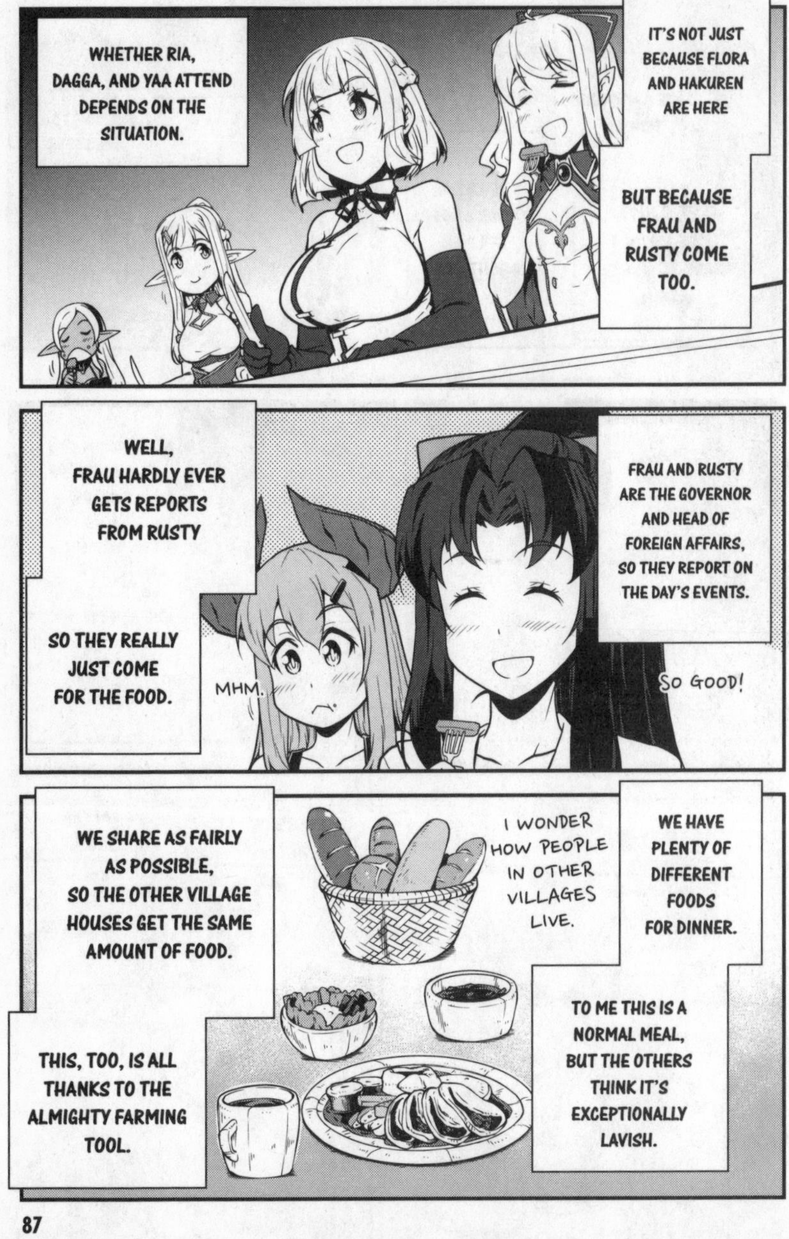
IT'S NOT JUST BECAUSE FLORA AND HAKUREN ARE HERE
BUT BECAUSE FRAU AND RUSTY COME TOO.
WHETHER RIA, DAGGA, AND YAA ATTEND DEPENDS ON THE SITUATION.
FRAU AND RUSTY ARE THE GOVERNOR AND HEAD OF FOREIGN AFFAIRS, SO THEY REPORT ON THE DAY'S EVENTS.
SO GOOD!
WELL, FRAU HARDLY EVER GETS REPORTS FROM RUSTY
MHM.
SO THEY REALLY JUST COME FOR THE FOOD.
WE HAVE PLENTY OF DIFFERENT FOODS FOR DINNER.
I WONDER HOW PEOPLE IN OTHER VILLAGES LIVE.
WE SHARE AS FAIRLY AS POSSIBLE, SO THE OTHER VILLAGE HOUSES GET THE SAME AMOUNT OF FOOD.
TO ME THIS IS A NORMAL MEAL, BUT THE OTHERS THINK IT'S EXCEPTIONALLY LAVISH.
THIS, TOO, IS ALL THANKS TO THE ALMIGHTY FARMING TOOL.

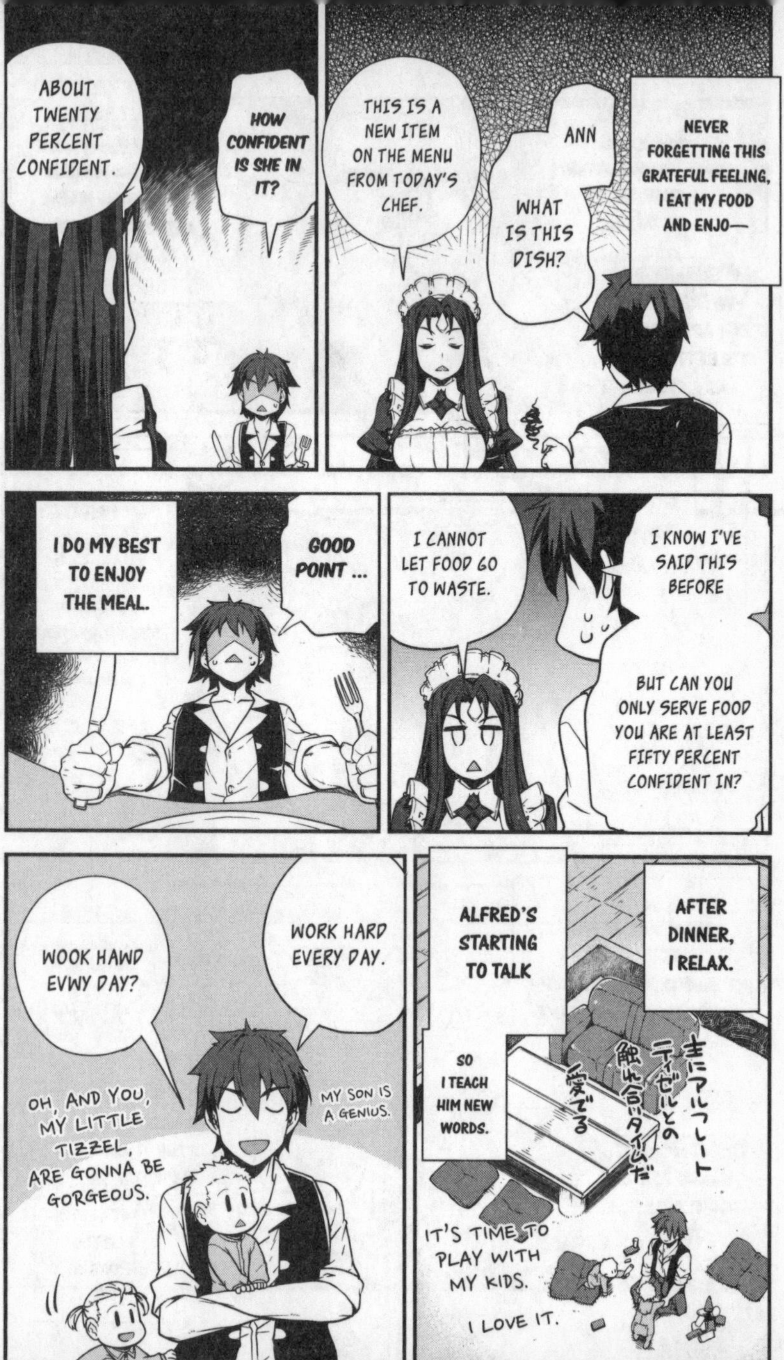
NEVER FORGETTING THIS GRATEFUL FEELING, I EAT MY FOOD AND ENJO—
ANN
WHAT IS THIS DISH?
THIS IS A NEW ITEM ON THE MENU FROM TODAY'S CHEF.
HOW CONFIDENT IS SHE IN IT?
ABOUT TWENTY PERCENT CONFIDENT.
I KNOW I'VE SAID THIS BEFORE
BUT CAN YOU ONLY SERVE FOOD YOU ARE AT LEAST FIFTY PERCENT CONFIDENT IN?
I CANNOT LET FOOD GO TO WASTE.
GOOD POINT ...
I DO MY BEST TO ENJOY THE MEAL.
AFTER DINNER, I RELAX.
主にアルフレートティゼルとの触れ合いタイムだ
愛でる
IT'S TIME TO PLAY WITH MY KIDS.
I LOVE IT.
ALFRED'S STARTING TO TALK
SO I TEACH HIM NEW WORDS.
WORK HARD EVERY DAY.
WOOK HAWD EVWY DAY?
MY SON IS A GENIUS.
OH, AND YOU, MY LITTLE TIZZEL, ARE GONNA BE GORGEOUS.

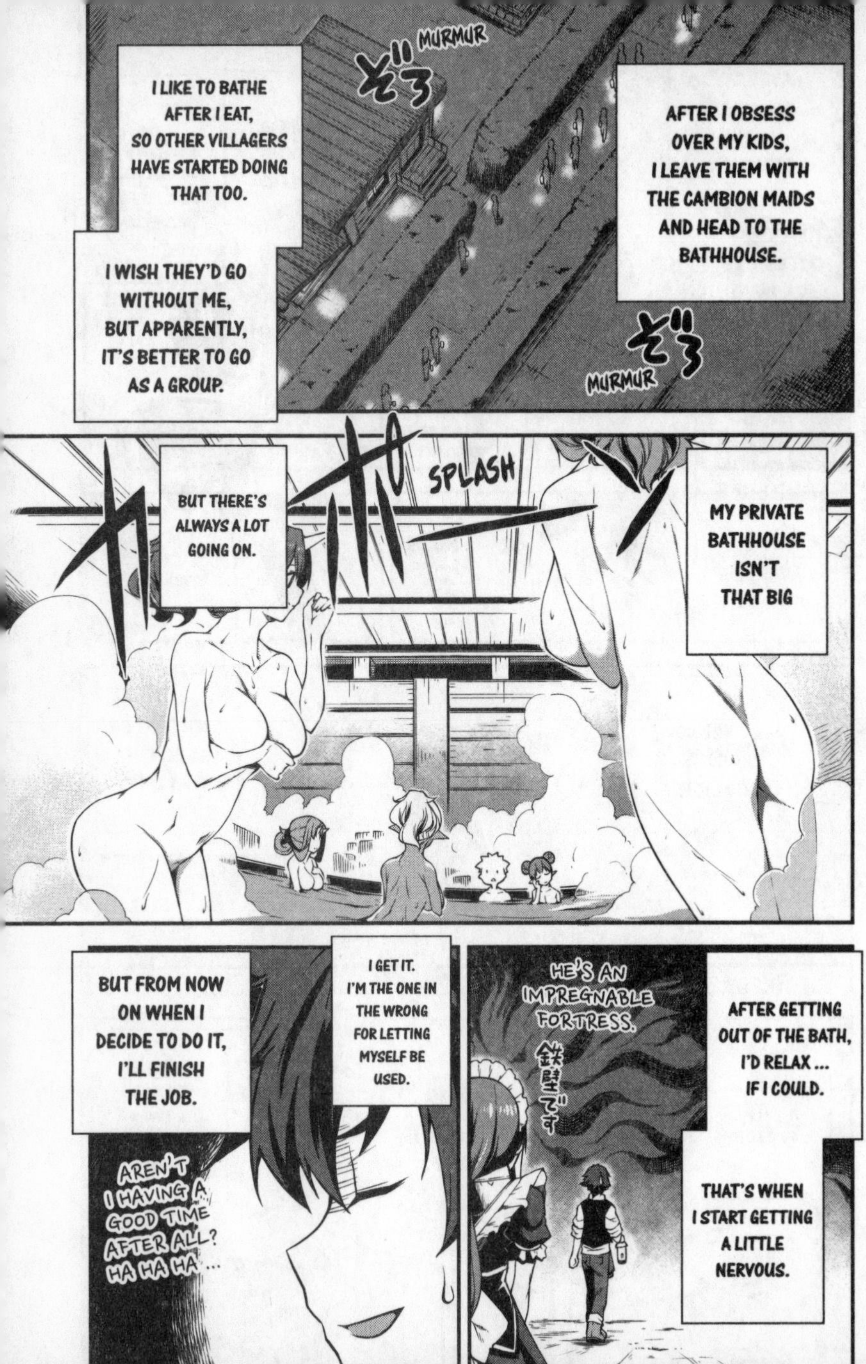
AFTER I OBSESS OVER MY KIDS, I LEAVE THEM WITH THE CAMBION MAIDS AND HEAD TO THE BATHHOUSE.
MURMUR
MURMUR
I LIKE TO BATHE AFTER I EAT, SO OTHER VILLAGERS HAVE STARTED DOING THAT TOO.
I WISH THEY'D GO WITHOUT ME, BUT APPARENTLY, IT'S BETTER TO GO AS A GROUP.
MY PRIVATE BATHHOUSE ISN'T THAT BIG
SPLASH
BUT THERE'S ALWAYS A LOT GOING ON.
AFTER GETTING OUT OF THE BATH, I'D RELAX ... IF I COULD.
HE'S AN IMPREGNABLE FORTRESS.
鉄壁です
THAT'S WHEN I START GETTING A LITTLE NERVOUS.
I GET IT. I'M THE ONE IN THE WRONG FOR LETTING MYSELF BE USED.
BUT FROM NOW ON WHEN I DECIDE TO DO IT, I'LL FINISH THE JOB.
AREN'T I HAVING A GOOD TIME AFTER ALL? HA HA HA ...

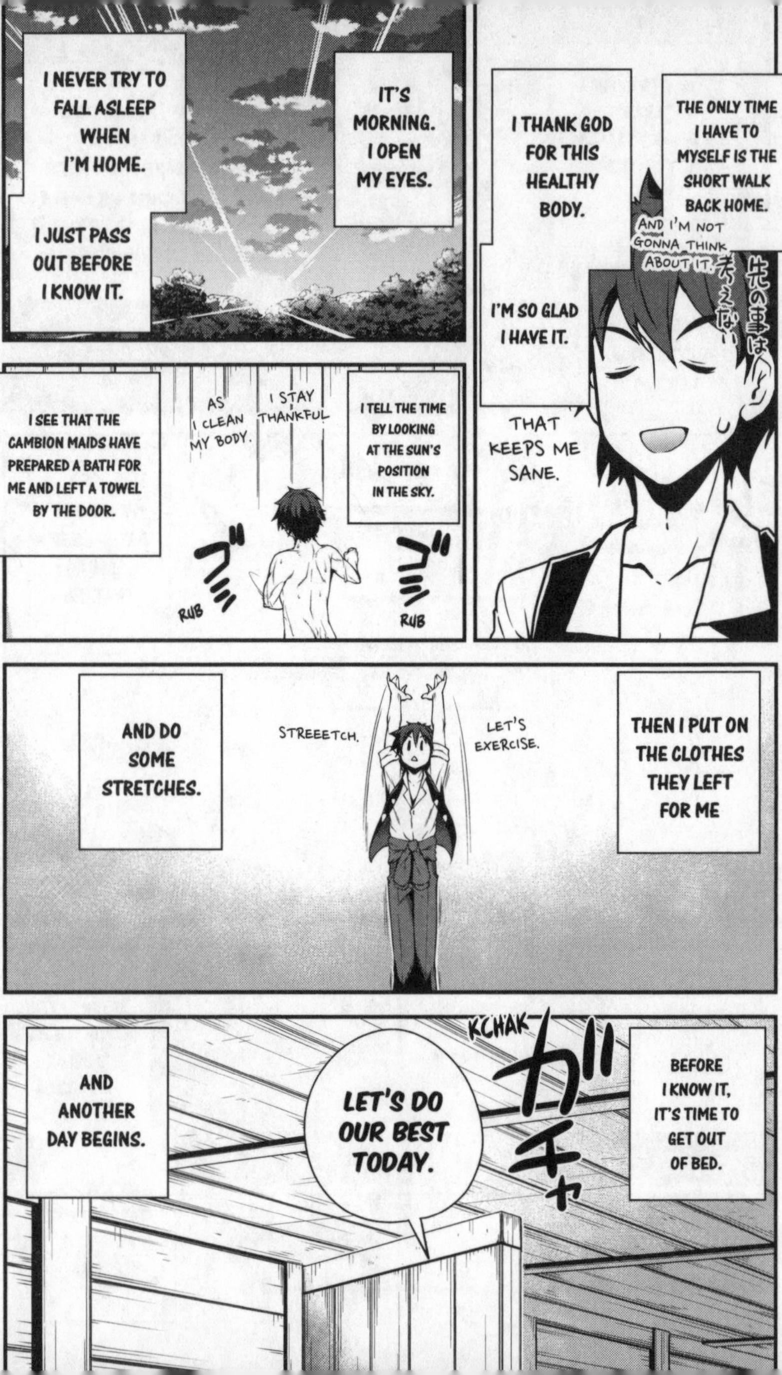
THE ONLY TIME I HAVE TO MYSELF IS THE SHORT WALK BACK HOME.
AND I'M NOT GONNA THINK ABOUT IT.
先の事は考えない
I THANK GOD FOR THIS HEALTHY BODY.
I'M SO GLAD I HAVE IT.
THAT KEEPS ME SANE.
IT'S MORNING. I OPEN MY EYES.
I NEVER TRY TO FALL ASLEEP WHEN I'M HOME.
I JUST PASS OUT BEFORE I KNOW IT.
I TELL THE TIME BY LOOKING AT THE SUN'S POSITION IN THE SKY.
ゴシ
RUB
I STAY THANKFUL
AS I CLEAN MY BODY.
ゴシ
RUB
I SEE THAT THE CAMBION MAIDS HAVE PREPARED A BATH FOR ME AND LEFT A TOWEL BY THE DOOR.
THEN I PUT ON THE CLOTHES THEY LEFT FOR ME
LET'S EXERCISE.
STREEETCH.
AND DO SOME STRETCHES.
BEFORE I KNOW IT, IT'S TIME TO GET OUT OF BED.
KCHAK
ガチャ
LET'S DO OUR BEST TODAY.
AND ANOTHER DAY BEGINS.

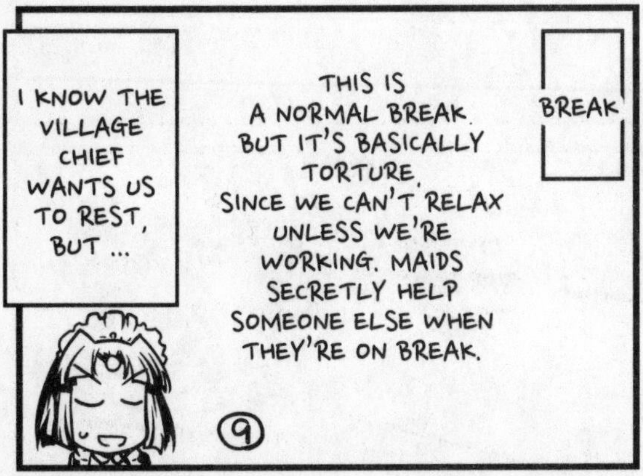
BREAK
THIS IS A NORMAL BREAK, BUT IT'S BASICALLY TORTURE, SINCE WE CAN'T RELAX UNLESS WE'RE WORKING. MAIDS SECRETLY HELP SOMEONE ELSE WHEN THEY'RE ON BREAK.
I KNOW THE VILLAGE CHIEF WANTS US TO REST, BUT ...
9

Farming life in another world.

CHAPTER 68: THAT TROUBLESOME YAA

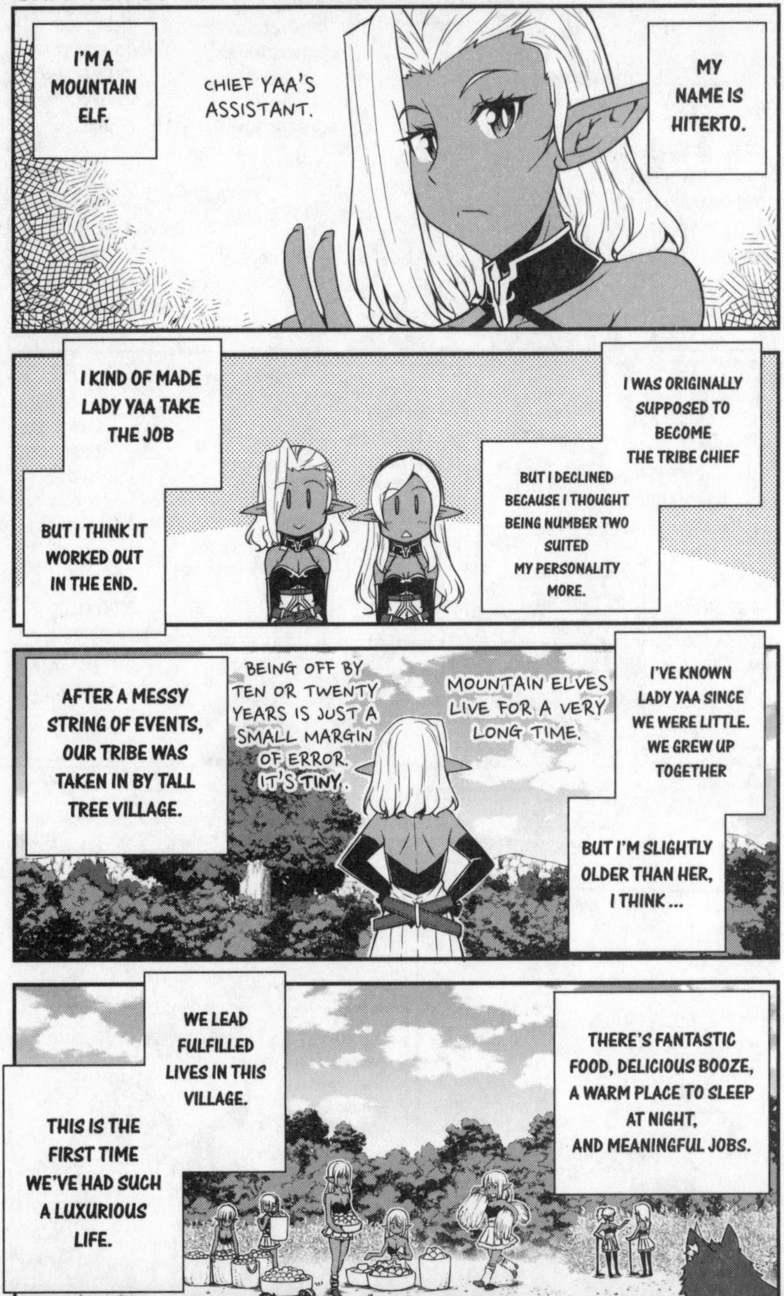

MY NAME IS HITERTO.
CHIEF YAA'S ASSISTANT.
I'M A MOUNTAIN ELF.
I WAS ORIGINALLY SUPPOSED TO BECOME THE TRIBE CHIEF
BUT I DECLINED BECAUSE I THOUGHT BEING NUMBER TWO SUITED MY PERSONALITY MORE.
I KIND OF MADE LADY YAA TAKE THE JOB
BUT I THINK IT WORKED OUT IN THE END.
I'VE KNOWN LADY YAA SINCE WE WERE LITTLE. WE GREW UP TOGETHER
BUT I'M SLIGHTLY OLDER THAN HER, I THINK ...
MOUNTAIN ELVES LIVE FOR A VERY LONG TIME.
BEING OFF BY TEN OR TWENTY YEARS IS JUST A SMALL MARGIN OF ERROR. IT'S TINY.
AFTER A MESSY STRING OF EVENTS, OUR TRIBE WAS TAKEN IN BY TALL TREE VILLAGE.
THERE'S FANTASTIC FOOD, DELICIOUS BOOZE, A WARM PLACE TO SLEEP AT NIGHT, AND MEANINGFUL JOBS.
WE LEAD FULFILLED LIVES IN THIS VILLAGE.
THIS IS THE FIRST TIME WE'VE HAD SUCH A LUXURIOUS LIFE.

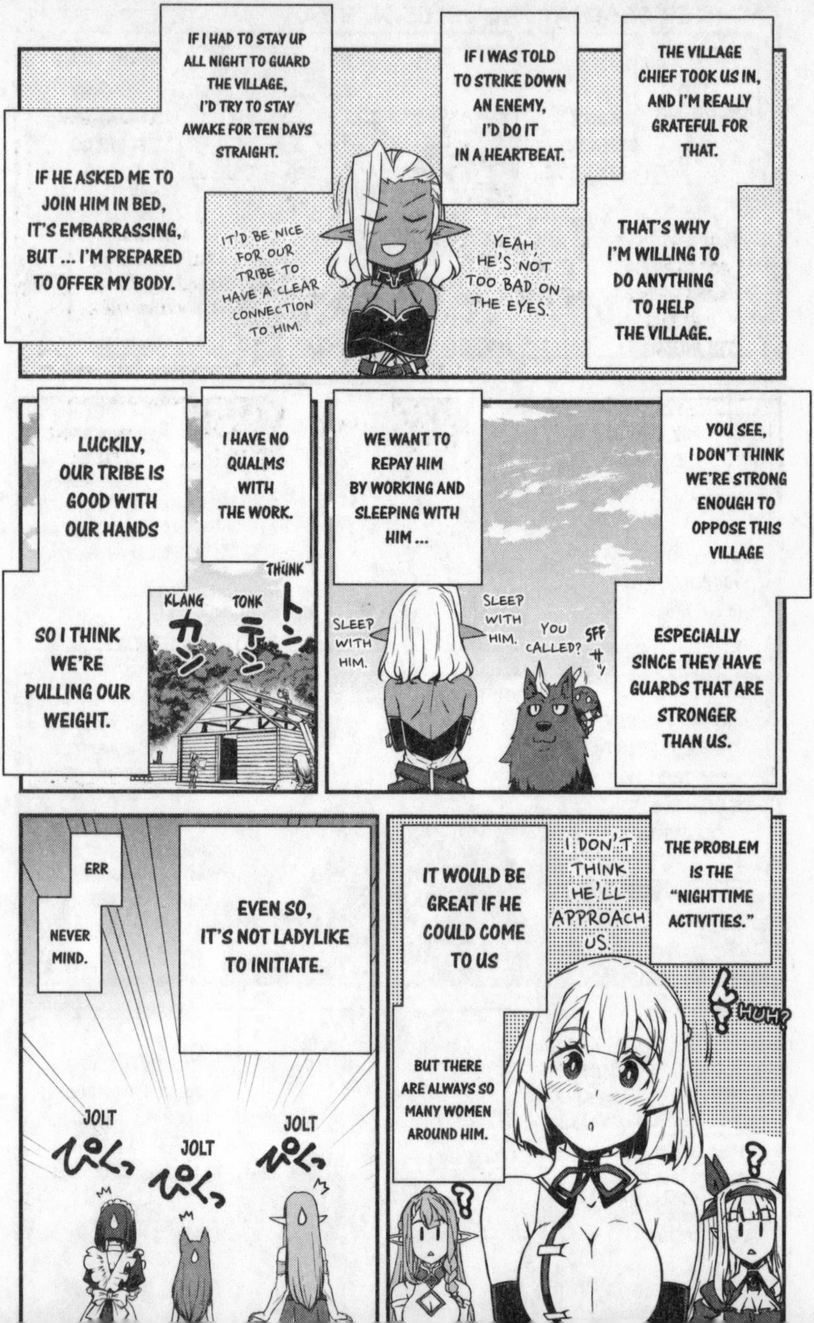

THE VILLAGE CHIEF TOOK US IN, AND I'M REALLY GRATEFUL FOR THAT.
IF I WAS TOLD TO STRIKE DOWN AN ENEMY, I'D DO IT IN A HEARTBEAT.
IF I HAD TO STAY UP ALL NIGHT TO GUARD THE VILLAGE, I'D TRY TO STAY AWAKE FOR TEN DAYS STRAIGHT.
THAT'S WHY I'M WILLING TO DO ANYTHING TO HELP THE VILLAGE.
YEAH, HE'S NOT TOO BAD ON THE EYES.
IT'D BE NICE FOR OUR TRIBE TO HAVE A CLEAR CONNECTION TO HIM.
IF HE ASKED ME TO JOIN HIM IN BED, IT'S EMBARRASSING, BUT ... I'M PREPARED TO OFFER MY BODY.
YOU SEE, I DON'T THINK WE'RE STRONG ENOUGH TO OPPOSE THIS VILLAGE
WE WANT TO REPAY HIM BY WORKING AND SLEEPING WITH HIM ...
ESPECIALLY SINCE THEY HAVE GUARDS THAT ARE STRONGER THAN US.
SFF
YOU CALLED?
SLEEP WITH HIM.
SLEEP WITH HIM.
I HAVE NO QUALMS WITH THE WORK.
LUCKILY, OUR TRIBE IS GOOD WITH OUR HANDS
THUNK
トン
TONK
テン
KLANG
カン
SO I THINK WE'RE PULLING OUR WEIGHT.
THE PROBLEM IS THE "NIGHTTIME ACTIVITIES."
I DON'T THINK HE'LL APPROACH US.
IT WOULD BE GREAT IF HE COULD COME TO US
HUH?
BUT THERE ARE ALWAYS SO MANY WOMEN AROUND HIM.
EVEN SO, IT'S NOT LADYLIKE TO INITIATE.
ERR
NEVER MIND.
JOLT
ぴくっ
JOLT
ぴくっ
JOLT
ぴくっ

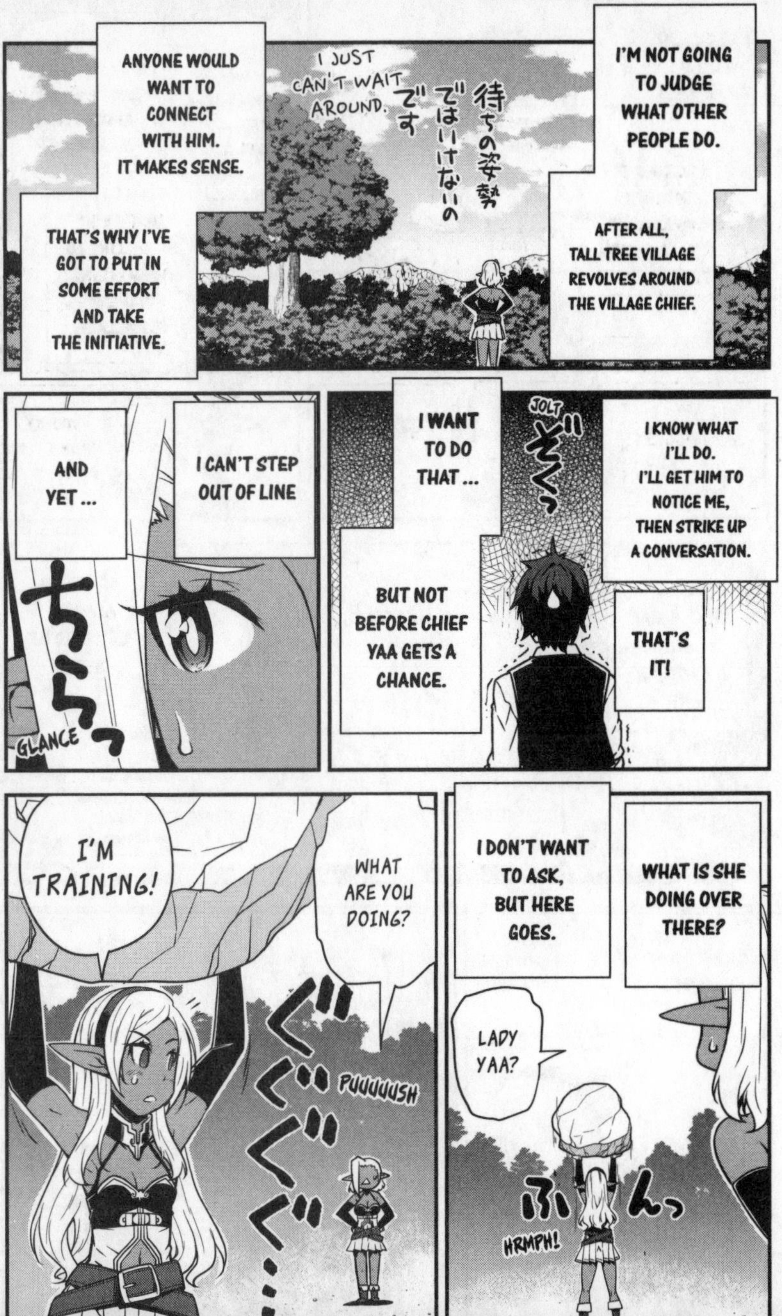
I'M NOT GOING TO JUDGE WHAT OTHER PEOPLE DO.
AFTER ALL, TALL TREE VILLAGE REVOLVES AROUND THE VILLAGE CHIEF.
待ちの姿勢ではいけないのです
I JUST CAN'T WAIT AROUND.
ANYONE WOULD WANT TO CONNECT WITH HIM. IT MAKES SENSE.
THAT'S WHY I'VE GOT TO PUT IN SOME EFFORT AND TAKE THE INITIATIVE.
I KNOW WHAT I'LL DO. I'LL GET HIM TO NOTICE ME, THEN STRIKE UP A CONVERSATION.
ぞくっ
JOLT
I WANT TO DO THAT ...
THAT'S IT!
BUT NOT BEFORE CHIEF YAA GETS A CHANCE.
I CAN'T STEP OUT OF LINE
AND YET ...
ちらっ
GLANCE
WHAT IS SHE DOING OVER THERE?
I DON'T WANT TO ASK, BUT HERE GOES.
LADY YAA?
ふんっ
HRMPH!
WHAT ARE YOU DOING?
I'M TRAINING!
ぐぐぐ…
PUUUUUSH

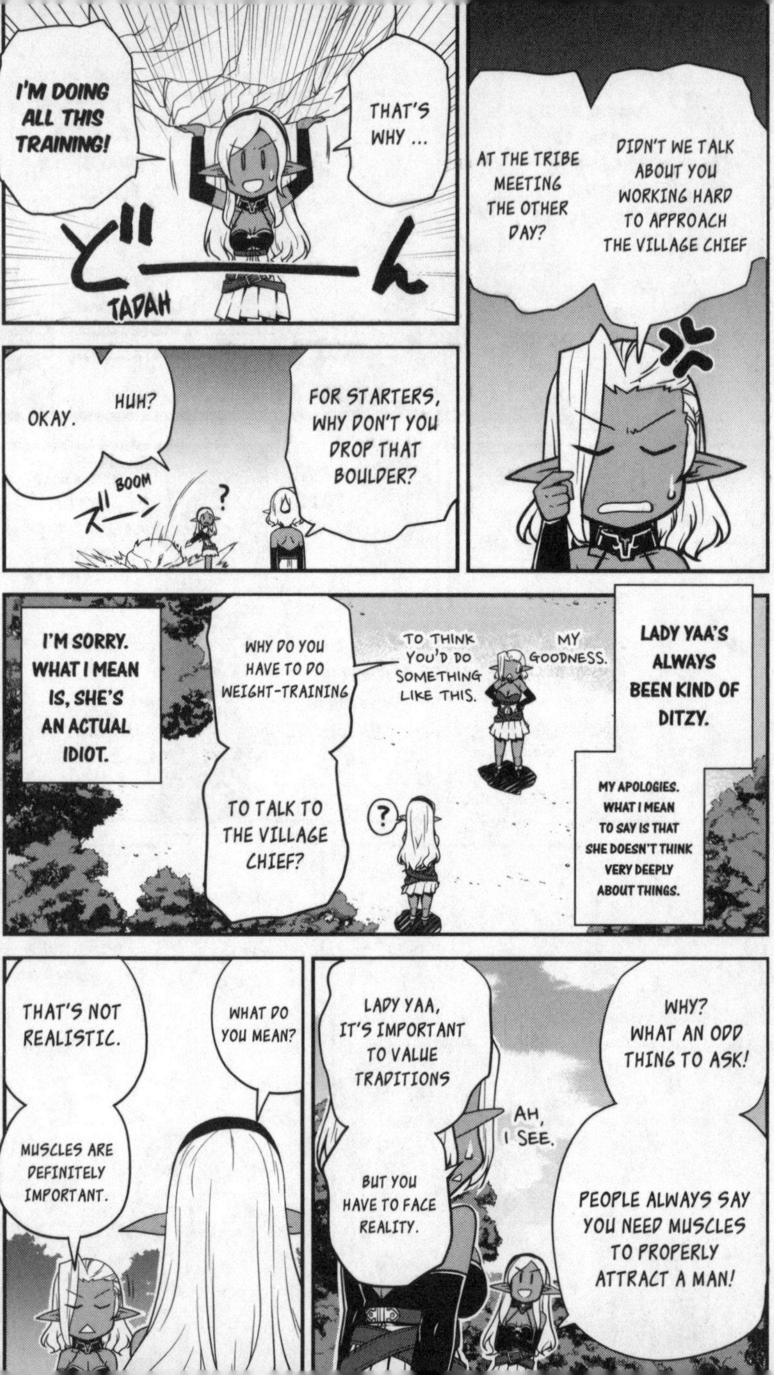
DIDN'T WE TALK ABOUT YOU WORKING HARD TO APPROACH THE VILLAGE CHIEF
AT THE TRIBE MEETING THE OTHER DAY?
THAT'S WHY ...
I'M DOING ALL THIS TRAINING!
どーん
TADAH
FOR STARTERS, WHY DON'T YOU DROP THAT BOULDER?
HUH?
OKAY.
BOOM
ズーン
?
LADY YAA'S ALWAYS BEEN KIND OF DITZY.
MY APOLOGIES. WHAT I MEAN TO SAY IS THAT SHE DOESN'T THINK VERY DEEPLY ABOUT THINGS.
MY GOODNESS.
TO THINK YOU'D DO SOMETHING LIKE THIS.
WHY DO YOU HAVE TO DO WEIGHT-TRAINING
TO TALK TO THE VILLAGE CHIEF?
?
I'M SORRY. WHAT I MEAN IS, SHE'S AN ACTUAL IDIOT.
WHY? WHAT AN ODD THING TO ASK!
PEOPLE ALWAYS SAY YOU NEED MUSCLES TO PROPERLY ATTRACT A MAN!
AH, I SEE.
LADY YAA, IT'S IMPORTANT TO VALUE TRADITIONS
BUT YOU HAVE TO FACE REALITY.
WHAT DO YOU MEAN?
THAT'S NOT REALISTIC.
MUSCLES ARE DEFINITELY IMPORTANT.

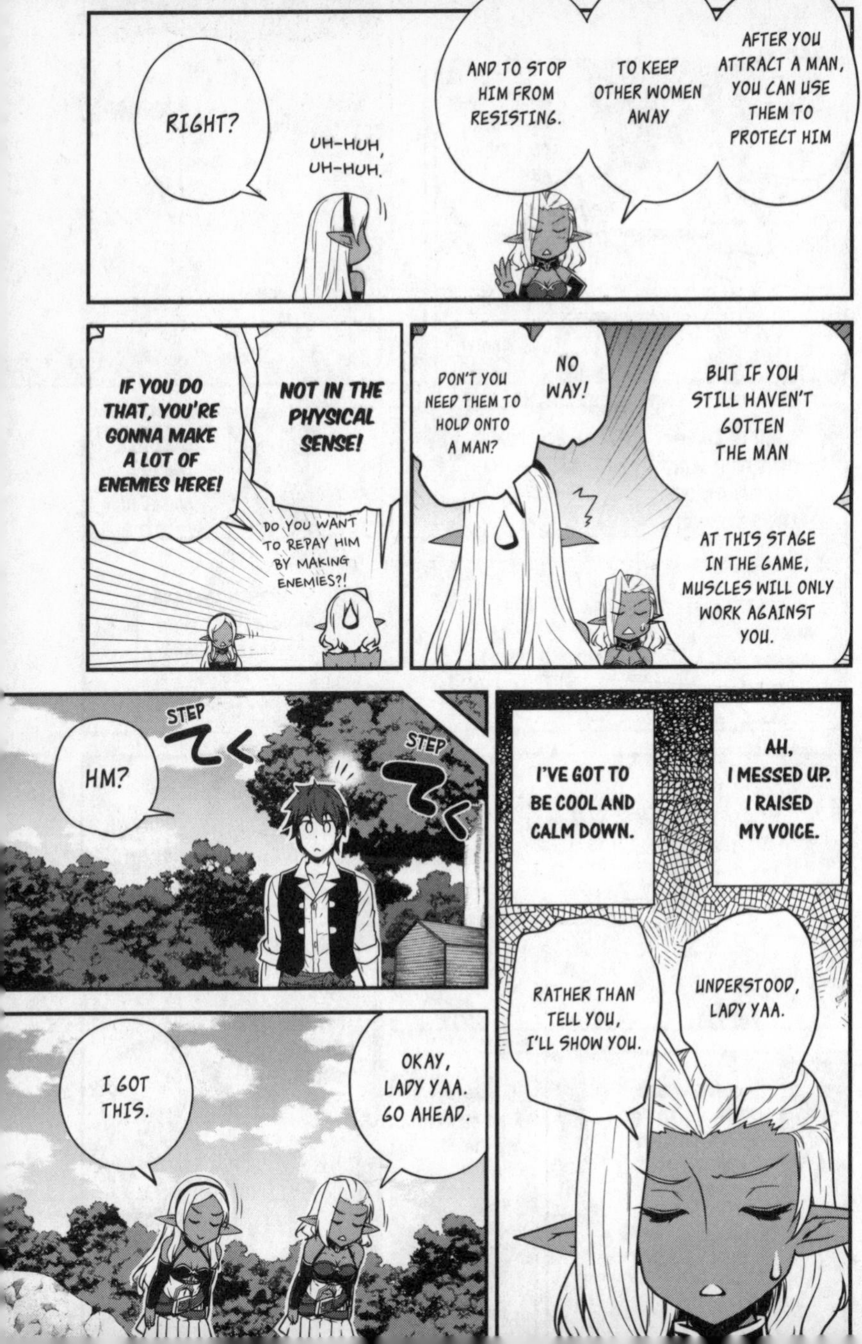
AFTER YOU ATTRACT A MAN, YOU CAN USE THEM TO PROTECT HIM
TO KEEP OTHER WOMEN AWAY
AND TO STOP HIM FROM RESISTING.
UH-HUH, UH-HUH.
RIGHT?
BUT IF YOU STILL HAVEN'T GOTTEN THE MAN
AT THIS STAGE IN THE GAME, MUSCLES WILL ONLY WORK AGAINST YOU.
NO WAY!
DON'T YOU NEED THEM TO HOLD ONTO A MAN?
NOT IN THE PHYSICAL SENSE!
IF YOU DO THAT, YOU'RE GONNA MAKE A LOT OF ENEMIES HERE!
DO YOU WANT TO REPAY HIM BY MAKING ENEMIES?!
AH, I MESSED UP. I RAISED MY VOICE.
I'VE GOT TO BE COOL AND CALM DOWN.
UNDERSTOOD, LADY YAA.
RATHER THAN TELL YOU, I'LL SHOW YOU.
STEP てく
STEP てく
HM?
OKAY, LADY YAA. GO AHEAD.
I GOT THIS.

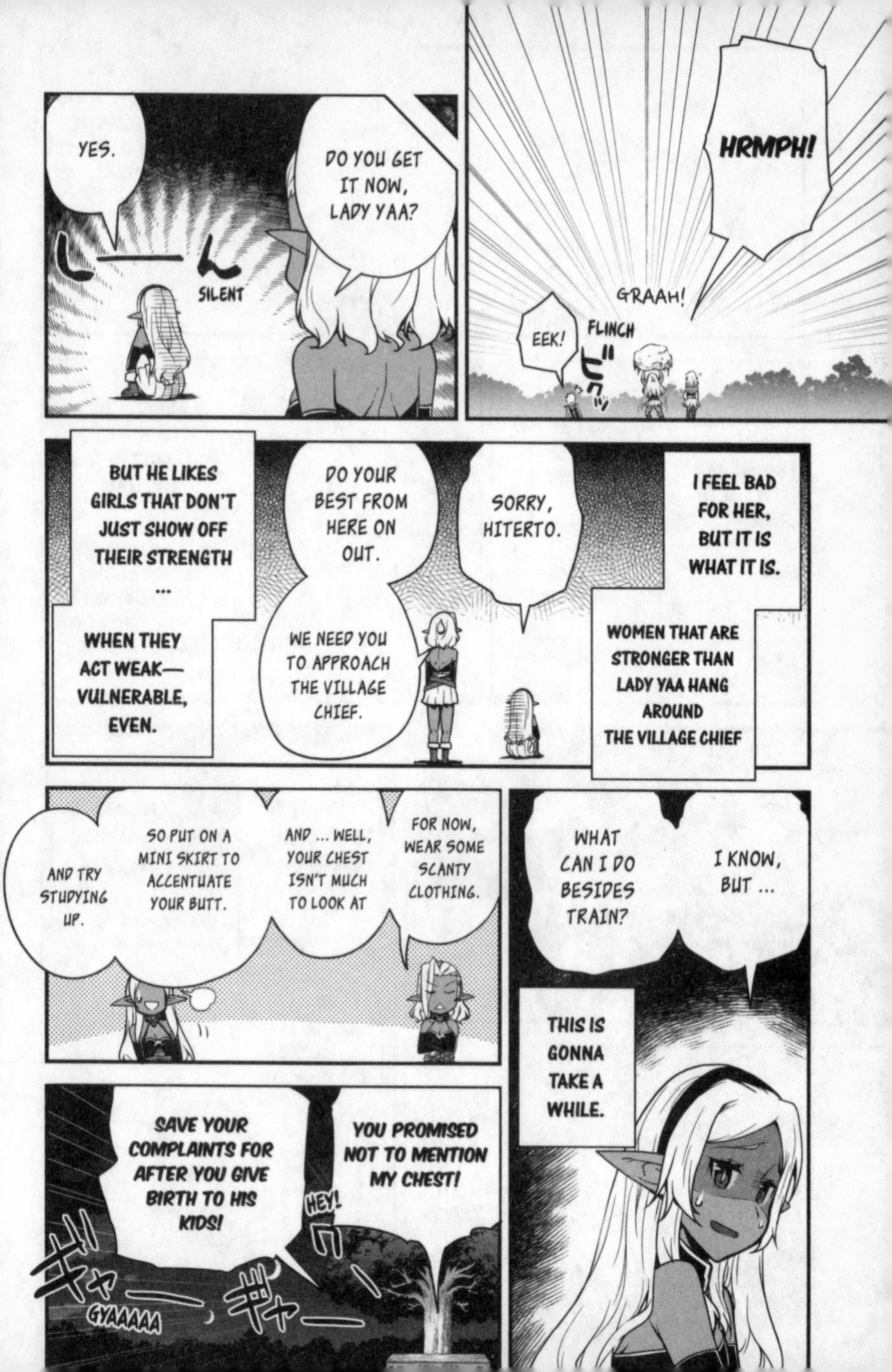
HRMPH!
GRAAH!
FLINCH
EEK!
DO YOU GET IT NOW, LADY YAA?
YES.
SILENT
I FEEL BAD FOR HER, BUT IT IS WHAT IT IS.
WOMEN THAT ARE STRONGER THAN LADY YAA HANG AROUND THE VILLAGE CHIEF
SORRY, HITERTO.
DO YOUR BEST FROM HERE ON OUT.
WE NEED YOU TO APPROACH THE VILLAGE CHIEF.
BUT HE LIKES GIRLS THAT DON'T JUST SHOW OFF THEIR STRENGTH ...
WHEN THEY ACT WEAK—VULNERABLE, EVEN.
I KNOW, BUT ...
WHAT CAN I DO BESIDES TRAIN?
THIS IS GONNA TAKE A WHILE.
FOR NOW, WEAR SOME SCANTY CLOTHING.
AND ... WELL, YOUR CHEST ISN'T MUCH TO LOOK AT
SO PUT ON A MINI SKIRT TO ACCENTUATE YOUR BUTT.
AND TRY STUDYING UP.
YOU PROMISED NOT TO MENTION MY CHEST!
HEY!
SAVE YOUR COMPLAINTS FOR AFTER YOU GIVE BIRTH TO HIS KIDS!
GYAAAAA

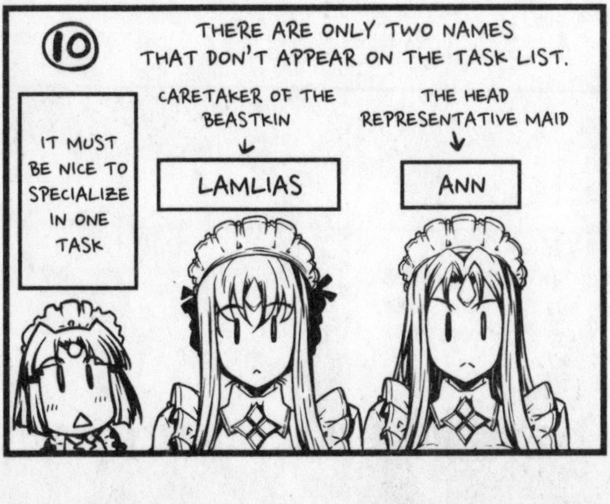
THERE ARE ONLY TWO NAMES THAT DON'T APPEAR ON THE TASK LIST.
10
THE HEAD REPRESENTATIVE MAID
ANN
CARETAKER OF THE BEASTKIN
LAMLIAS
IT MUST BE NICE TO SPECIALIZE IN ONE TASK

CHAPTER 69: FESTIVAL PREPARATIONS

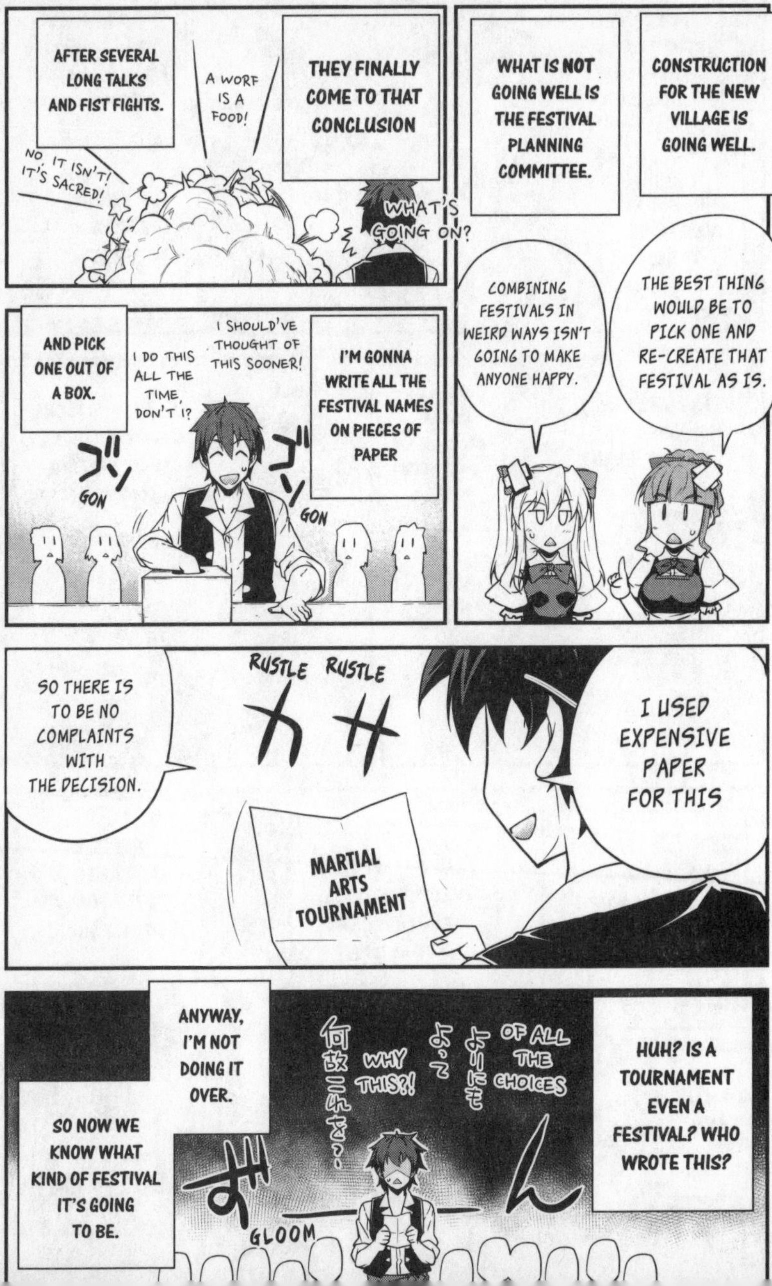
CONSTRUCTION FOR THE NEW VILLAGE IS GOING WELL.
WHAT IS NOT GOING WELL IS THE FESTIVAL PLANNING COMMITTEE.
THE BEST THING WOULD BE TO PICK ONE AND RE-CREATE THAT FESTIVAL AS IS.
COMBINING FESTIVALS IN WEIRD WAYS ISN'T GOING TO MAKE ANYONE HAPPY.
THEY FINALLY COME TO THAT CONCLUSION
A WORF IS A FOOD!
AFTER SEVERAL LONG TALKS AND FIST FIGHTS.
NO, IT ISN'T! IT'S SACRED!
WHAT'S GOING ON?
I'M GONNA WRITE ALL THE FESTIVAL NAMES ON PIECES OF PAPER
I SHOULD'VE THOUGHT OF THIS SOONER!
I DO THIS ALL THE TIME, DON'T I?
AND PICK ONE OUT OF A BOX.
ゴン GON
ゴン GON
I USED EXPENSIVE PAPER FOR THIS
カサ RUSTLE RUSTLE
SO THERE IS TO BE NO COMPLAINTS WITH THE DECISION.
MARTIAL ARTS TOURNAMENT
HUH? IS A TOURNAMENT EVEN A FESTIVAL? WHO WROTE THIS?
よりにもよって OF ALL THE CHOICES
何故これを?! WHY THIS?!
ANYWAY, I'M NOT DOING IT OVER.
SO NOW WE KNOW WHAT KIND OF FESTIVAL IT'S GOING TO BE.
ずーん GLOOM

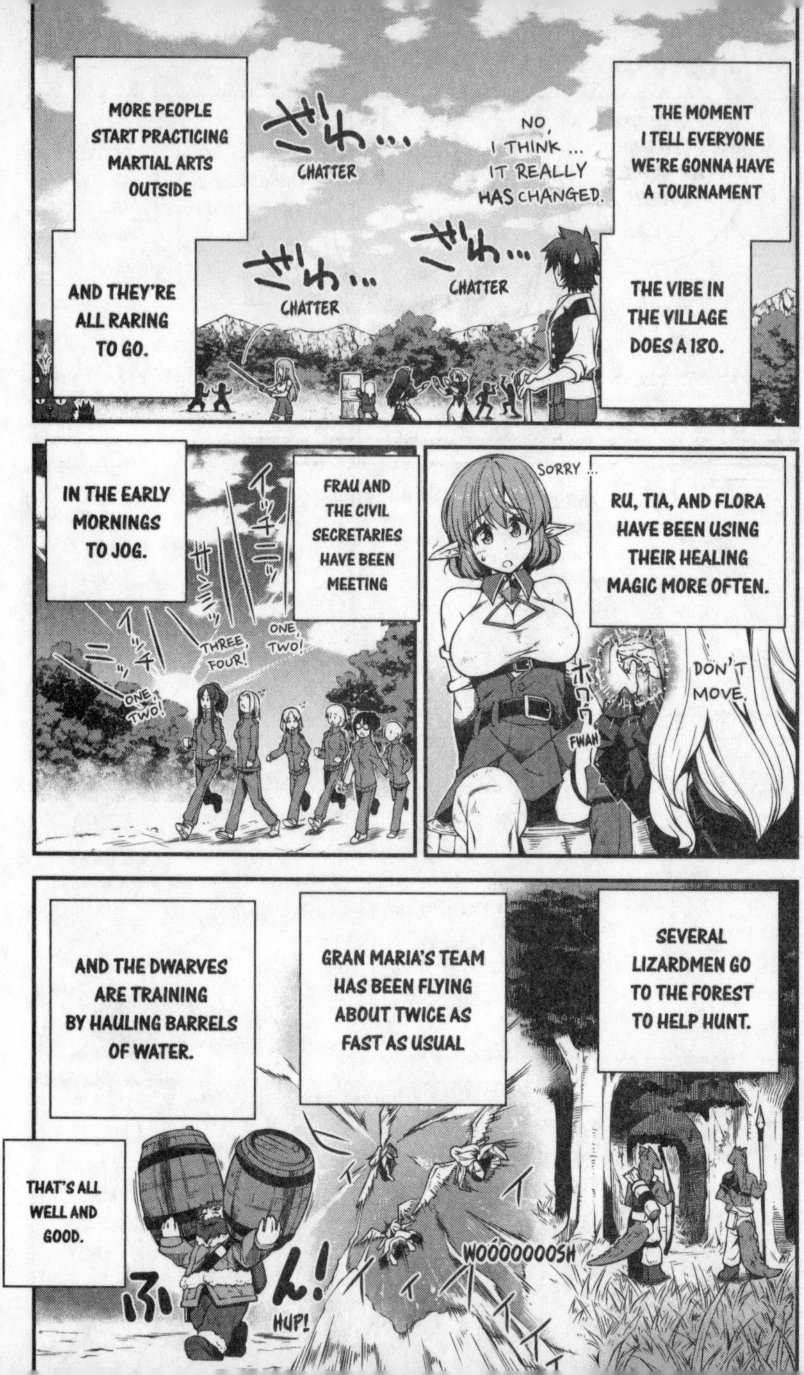
THE MOMENT I TELL EVERYONE WE'RE GONNA HAVE A TOURNAMENT
THE VIBE IN THE VILLAGE DOES A 180.
NO, I THINK ... IT REALLY HAS CHANGED.
ざわ…
CHATTER
ざわ…
CHATTER
ざわ…
CHATTER
MORE PEOPLE START PRACTICING MARTIAL ARTS OUTSIDE
AND THEY'RE ALL RARING TO GO.
RU, TIA, AND FLORA HAVE BEEN USING THEIR HEALING MAGIC MORE OFTEN.
SORRY ...
DON'T MOVE.
ホワワ
FWAH
FRAU AND THE CIVIL SECRETARIES HAVE BEEN MEETING
IN THE EARLY MORNINGS TO JOG.
イッチニーッ
ONE, TWO!
サンシッ
THREE, FOUR!
イッチニッ
ONE, TWO!
SEVERAL LIZARDMEN GO TO THE FOREST TO HELP HUNT.
GRAN MARIA'S TEAM HAS BEEN FLYING ABOUT TWICE AS FAST AS USUAL
WOOOOOOOSH
AND THE DWARVES ARE TRAINING BY HAULING BARRELS OF WATER.
THAT'S ALL WELL AND GOOD.
ふん!
HUP!

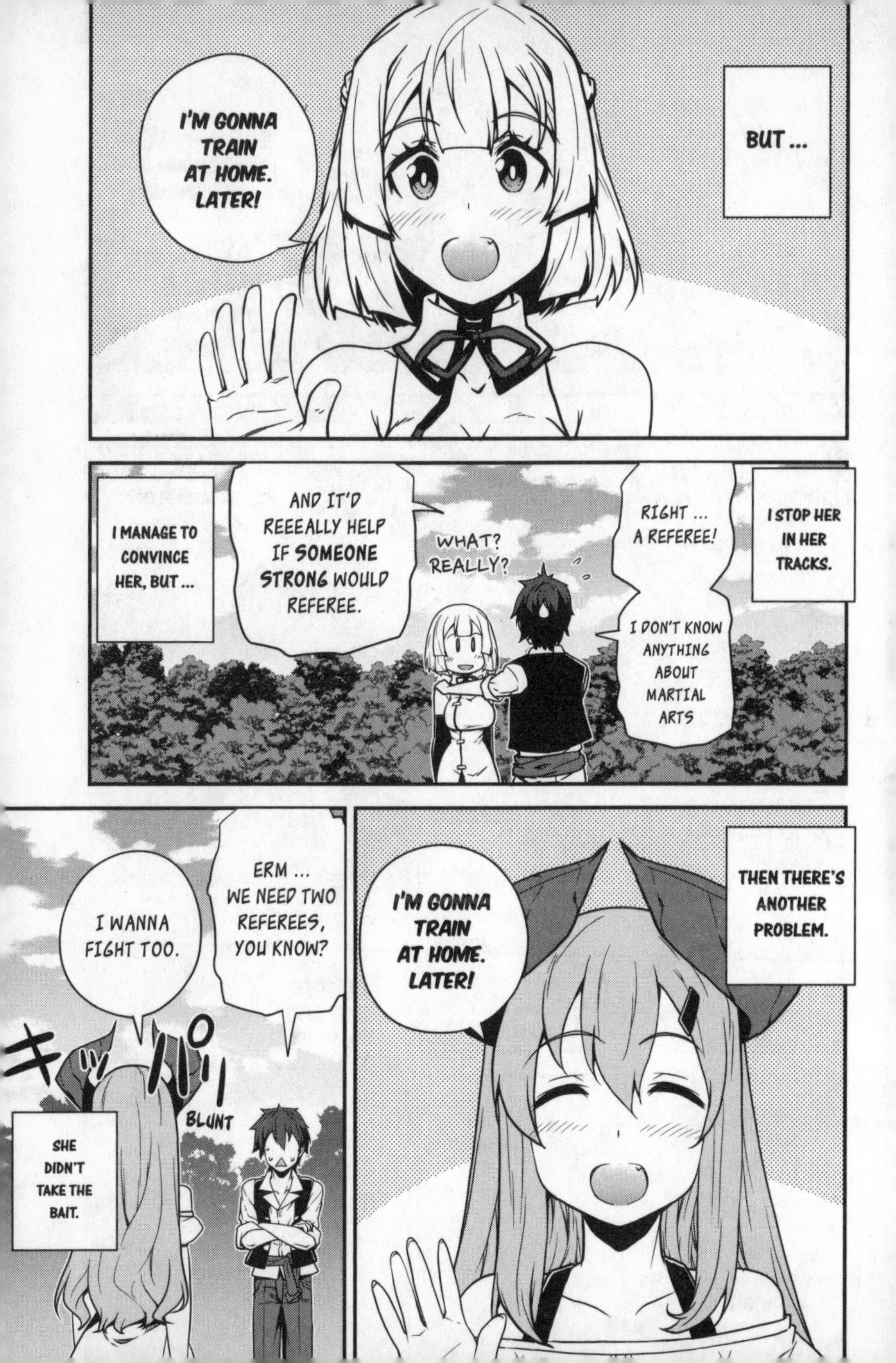

BUT ...
I'M GONNA TRAIN AT HOME. LATER!
I STOP HER IN HER TRACKS.
RIGHT ... A REFEREE!
I DON'T KNOW ANYTHING ABOUT MARTIAL ARTS
WHAT? REALLY?
AND IT'D REEEALLY HELP IF SOMEONE STRONG WOULD REFEREE.
I MANAGE TO CONVINCE HER, BUT ...
THEN THERE'S ANOTHER PROBLEM.
I'M GONNA TRAIN AT HOME. LATER!
ERM ... WE NEED TWO REFEREES, YOU KNOW?
I WANNA FIGHT TOO.
キッパリ
BLUNT
SHE DIDN'T TAKE THE BAIT.

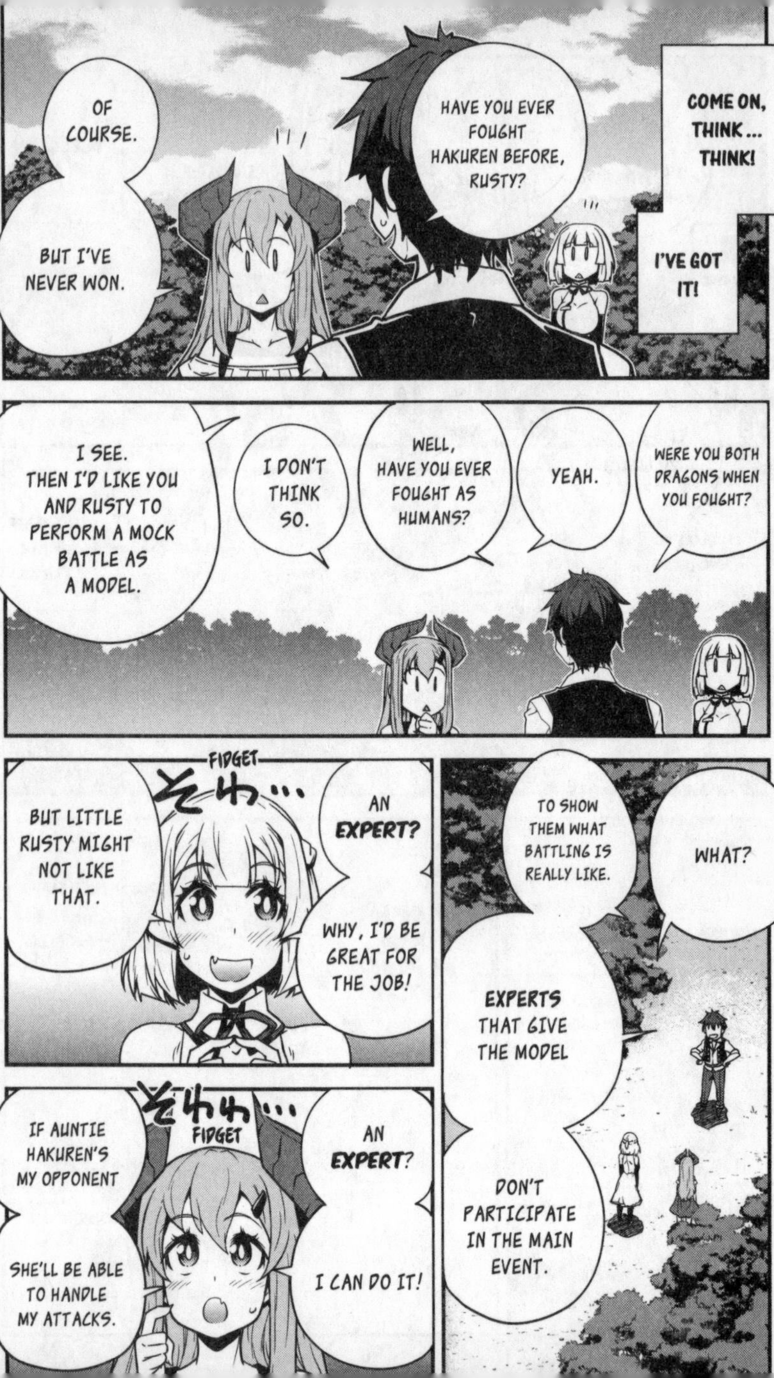
COME ON, THINK... THINK!
I'VE GOT IT!
HAVE YOU EVER FOUGHT HAKUREN BEFORE, RUSTY?
OF COURSE.
BUT I'VE NEVER WON.
WERE YOU BOTH DRAGONS WHEN YOU FOUGHT?
YEAH.
WELL, HAVE YOU EVER FOUGHT AS HUMANS?
I DON'T THINK SO.
I SEE. THEN I'D LIKE YOU AND RUSTY TO PERFORM A MOCK BATTLE AS A MODEL.
WHAT?
TO SHOW THEM WHAT BATTLING IS REALLY LIKE.
EXPERTS THAT GIVE THE MODEL
DON'T PARTICIPATE IN THE MAIN EVENT.
AN EXPERT?
WHY, I'D BE GREAT FOR THE JOB!
そわ…
FIDGET
BUT LITTLE RUSTY MIGHT NOT LIKE THAT.
そわわ…
FIDGET
AN EXPERT?
I CAN DO IT!
IF AUNTIE HAKUREN'S MY OPPONENT
SHE'LL BE ABLE TO HANDLE MY ATTACKS.

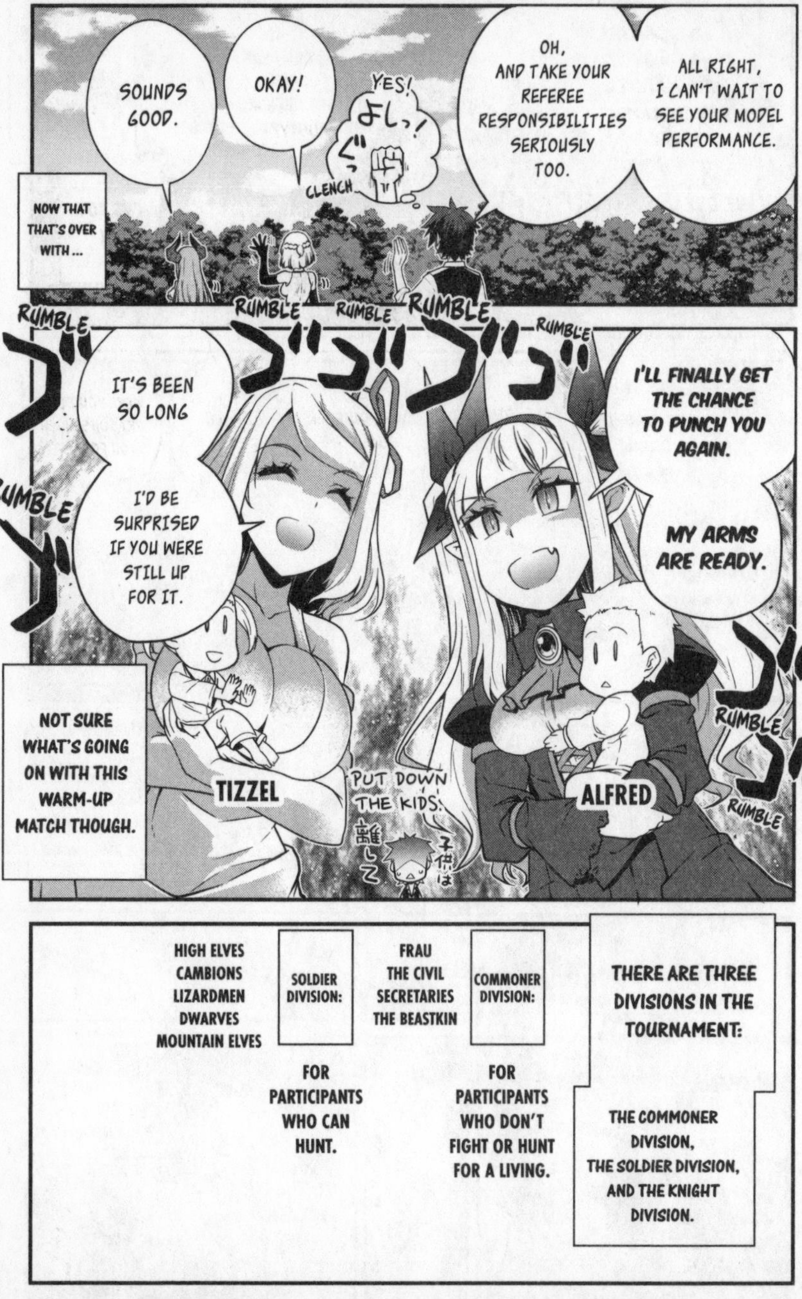
ALL RIGHT, I CAN'T WAIT TO SEE YOUR MODEL PERFORMANCE.
OH, AND TAKE YOUR REFEREE RESPONSIBILITIES SERIOUSLY TOO.
YES! よしっ!
ぐっ CLENCH
OKAY!
SOUNDS GOOD.
NOW THAT THAT'S OVER WITH ...
RUMBLE RUMBLE RUMBLE RUMBLE RUMBLE
I'LL FINALLY GET THE CHANCE TO PUNCH YOU AGAIN.
MY ARMS ARE READY.
IT'S BEEN SO LONG
I'D BE SURPRISED IF YOU WERE STILL UP FOR IT.
RUMBLE
RUMBLE RUMBLE
ALFRED
TIZZEL
PUT DOWN THE KIDS. 子供は離して
NOT SURE WHAT'S GOING ON WITH THIS WARM-UP MATCH THOUGH.
THERE ARE THREE DIVISIONS IN THE TOURNAMENT:
THE COMMONER DIVISION, THE SOLDIER DIVISION, AND THE KNIGHT DIVISION.
COMMONER DIVISION:
FRAU THE CIVIL SECRETARIES THE BEASTKIN
FOR PARTICIPANTS WHO DON'T FIGHT OR HUNT FOR A LIVING.
SOLDIER DIVISION:
HIGH ELVES CAMBIONS LIZARDMEN DWARVES MOUNTAIN ELVES
FOR PARTICIPANTS WHO CAN HUNT.

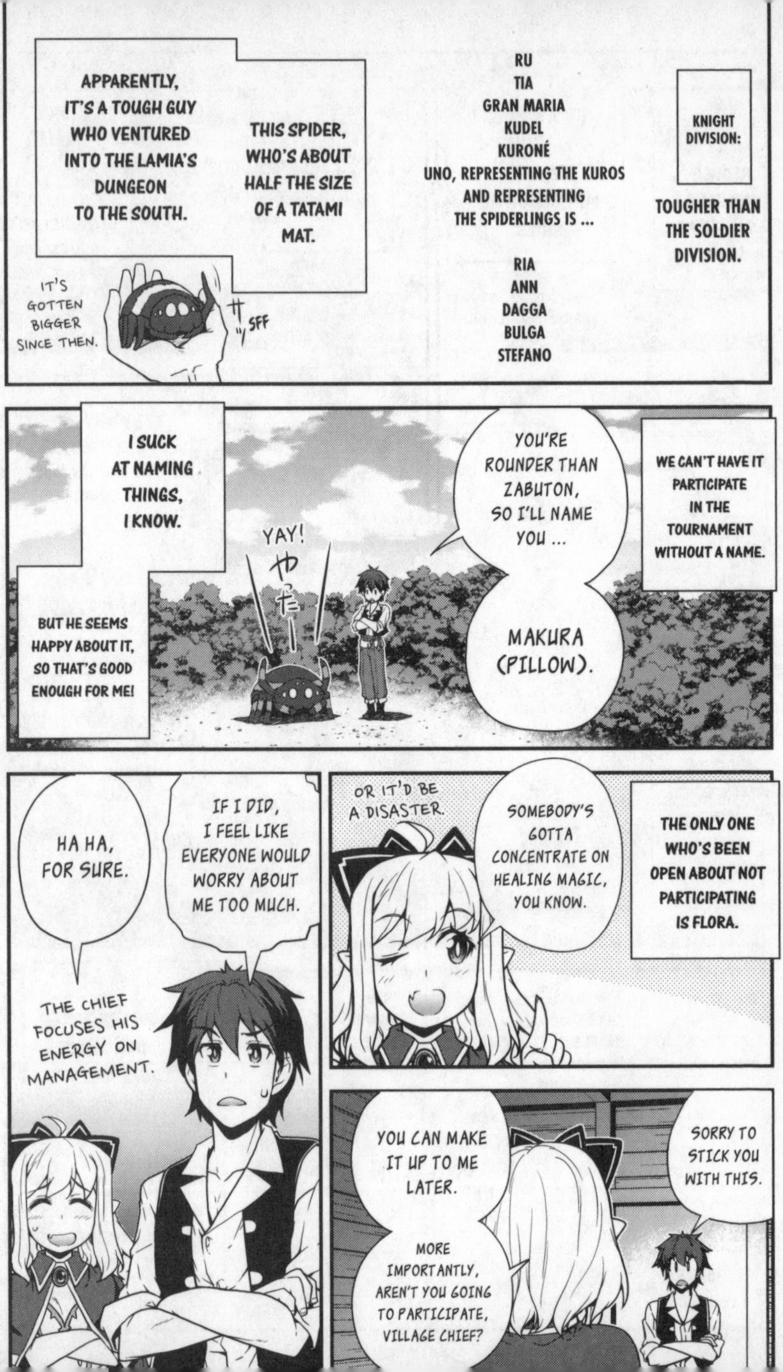
KNIGHT DIVISION:
TOUGHER THAN THE SOLDIER DIVISION.
RU
TIA
GRAN MARIA
KUDEL
KURONÉ
UNO, REPRESENTING THE KUROS
AND REPRESENTING THE SPIDERLINGS IS ...
RIA
ANN
DAGGA
BULGA
STEFANO
THIS SPIDER, WHO'S ABOUT HALF THE SIZE OF A TATAMI MAT.
APPARENTLY, IT'S A TOUGH GUY WHO VENTURED INTO THE LAMIA'S DUNGEON TO THE SOUTH.
SFF
IT'S GOTTEN BIGGER SINCE THEN.
WE CAN'T HAVE IT PARTICIPATE IN THE TOURNAMENT WITHOUT A NAME.
YOU'RE ROUNDER THAN ZABUTON, SO I'LL NAME YOU ...
MAKURA (PILLOW).
YAY!
やったー
I SUCK AT NAMING THINGS, I KNOW.
BUT HE SEEMS HAPPY ABOUT IT, SO THAT'S GOOD ENOUGH FOR ME!
THE ONLY ONE WHO'S BEEN OPEN ABOUT NOT PARTICIPATING IS FLORA.
SOMEBODY'S GOTTA CONCENTRATE ON HEALING MAGIC, YOU KNOW.
OR IT'D BE A DISASTER.
SORRY TO STICK YOU WITH THIS.
YOU CAN MAKE IT UP TO ME LATER.
MORE IMPORTANTLY, AREN'T YOU GOING TO PARTICIPATE, VILLAGE CHIEF?
IF I DID, I FEEL LIKE EVERYONE WOULD WORRY ABOUT ME TOO MUCH.
HA HA, FOR SURE.
THE CHIEF FOCUSES HIS ENERGY ON MANAGEMENT.

SOUTH OF THE RESIDENTIAL AREA, I SCALE BACK THE FOREST AND EXPAND THE EMPTY FIELD
SO I CAN MAKE A VENUE FOR THE TOURNAMENT.
FOREST
FRUITS
LAKE
GOLF COURSE
RESIDENTIAL AREA
FIELD
PLANNED TOURNAMENT VENUE
FOREST
IT'S A SQUARE STAGE THAT'S TWENTY METERS ON ALL SIDES.
I WANT TO REDUCE INJURIES AS MUCH AS I CAN.
THE SURROUNDING AREA WILL BE SOFT.
50 CM HIGH
20 M
I'LL MAKE A TON OF SEATS SO THE AUDIENCE CAN ENJOY A MEAL AND A SHOW.
SHAVED-DOWN LOG BENCHES
BIGGER TREES ELEVATE THE SPECTATOR.
通路
AISLE
YEAH, NOW THAT'S MORE LIKE IT.
AND NOT TOO FAR FROM HERE
THERE'S A PLACE TO COOK
AND TO EAT.
WE'LL ALSO NEED RESTROOMS.
A LOG CUT IN HALF
I'LL MAKE A WHOLE BUNCH.

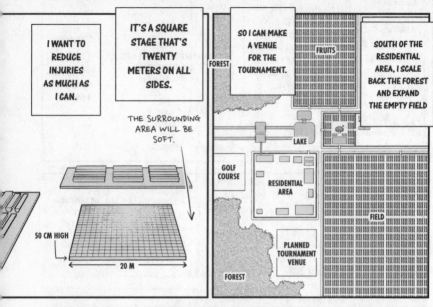

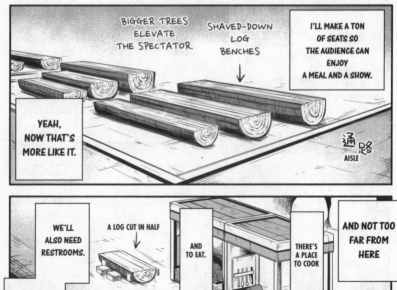

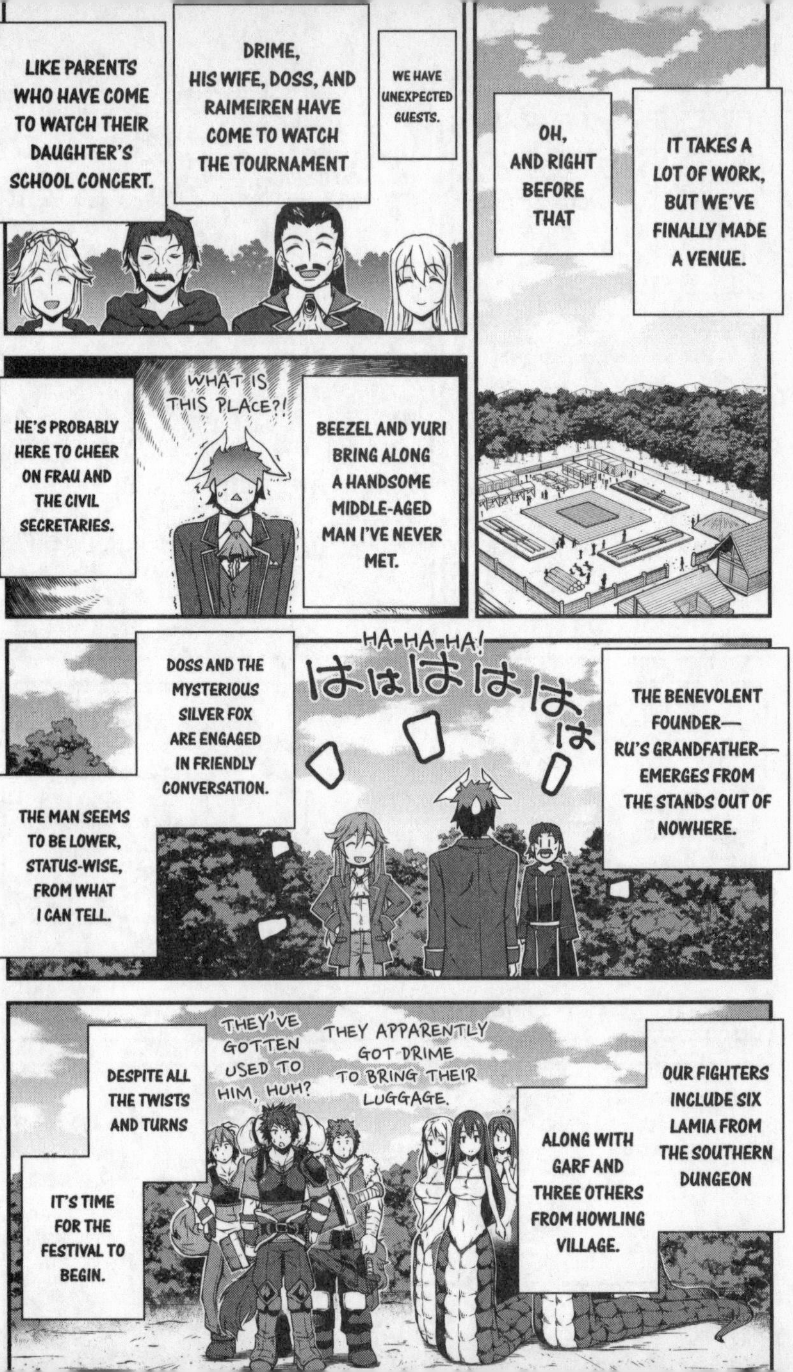
IT TAKES A LOT OF WORK, BUT WE'VE FINALLY MADE A VENUE.
OH, AND RIGHT BEFORE THAT
WE HAVE UNEXPECTED GUESTS.
DRIME, HIS WIFE, DOSS, AND RAIMEIREN HAVE COME TO WATCH THE TOURNAMENT
LIKE PARENTS WHO HAVE COME TO WATCH THEIR DAUGHTER'S SCHOOL CONCERT.
BEEZEL AND YURI BRING ALONG A HANDSOME MIDDLE-AGED MAN I'VE NEVER MET.
WHAT IS THIS PLACE?!
HE'S PROBABLY HERE TO CHEER ON FRAU AND THE CIVIL SECRETARIES.
THE BENEVOLENT FOUNDER—RU'S GRANDFATHER—EMERGES FROM THE STANDS OUT OF NOWHERE.
HA-HA-HA!
はははははは
DOSS AND THE MYSTERIOUS SILVER FOX ARE ENGAGED IN FRIENDLY CONVERSATION.
THE MAN SEEMS TO BE LOWER, STATUS-WISE, FROM WHAT I CAN TELL.
OUR FIGHTERS INCLUDE SIX LAMIA FROM THE SOUTHERN DUNGEON
ALONG WITH GARF AND THREE OTHERS FROM HOWLING VILLAGE.
THEY APPARENTLY GOT DRIME TO BRING THEIR LUGGAGE.
THEY'VE GOTTEN USED TO HIM, HUH?
DESPITE ALL THE TWISTS AND TURNS
IT'S TIME FOR THE FESTIVAL TO BEGIN.

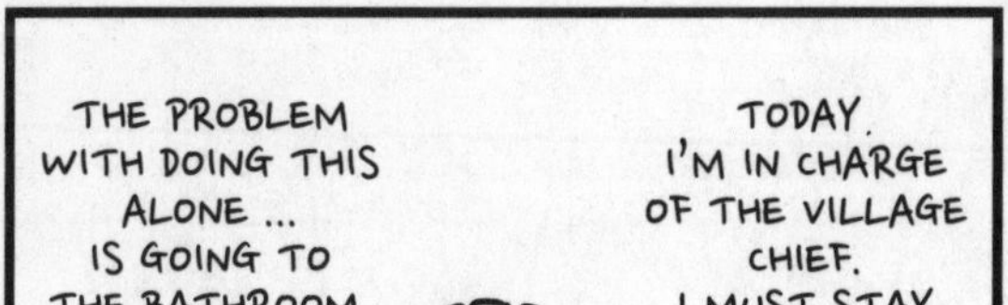

TODAY, I'M IN CHARGE OF THE VILLAGE CHIEF. I MUST STAY ALERT. I'M THE ONLY ONE ON CHIEF DUTY.
THE PROBLEM WITH DOING THIS ALONE ... IS GOING TO THE BATHROOM. I CAN ONLY GO WHEN HE DOES.
11

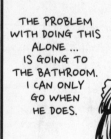

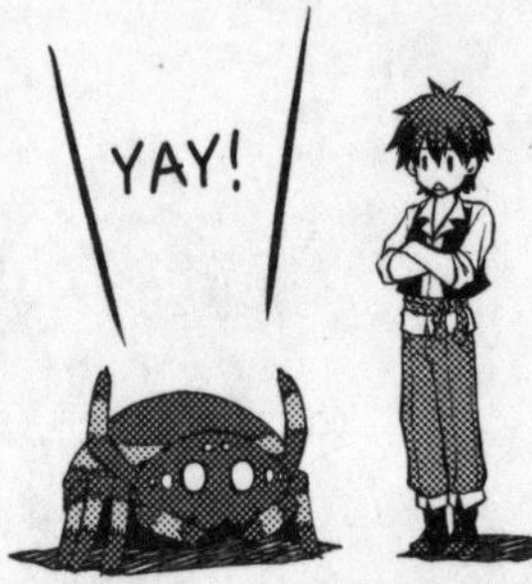
YAY!
Farming life in another world.

CHAPTER 70: MARTIAL ARTS TOURNAMENT, COMMONER DIVISION

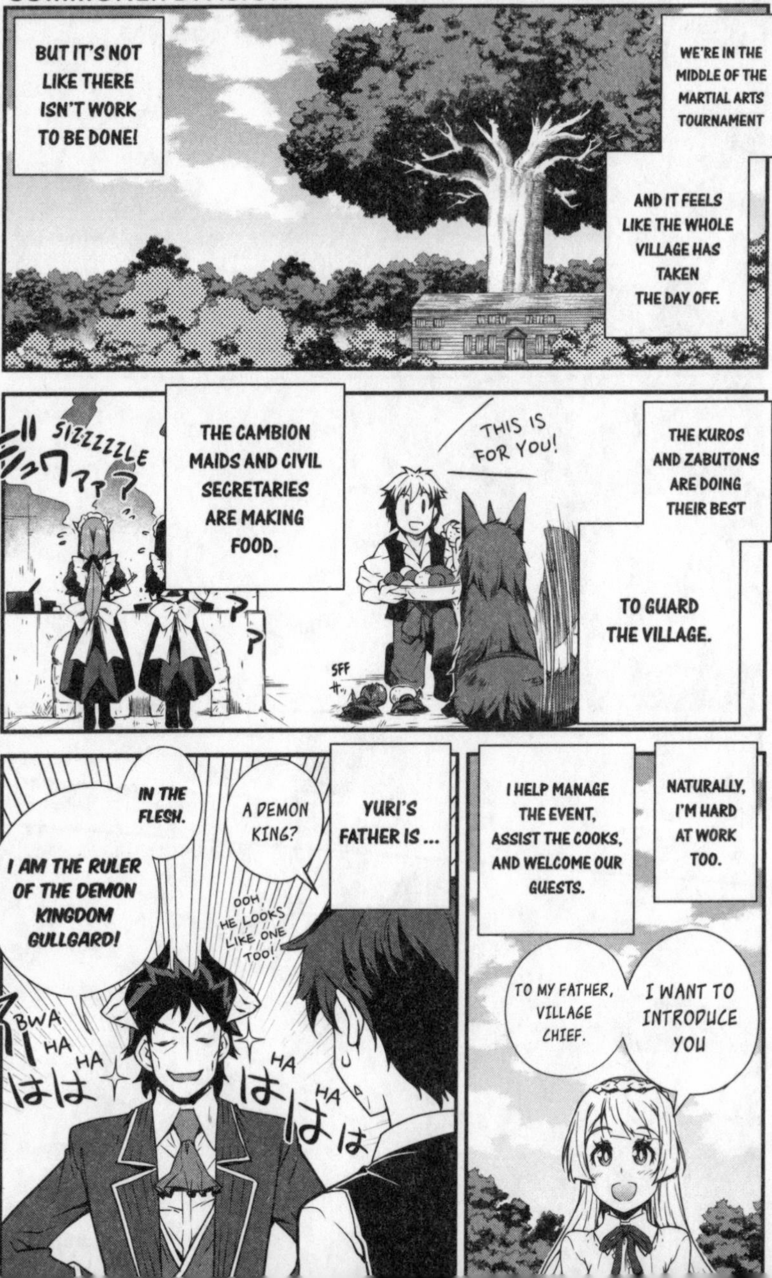
WE'RE IN THE MIDDLE OF THE MARTIAL ARTS TOURNAMENT
AND IT FEELS LIKE THE WHOLE VILLAGE HAS TAKEN THE DAY OFF.
BUT IT'S NOT LIKE THERE ISN'T WORK TO BE DONE!
THE KUROS AND ZABUTONS ARE DOING THEIR BEST
TO GUARD THE VILLAGE.
THIS IS FOR YOU!
SFF
THE CAMBION MAIDS AND CIVIL SECRETARIES ARE MAKING FOOD.
SIZZZZZZLE
NATURALLY, I'M HARD AT WORK TOO.
I HELP MANAGE THE EVENT, ASSIST THE COOKS, AND WELCOME OUR GUESTS.
I WANT TO INTRODUCE YOU
TO MY FATHER, VILLAGE CHIEF.
YURI'S FATHER IS ...
A DEMON KING?
IN THE FLESH.
I AM THE RULER OF THE DEMON KINGDOM GULLGARD!
OOH HE LOOKS LIKE ONE TOO!
BWA HA HA HA HA

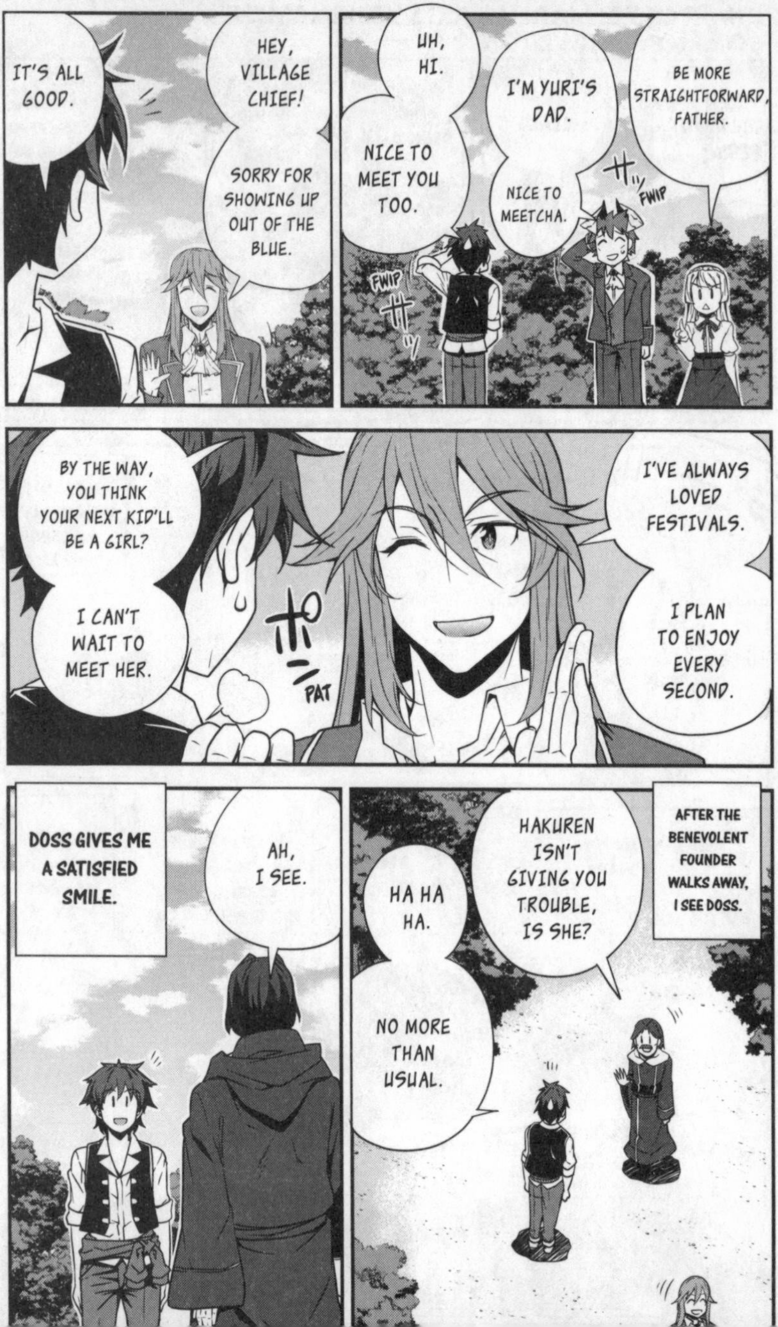
BE MORE STRAIGHTFORWARD, FATHER.
I'M YURI'S DAD.
NICE TO MEETCHA.
FWIP
UH, HI.
NICE TO MEET YOU TOO.
FWIP
HEY, VILLAGE CHIEF!
SORRY FOR SHOWING UP OUT OF THE BLUE.
IT'S ALL GOOD.
I'VE ALWAYS LOVED FESTIVALS.
I PLAN TO ENJOY EVERY SECOND.
BY THE WAY, YOU THINK YOUR NEXT KID'LL BE A GIRL?
I CAN'T WAIT TO MEET HER.
PAT
AFTER THE BENEVOLENT FOUNDER WALKS AWAY, I SEE DOSS.
HAKUREN ISN'T GIVING YOU TROUBLE, IS SHE?
HA HA HA.
NO MORE THAN USUAL.
AH, I SEE.
DOSS GIVES ME A SATISFIED SMILE.

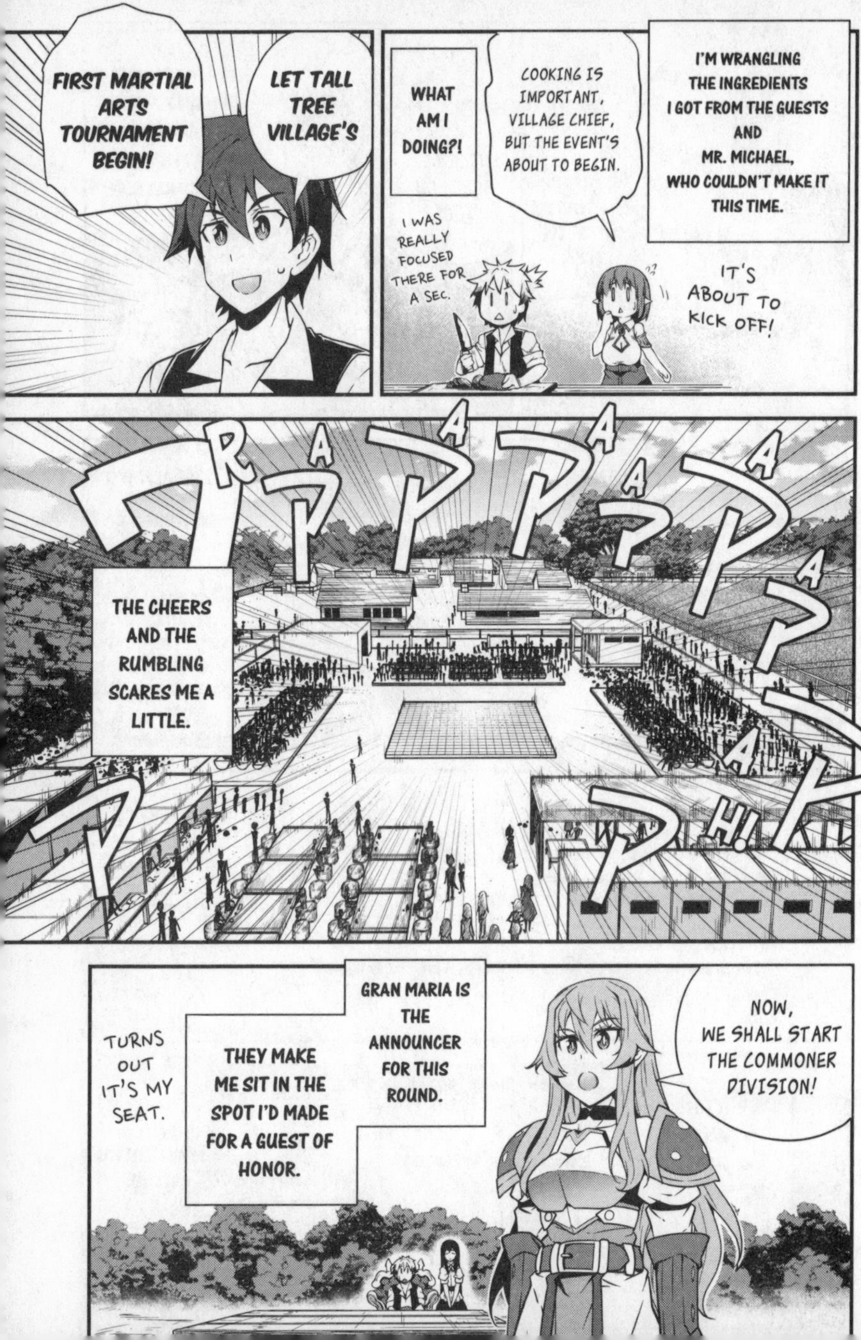
I'M WRANGLING THE INGREDIENTS I GOT FROM THE GUESTS AND MR. MICHAEL, WHO COULDN'T MAKE IT THIS TIME.
COOKING IS IMPORTANT, VILLAGE CHIEF, BUT THE EVENT'S ABOUT TO BEGIN.
WHAT AM I DOING?!
IT'S ABOUT TO KICK OFF!
I WAS REALLY FOCUSED THERE FOR A SEC.
LET TALL TREE VILLAGE'S
FIRST MARTIAL ARTS TOURNAMENT BEGIN!
RAAAAAAAAH!!
THE CHEERS AND THE RUMBLING SCARES ME A LITTLE.
NOW, WE SHALL START THE COMMONER DIVISION!
GRAN MARIA IS THE ANNOUNCER FOR THIS ROUND.
THEY MAKE ME SIT IN THE SPOT I'D MADE FOR A GUEST OF HONOR.
TURNS OUT IT'S MY SEAT.

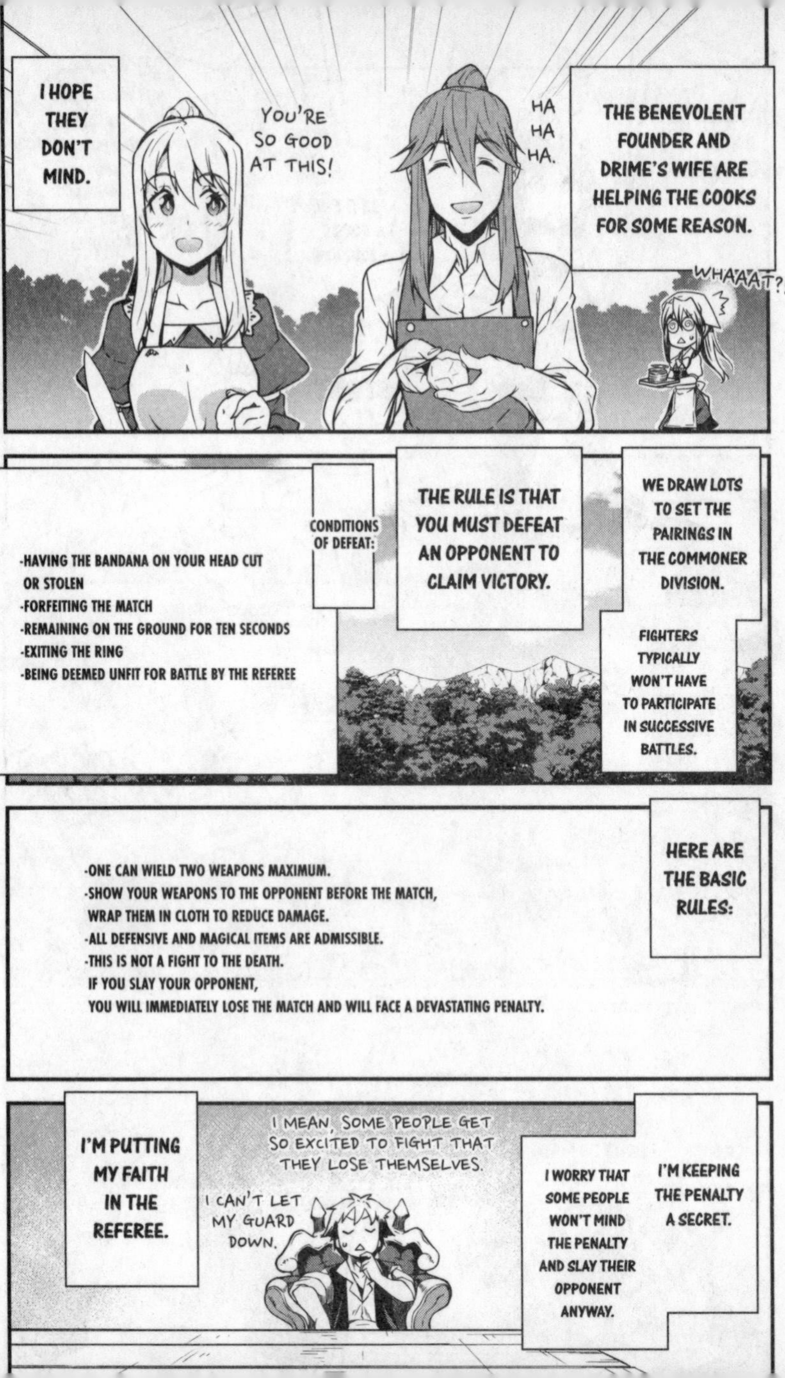
THE BENEVOLENT FOUNDER AND DRIME'S WIFE ARE HELPING THE COOKS FOR SOME REASON.
WHAAAT?!
HA HA HA.
YOU'RE SO GOOD AT THIS!
I HOPE THEY DON'T MIND.
WE DRAW LOTS TO SET THE PAIRINGS IN THE COMMONER DIVISION.
FIGHTERS TYPICALLY WON'T HAVE TO PARTICIPATE IN SUCCESSIVE BATTLES.
THE RULE IS THAT YOU MUST DEFEAT AN OPPONENT TO CLAIM VICTORY.
CONDITIONS OF DEFEAT:
-HAVING THE BANDANA ON YOUR HEAD CUT OR STOLEN
-FORFEITING THE MATCH
-REMAINING ON THE GROUND FOR TEN SECONDS
-EXITING THE RING
-BEING DEEMED UNFIT FOR BATTLE BY THE REFEREE
HERE ARE THE BASIC RULES:
-ONE CAN WIELD TWO WEAPONS MAXIMUM.
-SHOW YOUR WEAPONS TO THE OPPONENT BEFORE THE MATCH, WRAP THEM IN CLOTH TO REDUCE DAMAGE.
-ALL DEFENSIVE AND MAGICAL ITEMS ARE ADMISSIBLE.
-THIS IS NOT A FIGHT TO THE DEATH. IF YOU SLAY YOUR OPPONENT, YOU WILL IMMEDIATELY LOSE THE MATCH AND WILL FACE A DEVASTATING PENALTY.
I'M KEEPING THE PENALTY A SECRET.
I WORRY THAT SOME PEOPLE WON'T MIND THE PENALTY AND SLAY THEIR OPPONENT ANYWAY.
I MEAN, SOME PEOPLE GET SO EXCITED TO FIGHT THAT THEY LOSE THEMSELVES.
I CAN'T LET MY GUARD DOWN.
I'M PUTTING MY FAITH IN THE REFEREE.

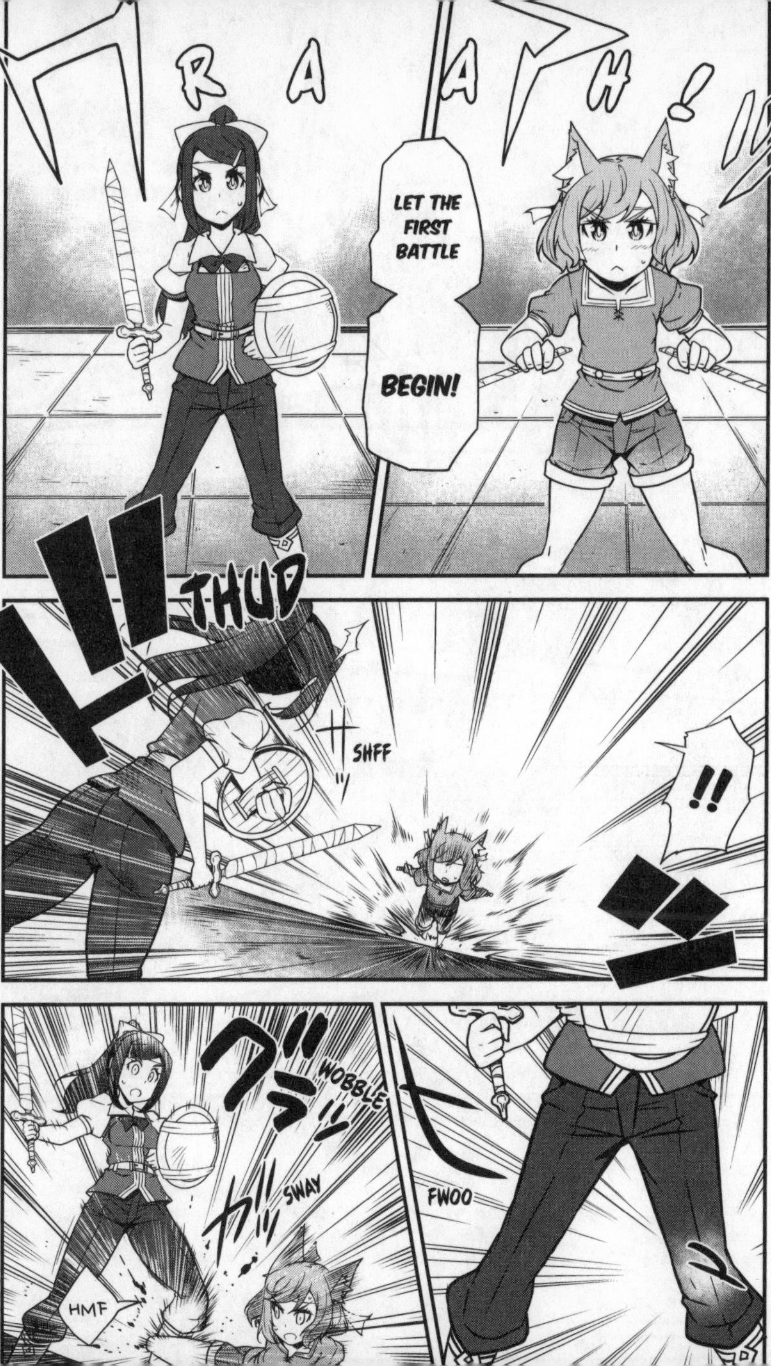
RAAH!!
LET THE FIRST BATTLE BEGIN!
THUD
!!
SHFF
FWOO
WOBBLE
SWAY
HMF

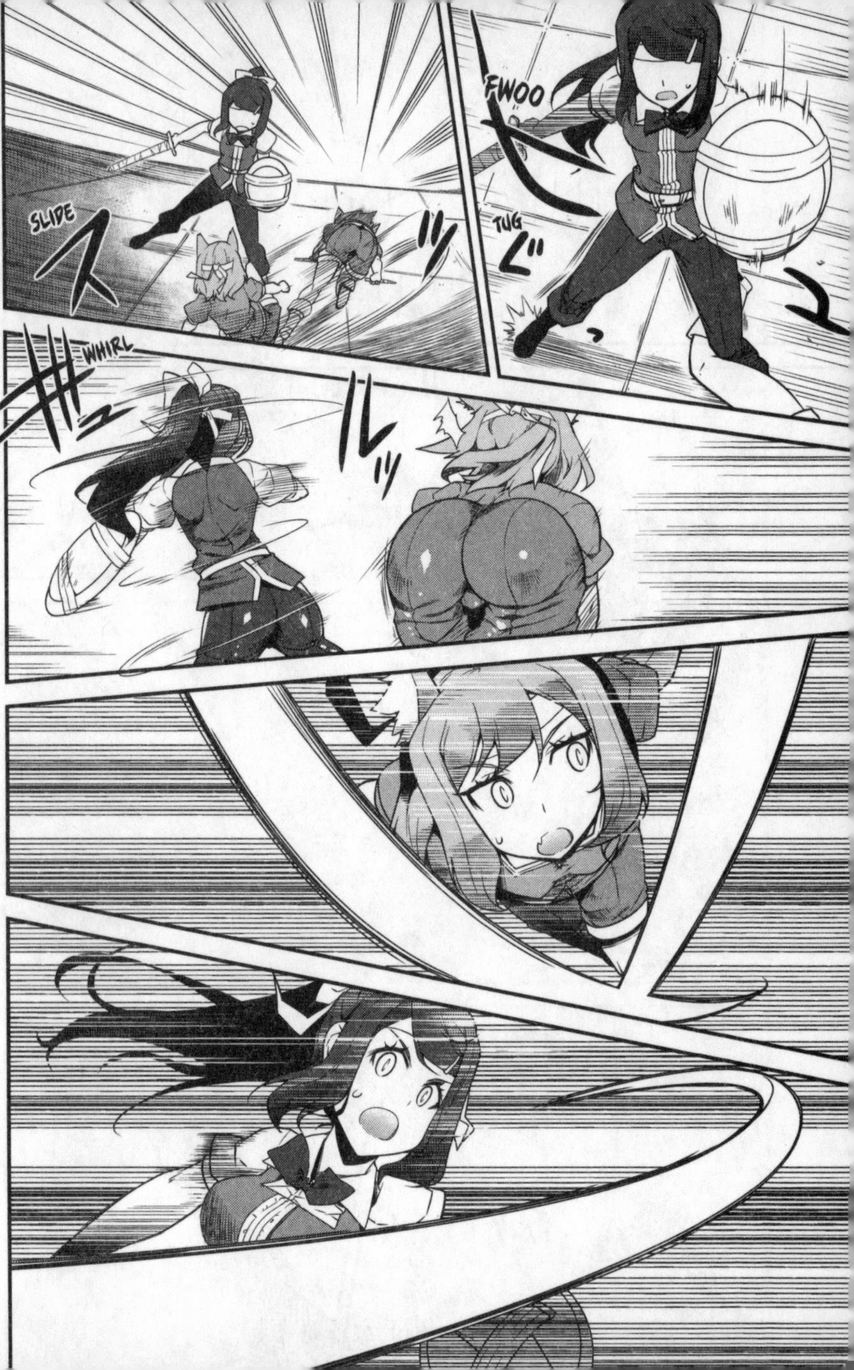
FWOO
TUG
SLIDE
WHIRL

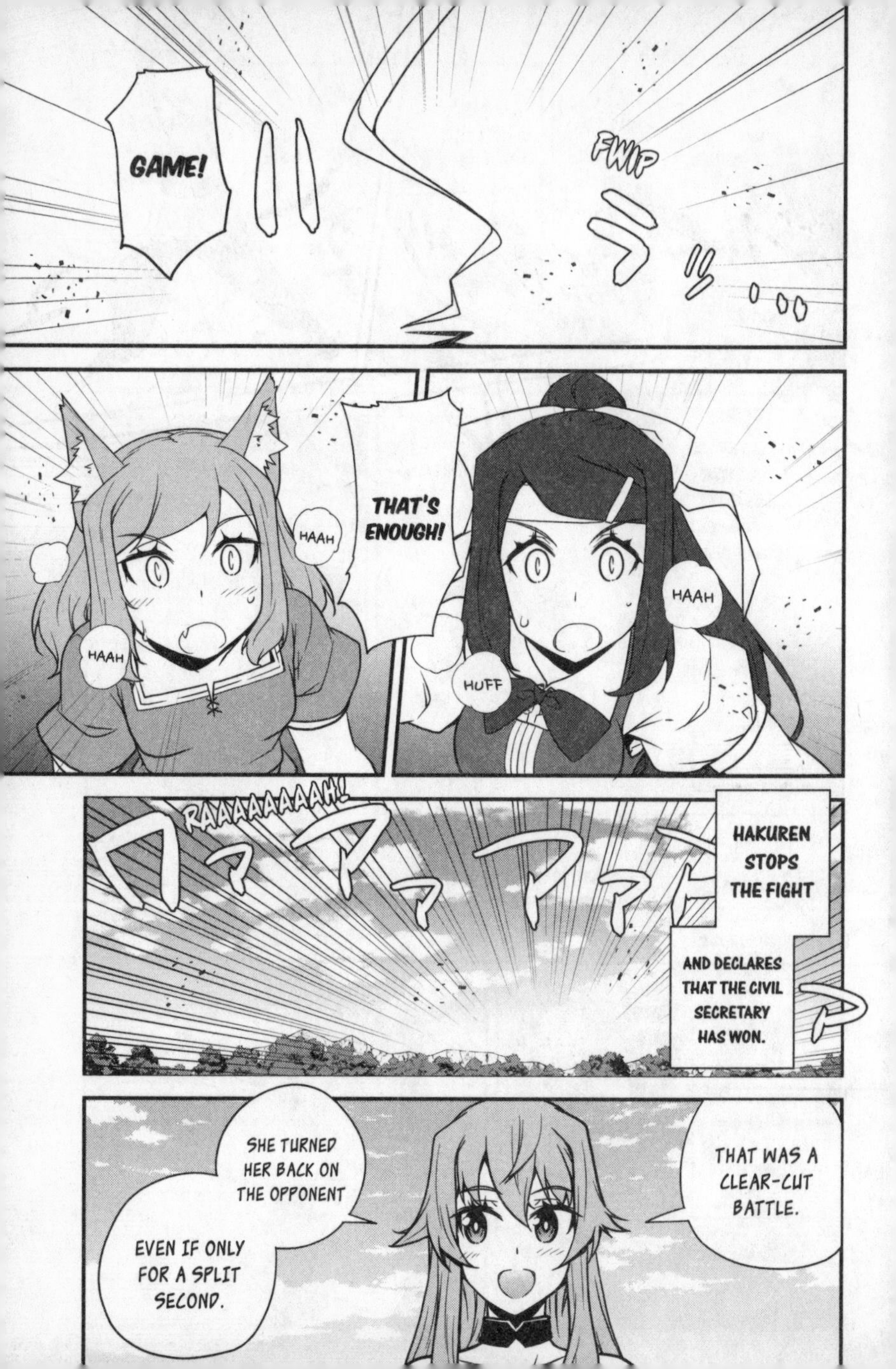
FWIP
GAME!
HAAH
HUFF
THAT'S ENOUGH!
HAAH
HAAH
HAKUREN STOPS THE FIGHT
AND DECLARES THAT THE CIVIL SECRETARY HAS WON.
RAAAAAAAAH!
THAT WAS A CLEAR-CUT BATTLE.
SHE TURNED HER BACK ON THE OPPONENT
EVEN IF ONLY FOR A SPLIT SECOND.

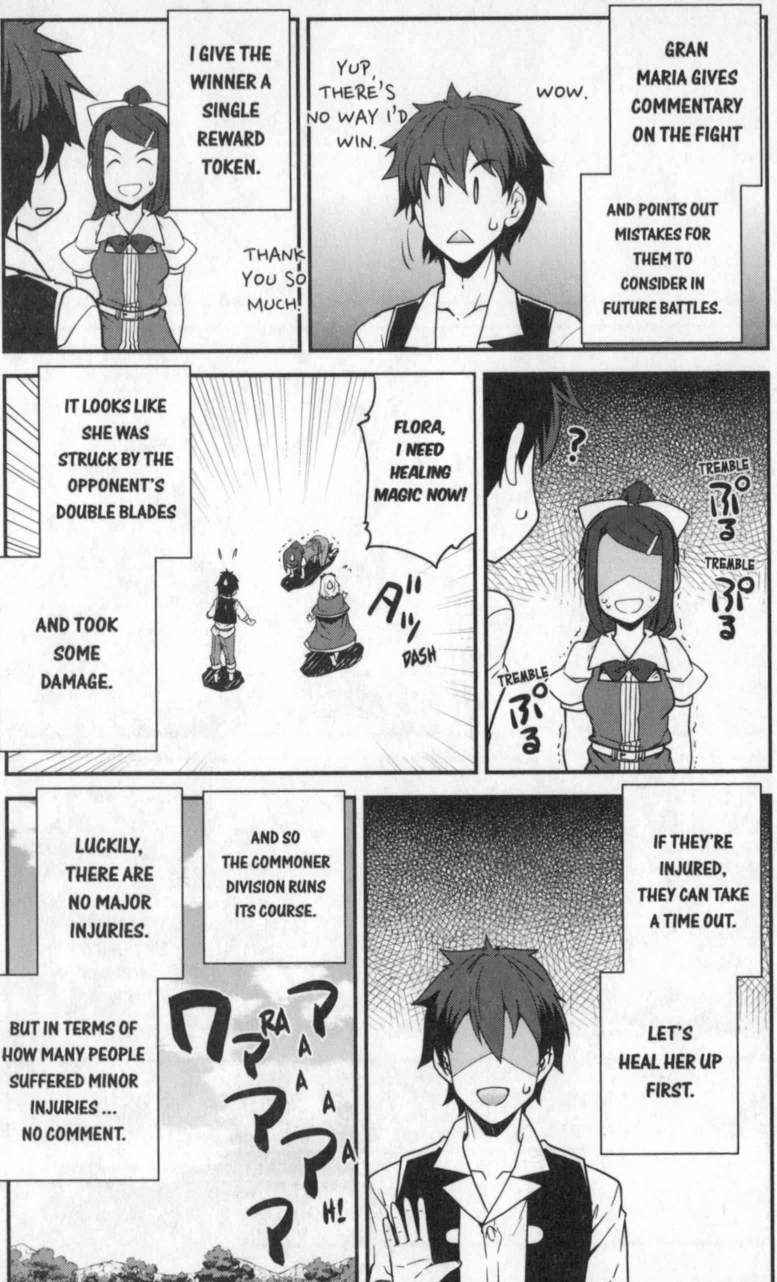
GRAN MARIA GIVES COMMENTARY ON THE FIGHT
AND POINTS OUT MISTAKES FOR THEM TO CONSIDER IN FUTURE BATTLES.
WOW.
YUP, THERE'S NO WAY I'D WIN.
I GIVE THE WINNER A SINGLE REWARD TOKEN.
THANK YOU SO MUCH!
?
TREMBLE
ぷる
TREMBLE
ぷる
TREMBLE
ぷる
FLORA, I NEED HEALING MAGIC NOW!
ダッ
DASH
IT LOOKS LIKE SHE WAS STRUCK BY THE OPPONENT'S DOUBLE BLADES
AND TOOK SOME DAMAGE.
IF THEY'RE INJURED, THEY CAN TAKE A TIME OUT.
LET'S HEAL HER UP FIRST.
AND SO THE COMMONER DIVISION RUNS ITS COURSE.
LUCKILY, THERE ARE NO MAJOR INJURIES.
BUT IN TERMS OF HOW MANY PEOPLE SUFFERED MINOR INJURIES ... NO COMMENT.
ワアアアア
RAAAAAH!

HE HAS SO MUCH PRIDE
THAT HE WON'T WEAR A DIAPER.

INSTEAD, HE'S GATHERING
BAMBOO CONTAINERS.

I DON'T WANT TO KNOW
HOW HE'S GOING TO
USE THEM.

Farming life in another world.

CHAPTER 71: MARTIAL ARTS TOURNAMENT, WARRIOR DIVISION PART 1

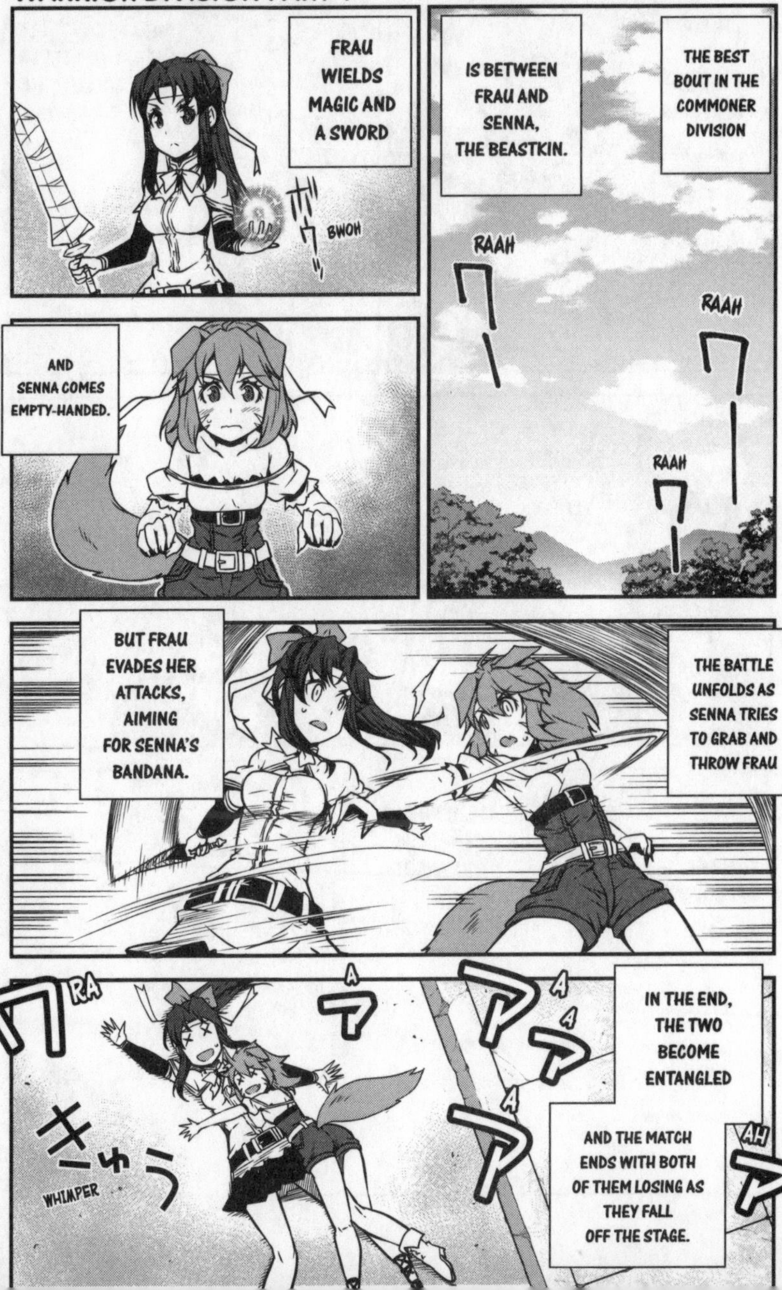
THE BEST BOUT IN THE COMMONER DIVISION
IS BETWEEN FRAU AND SENNA, THE BEASTKIN.
RAAH
RAAH
RAAH
FRAU WIELDS MAGIC AND A SWORD
BWOH
AND SENNA COMES EMPTY-HANDED.
THE BATTLE UNFOLDS AS SENNA TRIES TO GRAB AND THROW FRAU
BUT FRAU EVADES HER ATTACKS, AIMING FOR SENNA'S BANDANA.
IN THE END, THE TWO BECOME ENTANGLED
AND THE MATCH ENDS WITH BOTH OF THEM LOSING AS THEY FALL OFF THE STAGE.
AH
A
A
A
A
RA
WHIMPER

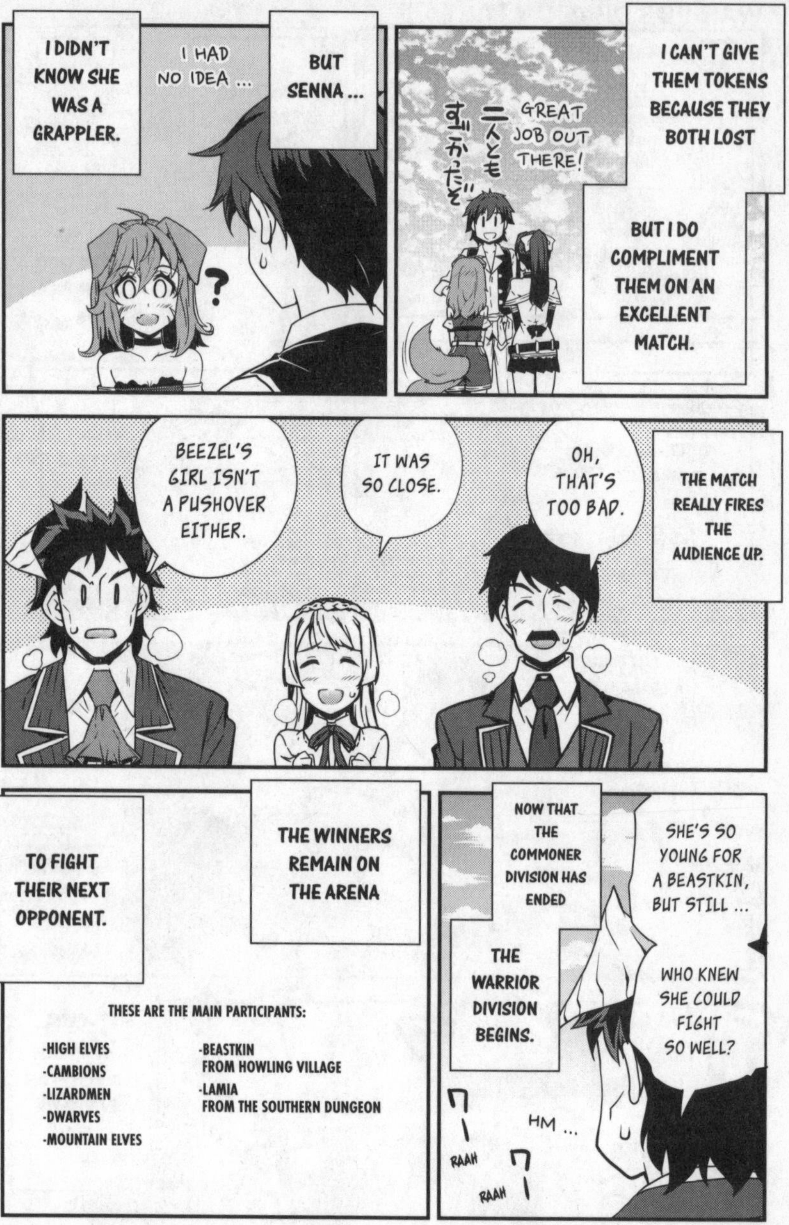
I CAN'T GIVE THEM TOKENS BECAUSE THEY BOTH LOST
二人ともすごかったぞ
GREAT JOB OUT THERE!
BUT I DO COMPLIMENT THEM ON AN EXCELLENT MATCH.
BUT SENNA ...
I HAD NO IDEA ...
I DIDN'T KNOW SHE WAS A GRAPPLER.
?
THE MATCH REALLY FIRES THE AUDIENCE UP.
OH, THAT'S TOO BAD.
IT WAS SO CLOSE.
BEEZEL'S GIRL ISN'T A PUSHOVER EITHER.
NOW THAT THE COMMONER DIVISION HAS ENDED
SHE'S SO YOUNG FOR A BEASTKIN, BUT STILL ...
THE WARRIOR DIVISION BEGINS.
WHO KNEW SHE COULD FIGHT SO WELL?
HM ...
ワー
RAAH
ワー
RAAH
THE WINNERS REMAIN ON THE ARENA
TO FIGHT THEIR NEXT OPPONENT.
THESE ARE THE MAIN PARTICIPANTS:
-HIGH ELVES
-CAMBIONS
-LIZARDMEN
-DWARVES
-MOUNTAIN ELVES
-BEASTKIN FROM HOWLING VILLAGE
-LAMIA FROM THE SOUTHERN DUNGEON

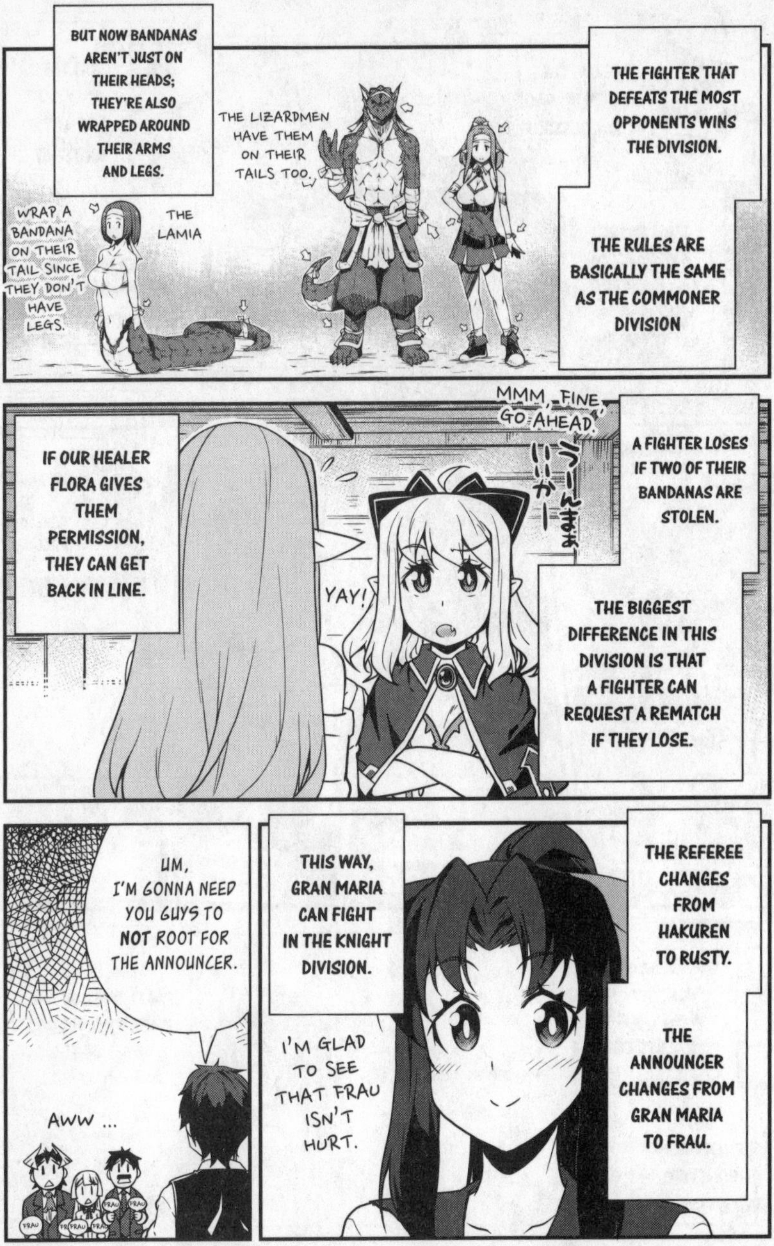
THE FIGHTER THAT DEFEATS THE MOST OPPONENTS WINS THE DIVISION.
THE RULES ARE BASICALLY THE SAME AS THE COMMONER DIVISION
BUT NOW BANDANAS AREN'T JUST ON THEIR HEADS; THEY'RE ALSO WRAPPED AROUND THEIR ARMS AND LEGS.
THE LIZARDMEN HAVE THEM ON THEIR TAILS TOO.
THE LAMIA
WRAP A BANDANA ON THEIR TAIL SINCE THEY DON'T HAVE LEGS.
A FIGHTER LOSES IF TWO OF THEIR BANDANAS ARE STOLEN.
THE BIGGEST DIFFERENCE IN THIS DIVISION IS THAT A FIGHTER CAN REQUEST A REMATCH IF THEY LOSE.
MMM, FINE, GO AHEAD.
うーんまぁいいかー
YAY!
IF OUR HEALER FLORA GIVES THEM PERMISSION, THEY CAN GET BACK IN LINE.
THE REFEREE CHANGES FROM HAKUREN TO RUSTY.
THE ANNOUNCER CHANGES FROM GRAN MARIA TO FRAU.
THIS WAY, GRAN MARIA CAN FIGHT IN THE KNIGHT DIVISION.
I'M GLAD TO SEE THAT FRAU ISN'T HURT.
UM, I'M GONNA NEED YOU GUYS TO NOT ROOT FOR THE ANNOUNCER.
AWW ...

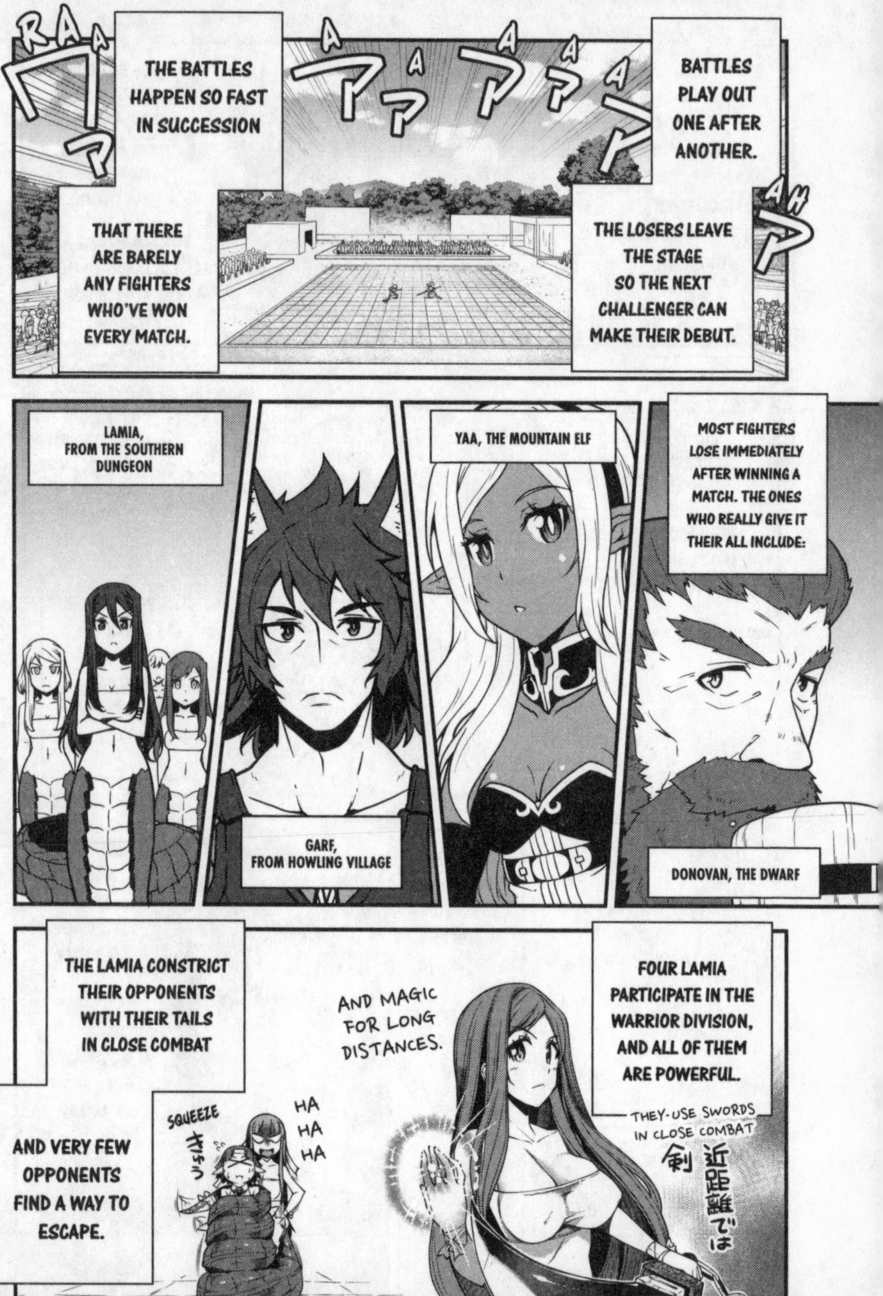
RAAAAAAAAAH
BATTLES PLAY OUT ONE AFTER ANOTHER.
THE LOSERS LEAVE THE STAGE SO THE NEXT CHALLENGER CAN MAKE THEIR DEBUT.
THE BATTLES HAPPEN SO FAST IN SUCCESSION
THAT THERE ARE BARELY ANY FIGHTERS WHO'VE WON EVERY MATCH.
MOST FIGHTERS LOSE IMMEDIATELY AFTER WINNING A MATCH. THE ONES WHO REALLY GIVE IT THEIR ALL INCLUDE:
DONOVAN, THE DWARF
YAA, THE MOUNTAIN ELF
GARF, FROM HOWLING VILLAGE
LAMIA, FROM THE SOUTHERN DUNGEON
FOUR LAMIA PARTICIPATE IN THE WARRIOR DIVISION, AND ALL OF THEM ARE POWERFUL.
THEY USE SWORDS IN CLOSE COMBAT
近距離では剣
AND MAGIC FOR LONG DISTANCES.
THE LAMIA CONSTRICT THEIR OPPONENTS WITH THEIR TAILS IN CLOSE COMBAT
HA HA HA
SQUEEZE
AND VERY FEW OPPONENTS FIND A WAY TO ESCAPE.

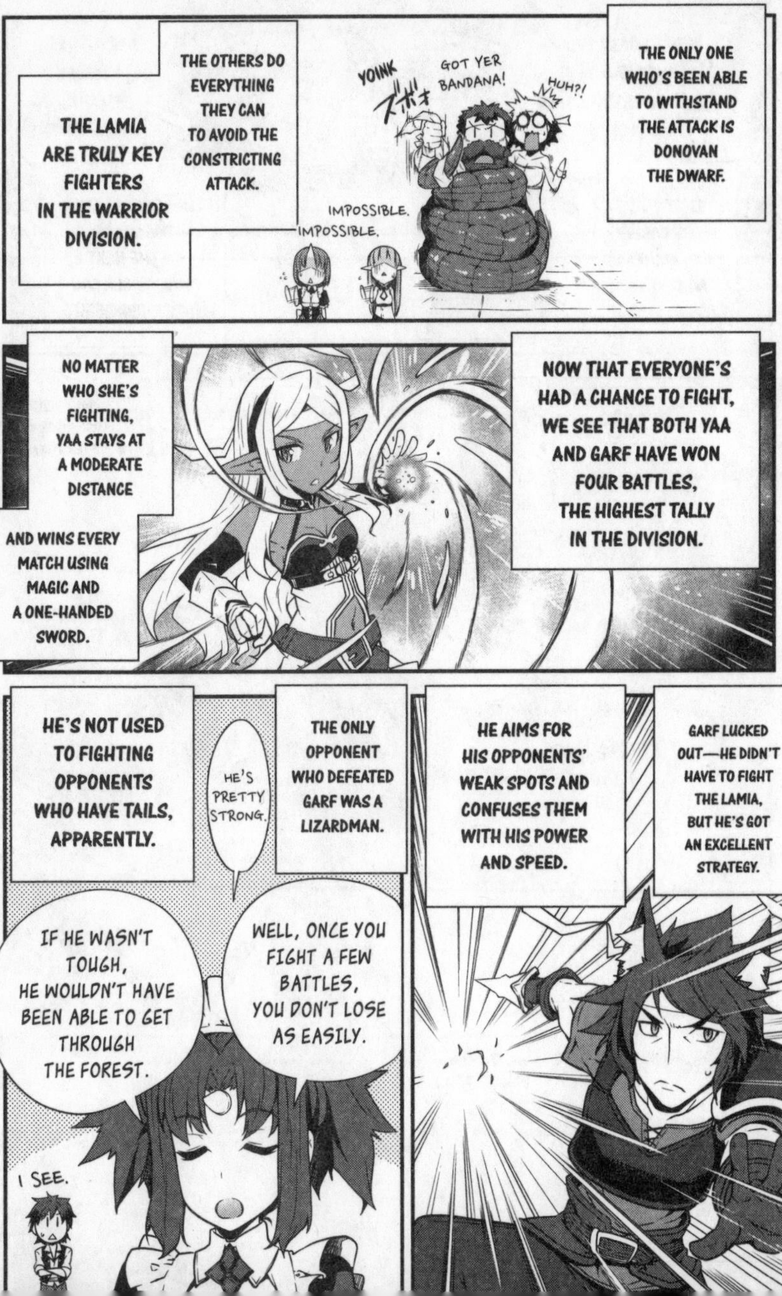
THE ONLY ONE WHO'S BEEN ABLE TO WITHSTAND THE ATTACK IS DONOVAN THE DWARF.
HUH?!
GOT YER BANDANA!
YOINK
ズボォ
THE OTHERS DO EVERYTHING THEY CAN TO AVOID THE CONSTRICTING ATTACK.
THE LAMIA ARE TRULY KEY FIGHTERS IN THE WARRIOR DIVISION.
IMPOSSIBLE.
IMPOSSIBLE.
NOW THAT EVERYONE'S HAD A CHANCE TO FIGHT, WE SEE THAT BOTH YAA AND GARF HAVE WON FOUR BATTLES, THE HIGHEST TALLY IN THE DIVISION.
NO MATTER WHO SHE'S FIGHTING, YAA STAYS AT A MODERATE DISTANCE
AND WINS EVERY MATCH USING MAGIC AND A ONE-HANDED SWORD.
GARF LUCKED OUT—HE DIDN'T HAVE TO FIGHT THE LAMIA, BUT HE'S GOT AN EXCELLENT STRATEGY.
HE AIMS FOR HIS OPPONENTS' WEAK SPOTS AND CONFUSES THEM WITH HIS POWER AND SPEED.
THE ONLY OPPONENT WHO DEFEATED GARF WAS A LIZARDMAN.
HE'S PRETTY STRONG.
HE'S NOT USED TO FIGHTING OPPONENTS WHO HAVE TAILS, APPARENTLY.
WELL, ONCE YOU FIGHT A FEW BATTLES, YOU DON'T LOSE AS EASILY.
IF HE WASN'T TOUGH, HE WOULDN'T HAVE BEEN ABLE TO GET THROUGH THE FOREST.
I SEE.

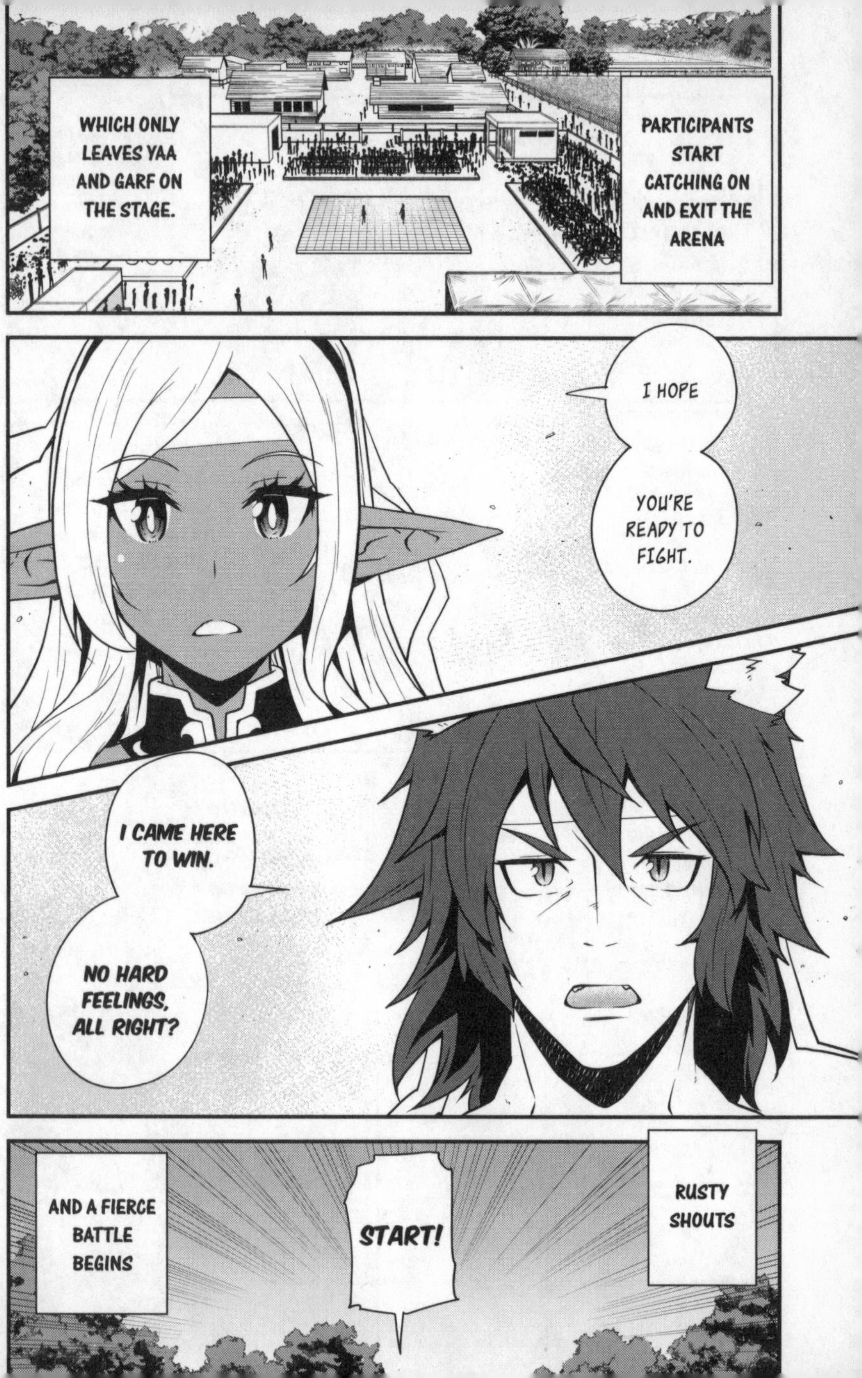
PARTICIPANTS START CATCHING ON AND EXIT THE ARENA
WHICH ONLY LEAVES YAA AND GARF ON THE STAGE.
I HOPE
YOU'RE READY TO FIGHT.
I CAME HERE TO WIN.
NO HARD FEELINGS, ALL RIGHT?
RUSTY SHOUTS
START!
AND A FIERCE BATTLE BEGINS

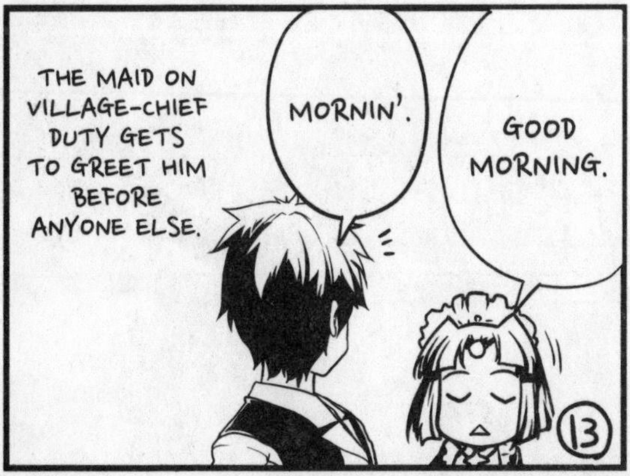
GOOD MORNING.
MORNIN'.
THE MAID ON VILLAGE-CHIEF DUTY GETS TO GREET HIM BEFORE ANYONE ELSE.
13

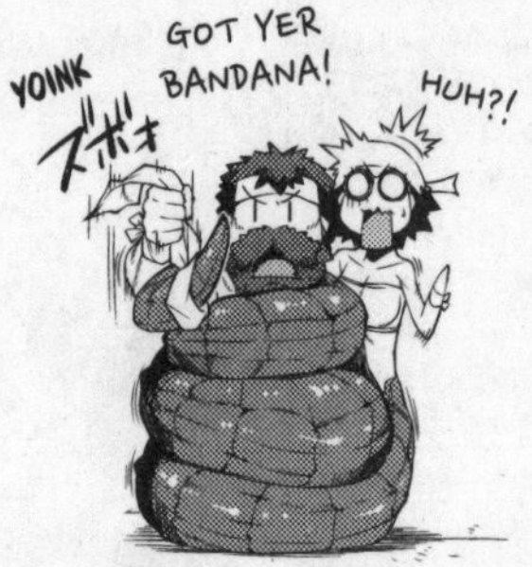
GOT YER BANDANA!
HUH?!
YOINK
ズボォ

Farming life in another world.

CHAPTER 72: MARTIAL ARTS TOURNAMENT, WARRIOR DIVISION PART 2

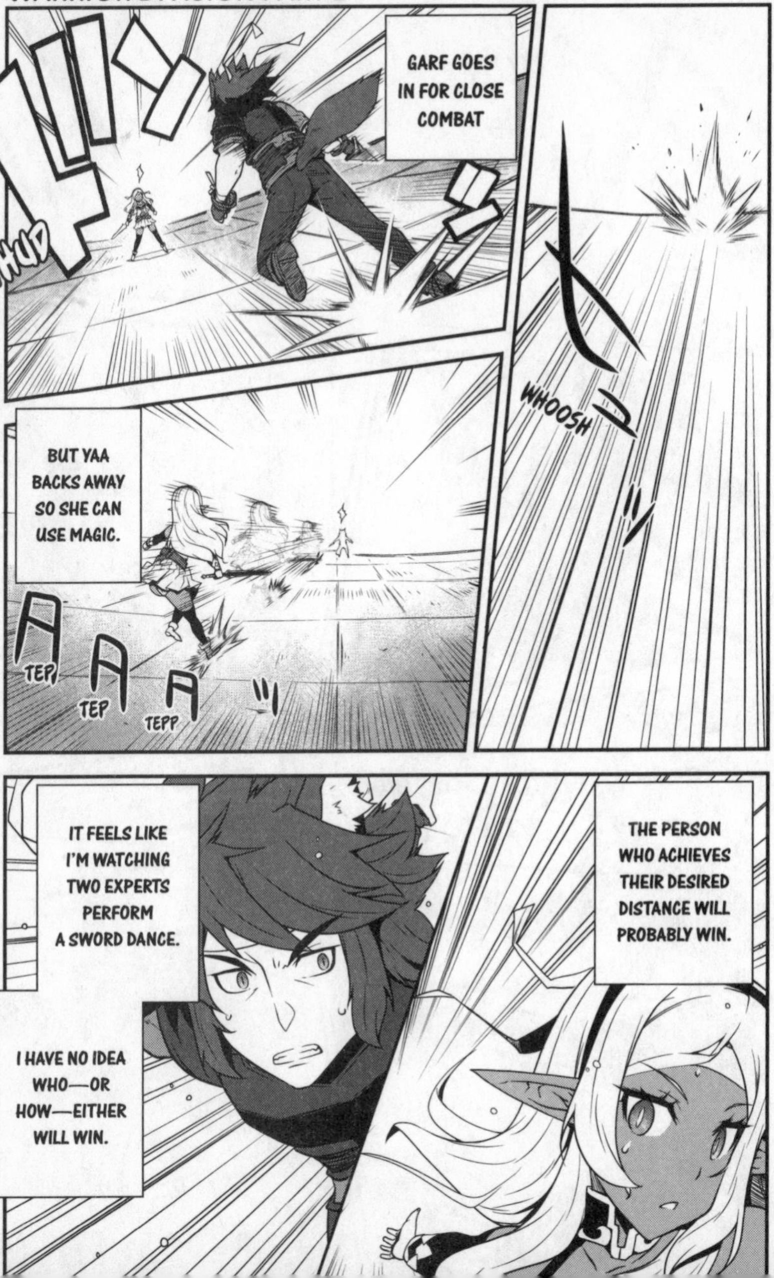
WHOOSH
GARF GOES IN FOR CLOSE COMBAT
THUD
BUT YAA BACKS AWAY SO SHE CAN USE MAGIC.
TEP
TEP
TEPP
THE PERSON WHO ACHIEVES THEIR DESIRED DISTANCE WILL PROBABLY WIN.
IT FEELS LIKE I'M WATCHING TWO EXPERTS PERFORM A SWORD DANCE.
I HAVE NO IDEA WHO—OR HOW—EITHER WILL WIN.

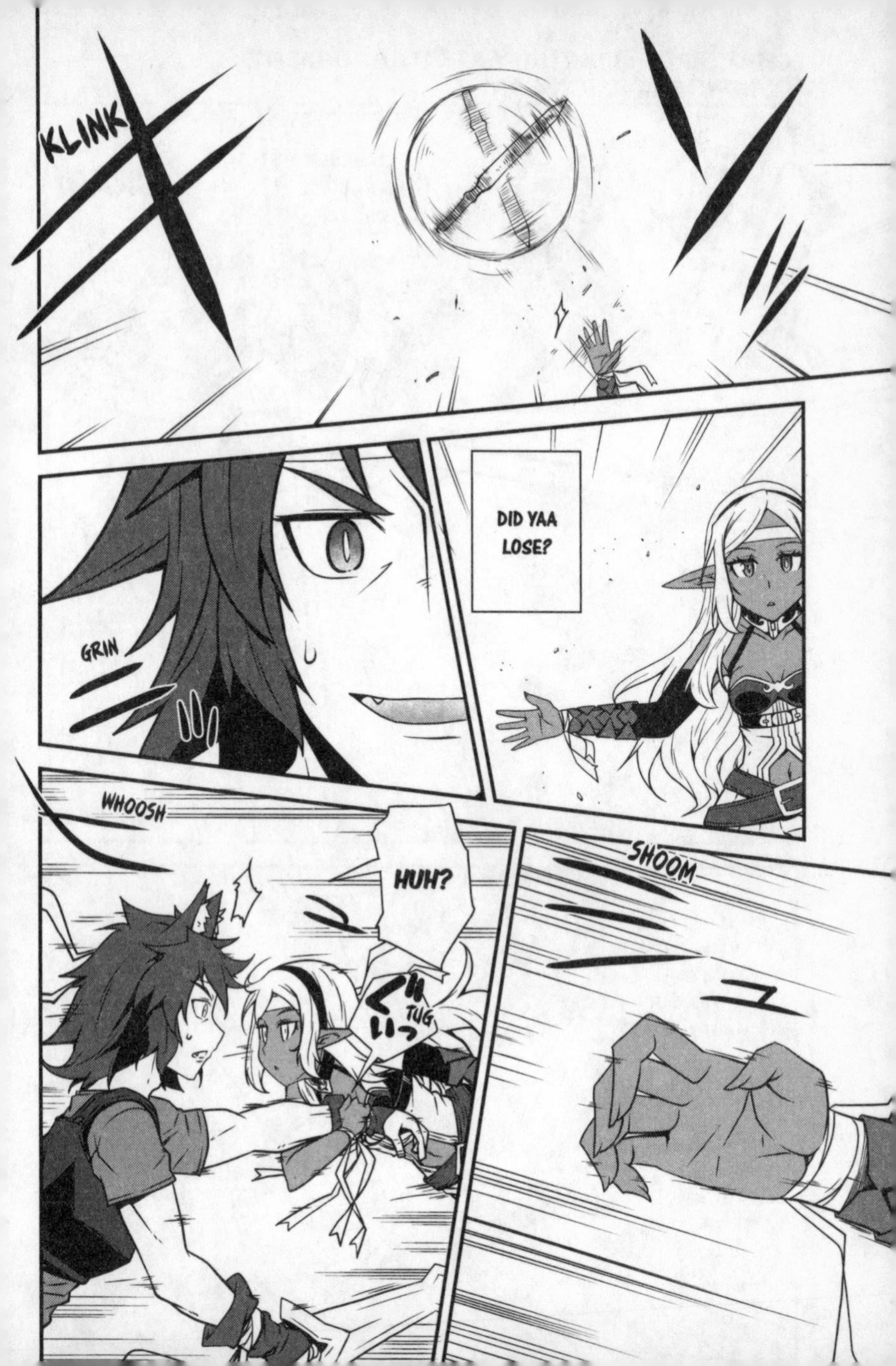
KLINK
DID YAA LOSE?
GRIN
SHOOM
WHOOSH
HUH?
TUG

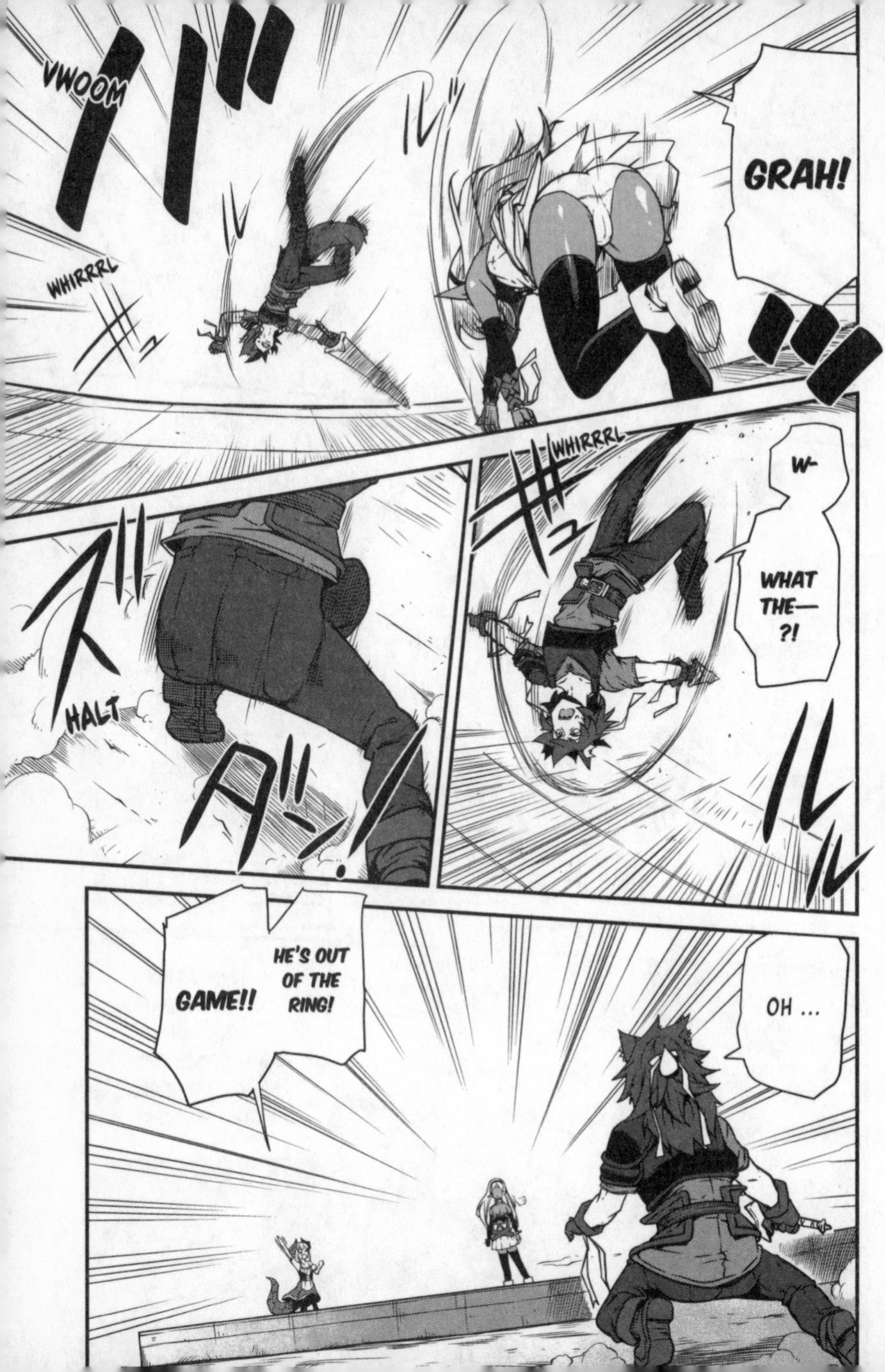
GRAH!
VWOOM
WHIRRRL
WHIRRRL
W-
WHAT THE—?!
HALT
OH ...
HE'S OUT OF THE RING!
GAME!!

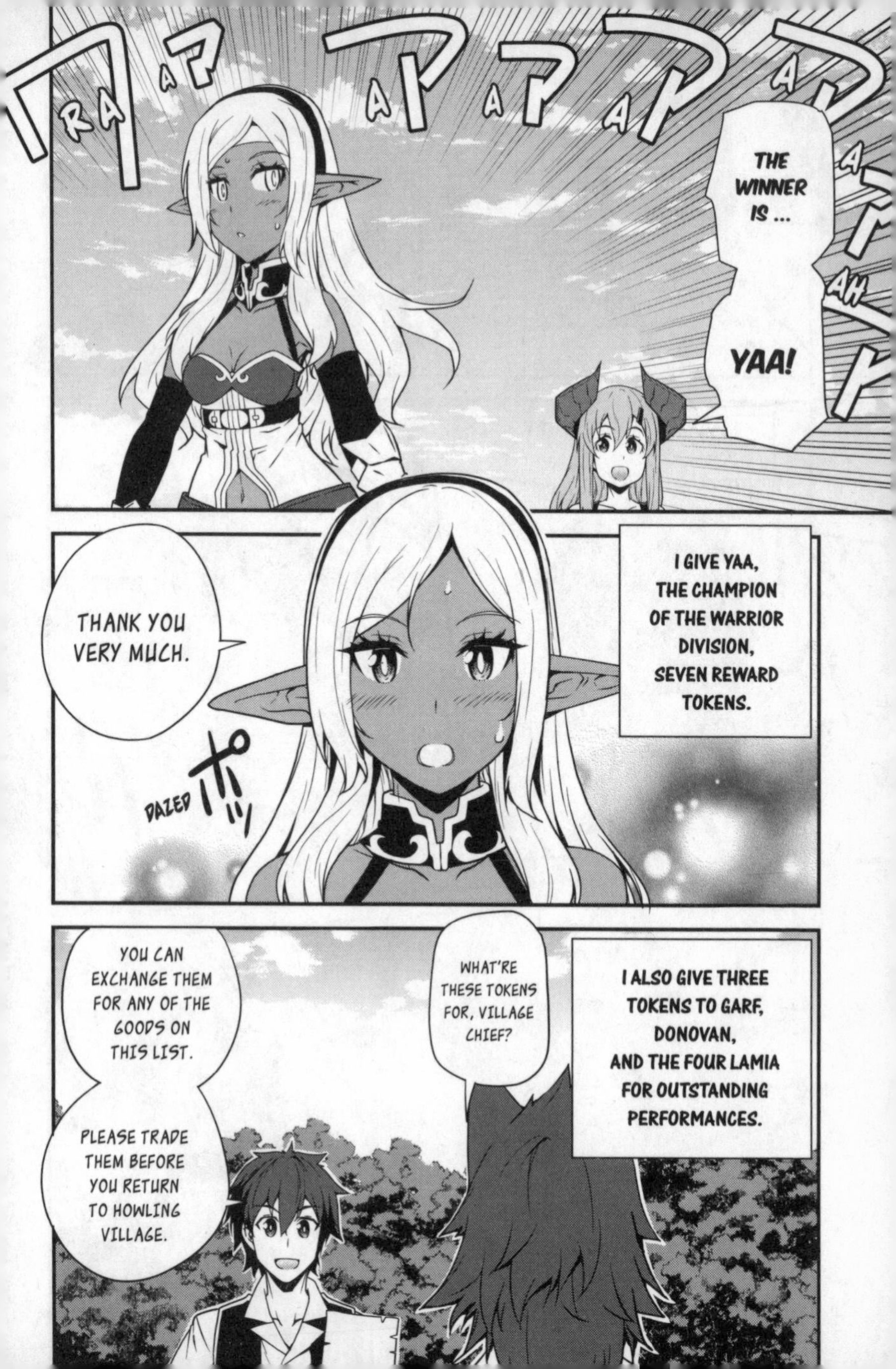
THE WINNER IS ... YAA!
RA A A A A A A AH
I GIVE YAA, THE CHAMPION OF THE WARRIOR DIVISION, SEVEN REWARD TOKENS.
THANK YOU VERY MUCH.
DAZED
I ALSO GIVE THREE TOKENS TO GARF, DONOVAN, AND THE FOUR LAMIA FOR OUTSTANDING PERFORMANCES.
WHAT'RE THESE TOKENS FOR, VILLAGE CHIEF?
YOU CAN EXCHANGE THEM FOR ANY OF THE GOODS ON THIS LIST.
PLEASE TRADE THEM BEFORE YOU RETURN TO HOWLING VILLAGE.

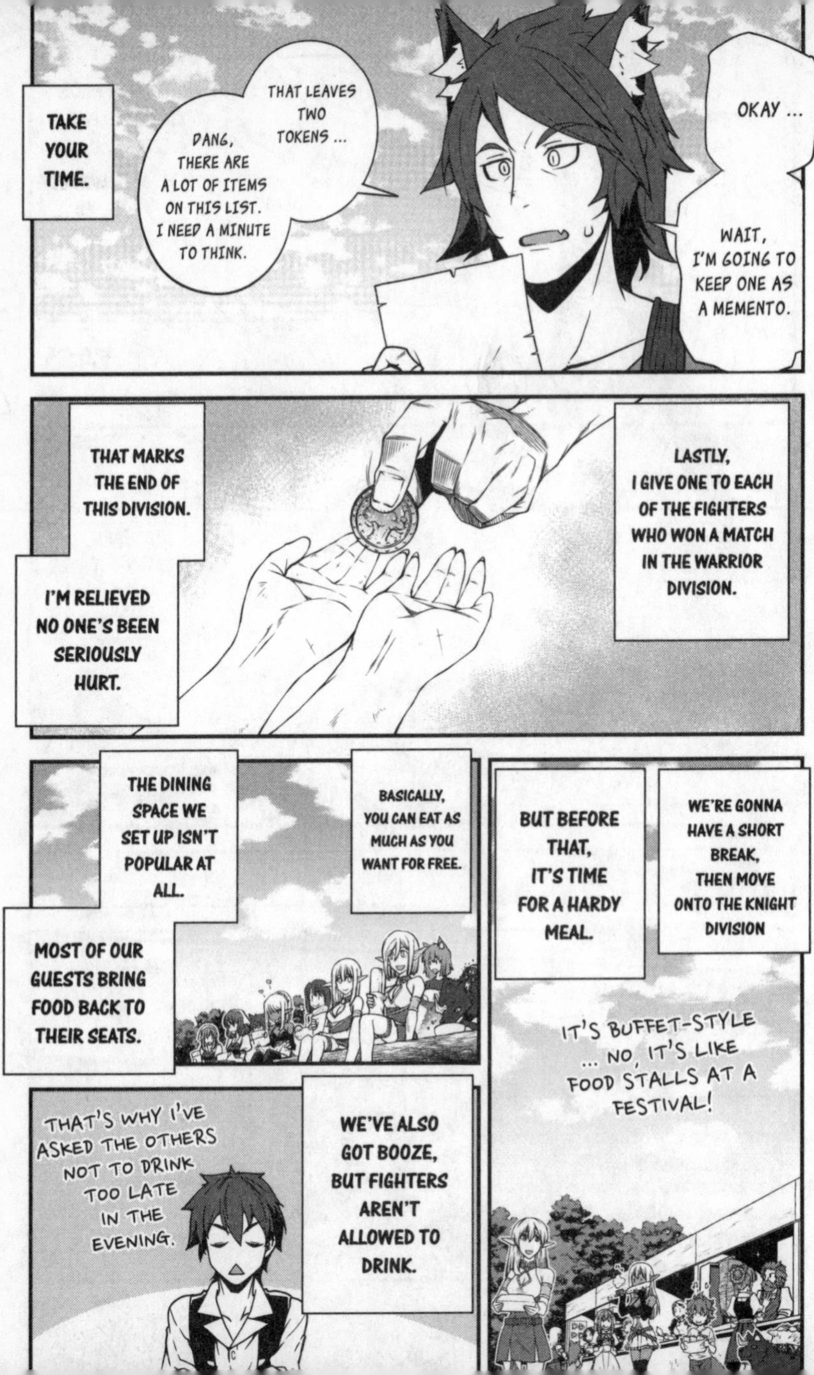
OKAY ...
WAIT, I'M GOING TO KEEP ONE AS A MEMENTO.
THAT LEAVES TWO TOKENS ...
DANG, THERE ARE A LOT OF ITEMS ON THIS LIST. I NEED A MINUTE TO THINK.
TAKE YOUR TIME.
LASTLY, I GIVE ONE TO EACH OF THE FIGHTERS WHO WON A MATCH IN THE WARRIOR DIVISION.
THAT MARKS THE END OF THIS DIVISION.
I'M RELIEVED NO ONE'S BEEN SERIOUSLY HURT.
WE'RE GONNA HAVE A SHORT BREAK, THEN MOVE ONTO THE KNIGHT DIVISION
BUT BEFORE THAT, IT'S TIME FOR A HARDY MEAL.
IT'S BUFFET-STYLE ... NO, IT'S LIKE FOOD STALLS AT A FESTIVAL!
BASICALLY, YOU CAN EAT AS MUCH AS YOU WANT FOR FREE.
THE DINING SPACE WE SET UP ISN'T POPULAR AT ALL.
MOST OF OUR GUESTS BRING FOOD BACK TO THEIR SEATS.
WE'VE ALSO GOT BOOZE, BUT FIGHTERS AREN'T ALLOWED TO DRINK.
THAT'S WHY I'VE ASKED THE OTHERS NOT TO DRINK TOO LATE IN THE EVENING.

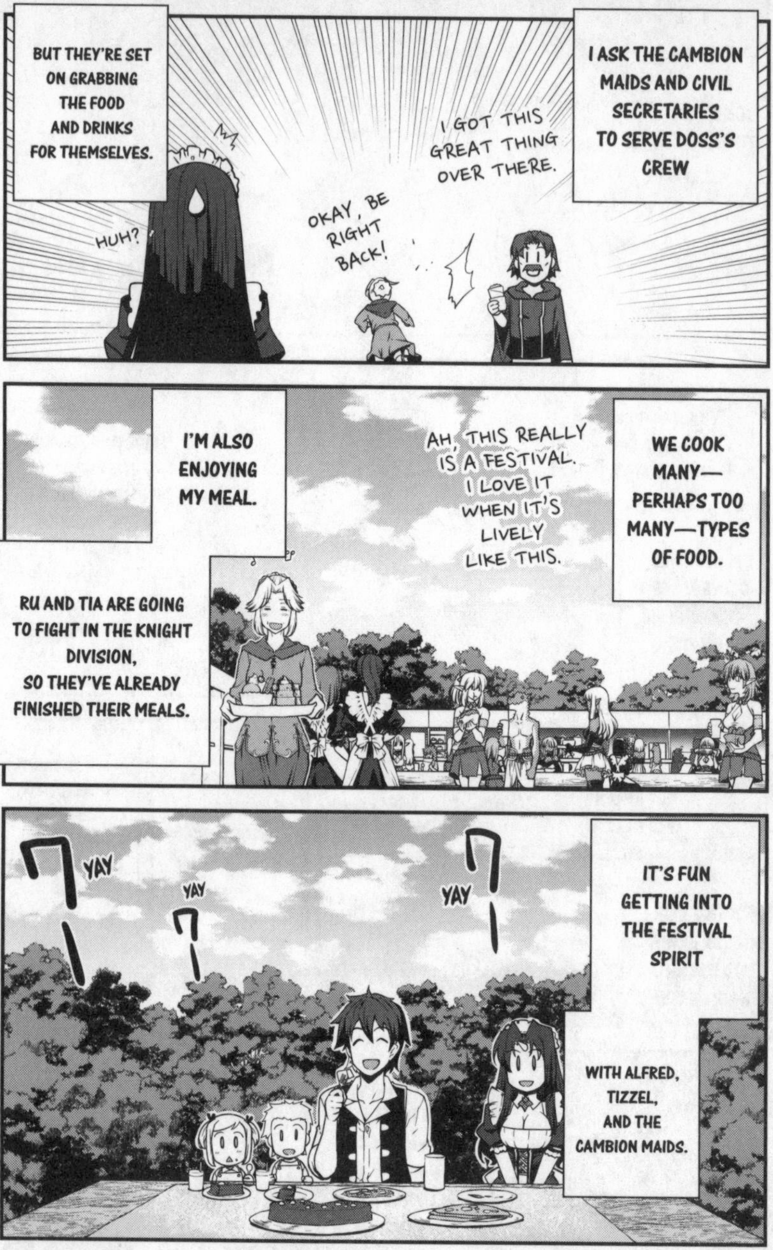
I ASK THE CAMBION MAIDS AND CIVIL SECRETARIES TO SERVE DOSS'S CREW
I GOT THIS GREAT THING OVER THERE.
OKAY, BE RIGHT BACK!
HUH?
BUT THEY'RE SET ON GRABBING THE FOOD AND DRINKS FOR THEMSELVES.
WE COOK MANY—PERHAPS TOO MANY—TYPES OF FOOD.
AH, THIS REALLY IS A FESTIVAL. I LOVE IT WHEN IT'S LIVELY LIKE THIS.
I'M ALSO ENJOYING MY MEAL.
RU AND TIA ARE GOING TO FIGHT IN THE KNIGHT DIVISION, SO THEY'VE ALREADY FINISHED THEIR MEALS.
IT'S FUN GETTING INTO THE FESTIVAL SPIRIT
WITH ALFRED, TIZZEL, AND THE CAMBION MAIDS.
YAY
YAY
YAY

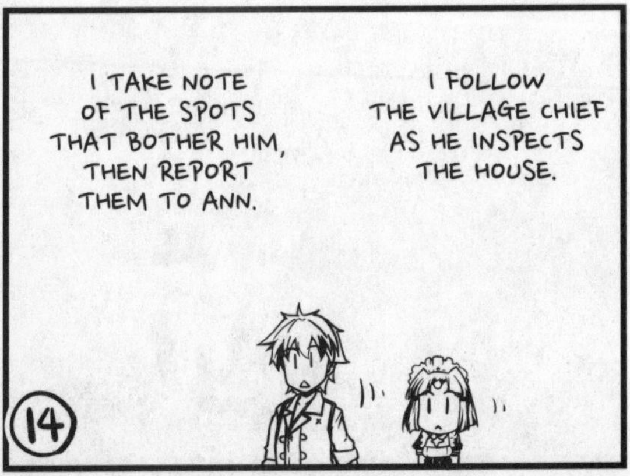
I FOLLOW THE VILLAGE CHIEF AS HE INSPECTS THE HOUSE.
I TAKE NOTE OF THE SPOTS THAT BOTHER HIM, THEN REPORT THEM TO ANN.
14

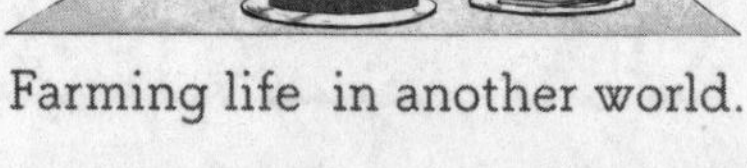

Farming life in another world.

CHAPTER 73: MARTIAL ARTS TOURNAMENT, KNIGHT DIVISION, ROUND 1 PART 1

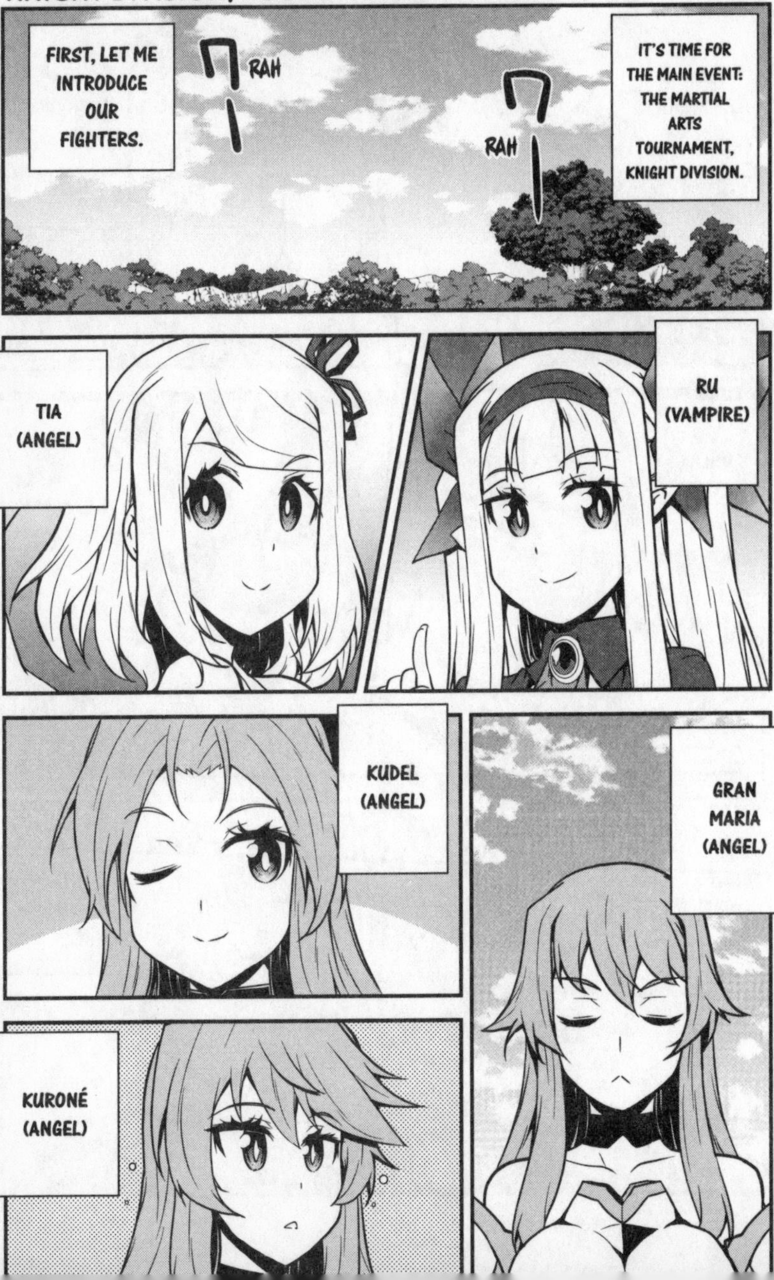
IT'S TIME FOR THE MAIN EVENT: THE MARTIAL ARTS TOURNAMENT, KNIGHT DIVISION.
RAH
RAH
FIRST, LET ME INTRODUCE OUR FIGHTERS.
RU (VAMPIRE)
TIA (ANGEL)
GRAN MARIA (ANGEL)
KUDEL (ANGEL)
KURONÉ (ANGEL)

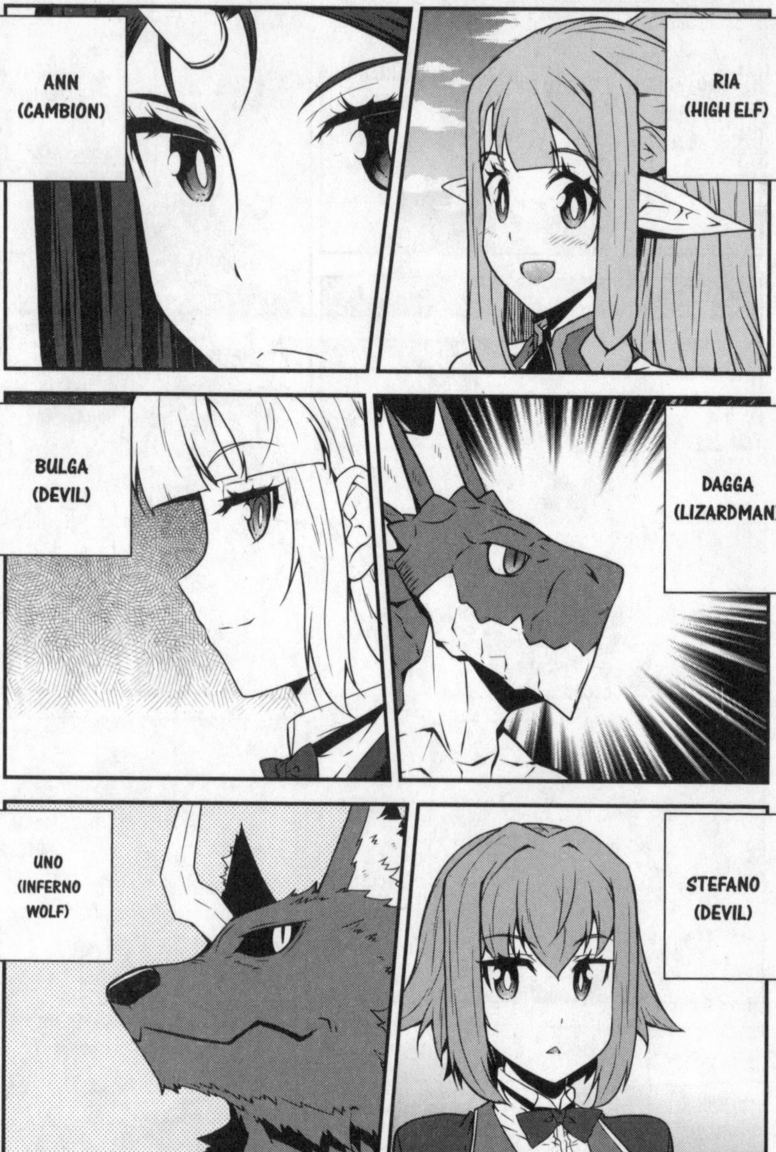
RIA (HIGH ELF)
ANN (CAMBION)
DAGGA (LIZARDMAN)
BULGA (DEVIL)
STEFANO (DEVIL)
UNO (INFERNO WOLF)

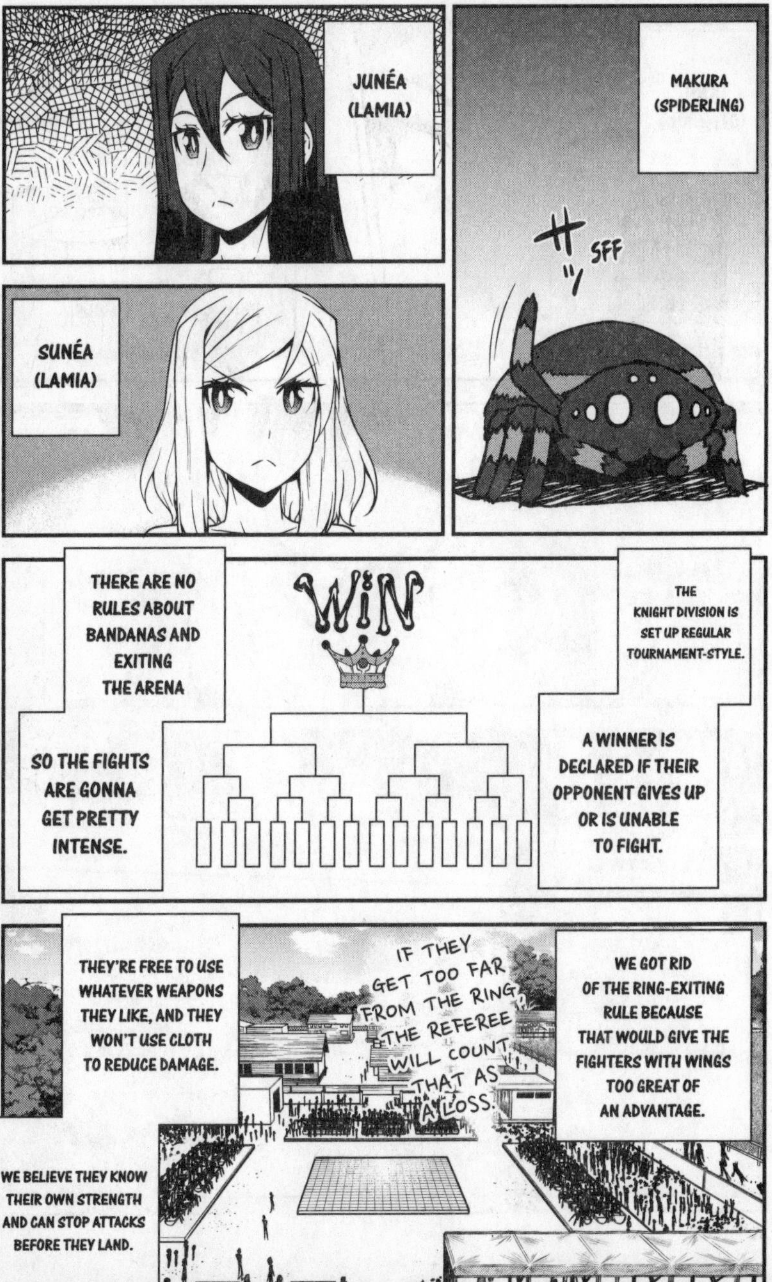
MAKURA (SPIDERLING)
SFF
JUNÉA (LAMIA)
SUNÉA (LAMIA)
THE KNIGHT DIVISION IS SET UP REGULAR TOURNAMENT-STYLE.
A WINNER IS DECLARED IF THEIR OPPONENT GIVES UP OR IS UNABLE TO FIGHT.
WIN
THERE ARE NO RULES ABOUT BANDANAS AND EXITING THE ARENA
SO THE FIGHTS ARE GONNA GET PRETTY INTENSE.
WE GOT RID OF THE RING-EXITING RULE BECAUSE THAT WOULD GIVE THE FIGHTERS WITH WINGS TOO GREAT OF AN ADVANTAGE.
IF THEY GET TOO FAR FROM THE RING, THE REFEREE WILL COUNT THAT AS A LOSS.
THEY'RE FREE TO USE WHATEVER WEAPONS THEY LIKE, AND THEY WON'T USE CLOTH TO REDUCE DAMAGE.
WE BELIEVE THEY KNOW THEIR OWN STRENGTH AND CAN STOP ATTACKS BEFORE THEY LAND.

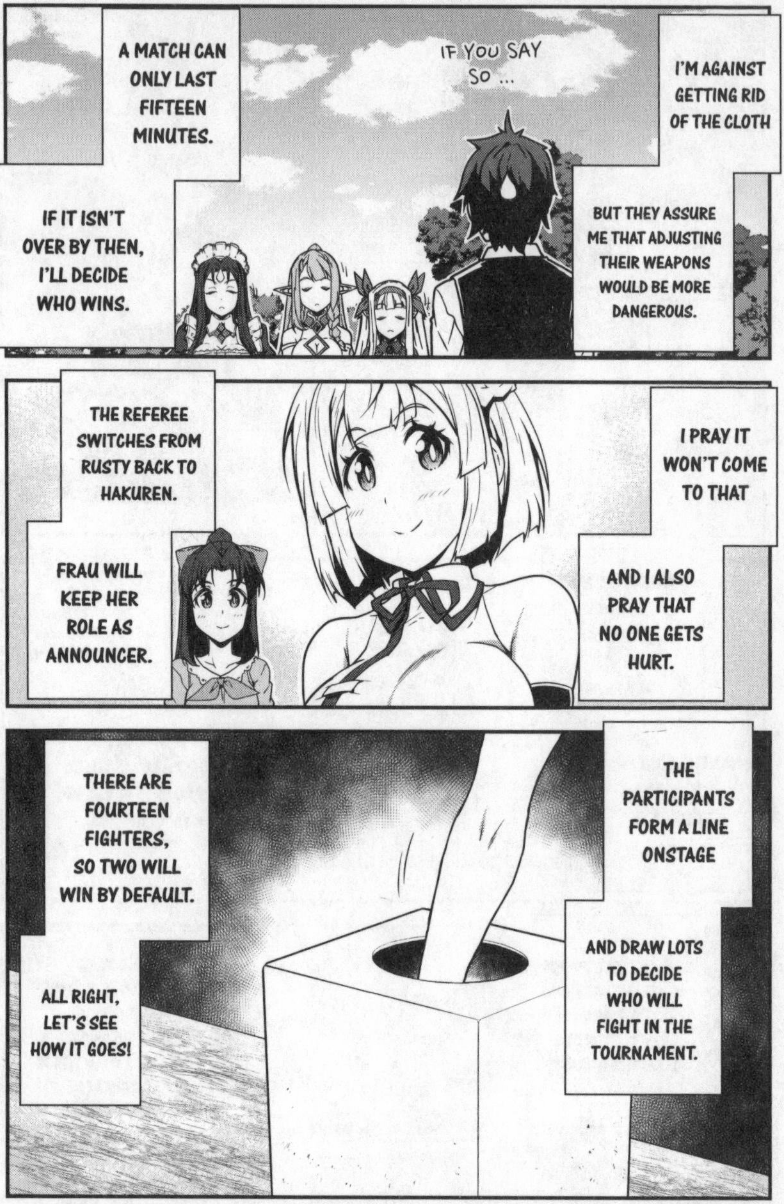
I'M AGAINST GETTING RID OF THE CLOTH
BUT THEY ASSURE ME THAT ADJUSTING THEIR WEAPONS WOULD BE MORE DANGEROUS.
IF YOU SAY SO ...
A MATCH CAN ONLY LAST FIFTEEN MINUTES.
IF IT ISN'T OVER BY THEN, I'LL DECIDE WHO WINS.
I PRAY IT WON'T COME TO THAT
AND I ALSO PRAY THAT NO ONE GETS HURT.
THE REFEREE SWITCHES FROM RUSTY BACK TO HAKUREN.
FRAU WILL KEEP HER ROLE AS ANNOUNCER.
THE PARTICIPANTS FORM A LINE ONSTAGE
AND DRAW LOTS TO DECIDE WHO WILL FIGHT IN THE TOURNAMENT.
THERE ARE FOURTEEN FIGHTERS, SO TWO WILL WIN BY DEFAULT.
ALL RIGHT, LET'S SEE HOW IT GOES!

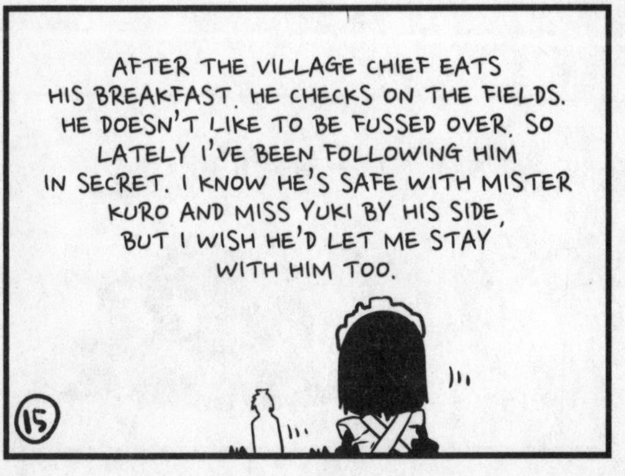
AFTER THE VILLAGE CHIEF EATS HIS BREAKFAST, HE CHECKS ON THE FIELDS. HE DOESN'T LIKE TO BE FUSSED OVER, SO LATELY I'VE BEEN FOLLOWING HIM IN SECRET. I KNOW HE'S SAFE WITH MISTER KURO AND MISS YUKI BY HIS SIDE, BUT I WISH HE'D LET ME STAY WITH HIM TOO.
15

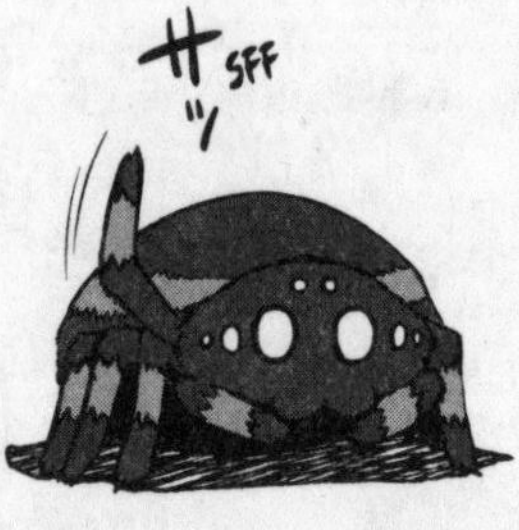
SFF

Farming life in another world.

CHAPTER 74: MARTIAL ARTS TOURNAMENT, KNIGHT DIVISION, ROUND 1 PART 2

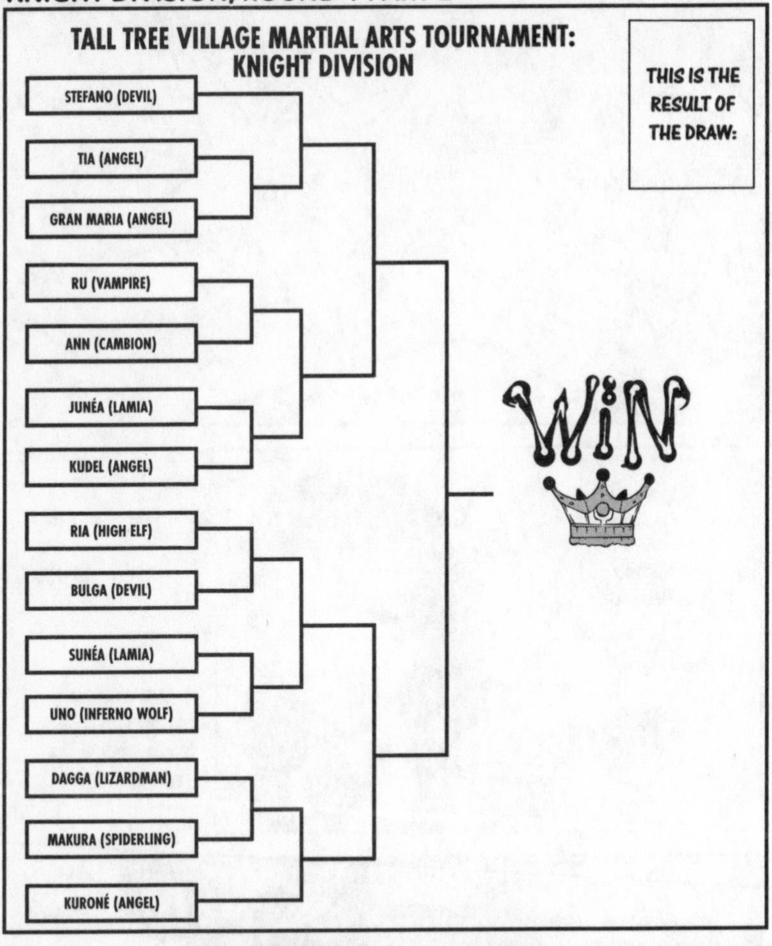

THIS IS THE RESULT OF THE DRAW:
TALL TREE VILLAGE MARTIAL ARTS TOURNAMENT: KNIGHT DIVISION
STEFANO (DEVIL)
TIA (ANGEL)
GRAN MARIA (ANGEL)
RU (VAMPIRE)
ANN (CAMBION)
JUNÉA (LAMIA)
KUDEL (ANGEL)
RIA (HIGH ELF)
BULGA (DEVIL)
SUNÉA (LAMIA)
UNO (INFERNO WOLF)
DAGGA (LIZARDMAN)
MAKURA (SPIDERLING)
KURONÉ (ANGEL)
WiN

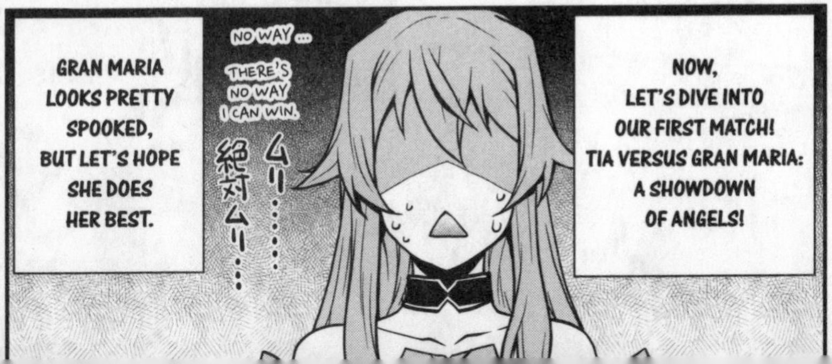

NOW, LET'S DIVE INTO OUR FIRST MATCH! TIA VERSUS GRAN MARIA: A SHOWDOWN OF ANGELS!
NO WAY...
THERE'S NO WAY I CAN WIN.
ムリ……
絶対ムリ…
GRAN MARIA LOOKS PRETTY SPOOKED, BUT LET'S HOPE SHE DOES HER BEST.

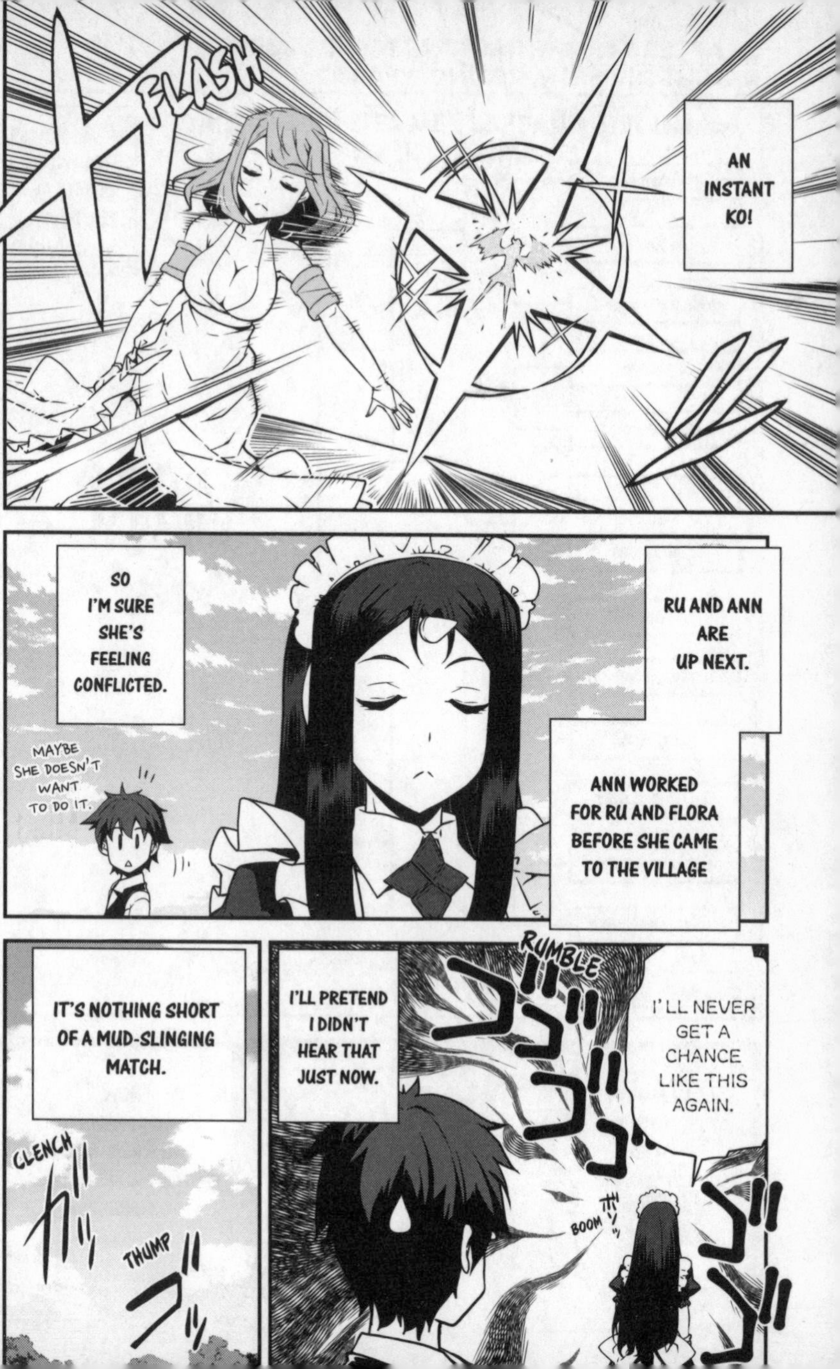
AN INSTANT KO!
FLASH
RU AND ANN ARE UP NEXT.
ANN WORKED FOR RU AND FLORA BEFORE SHE CAME TO THE VILLAGE
SO I'M SURE SHE'S FEELING CONFLICTED.
MAYBE SHE DOESN'T WANT TO DO IT.
RUMBLE
I'LL NEVER GET A CHANCE LIKE THIS AGAIN.
I'LL PRETEND I DIDN'T HEAR THAT JUST NOW.
BOOM
IT'S NOTHING SHORT OF A MUD-SLINGING MATCH.
CLENCH
THUMP

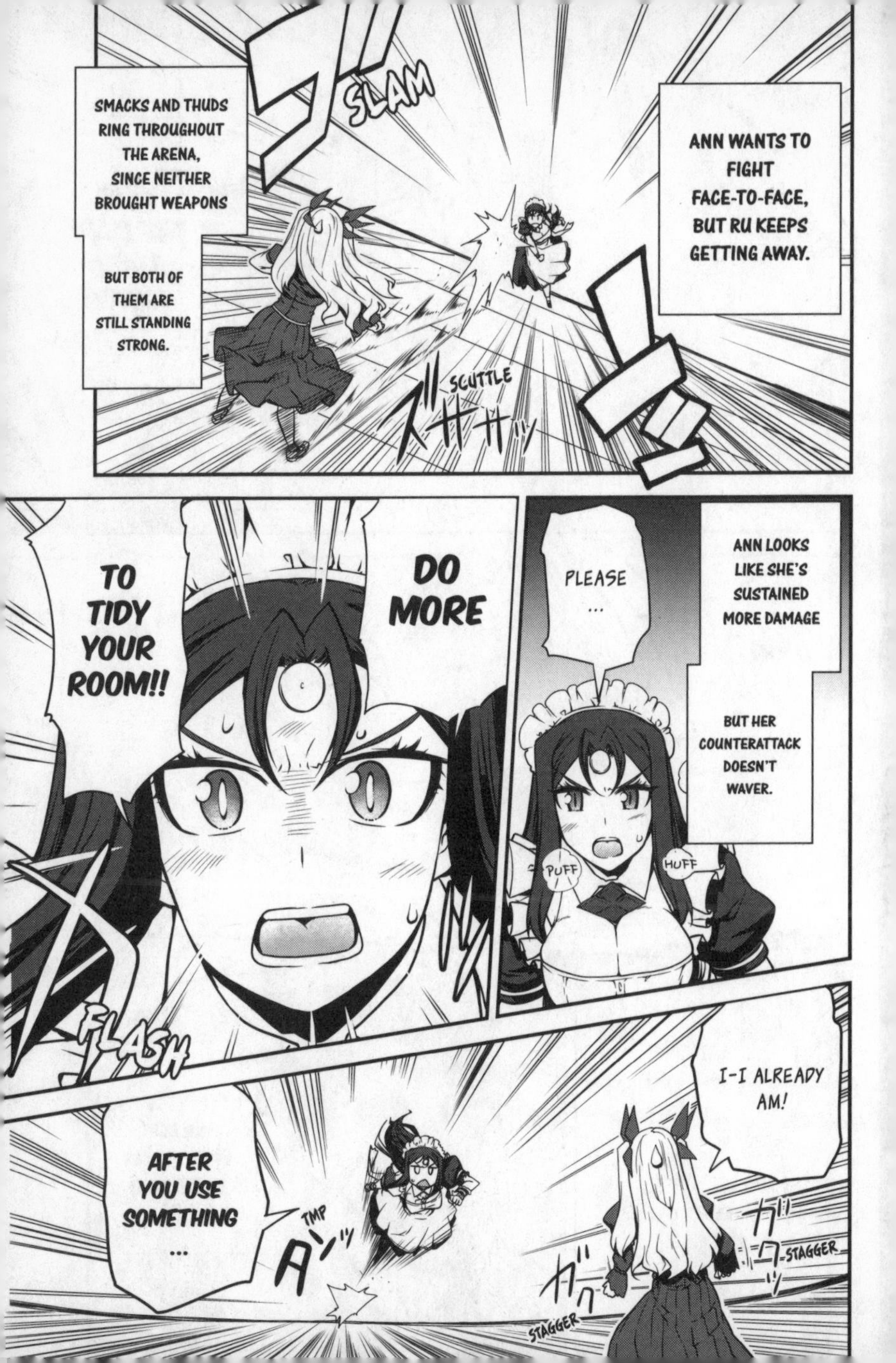
ANN WANTS TO FIGHT FACE-TO-FACE, BUT RU KEEPS GETTING AWAY.
SLAM
SMACKS AND THUDS RING THROUGHOUT THE ARENA, SINCE NEITHER BROUGHT WEAPONS
BUT BOTH OF THEM ARE STILL STANDING STRONG.
SCUTTLE
ANN LOOKS LIKE SHE'S SUSTAINED MORE DAMAGE
PLEASE ...
BUT HER COUNTERATTACK DOESN'T WAVER.
HUFF
PUFF
DO MORE
TO TIDY YOUR ROOM!!
FLASH
I-I ALREADY AM!
STAGGER
AFTER YOU USE SOMETHING ...
TMP
STAGGER

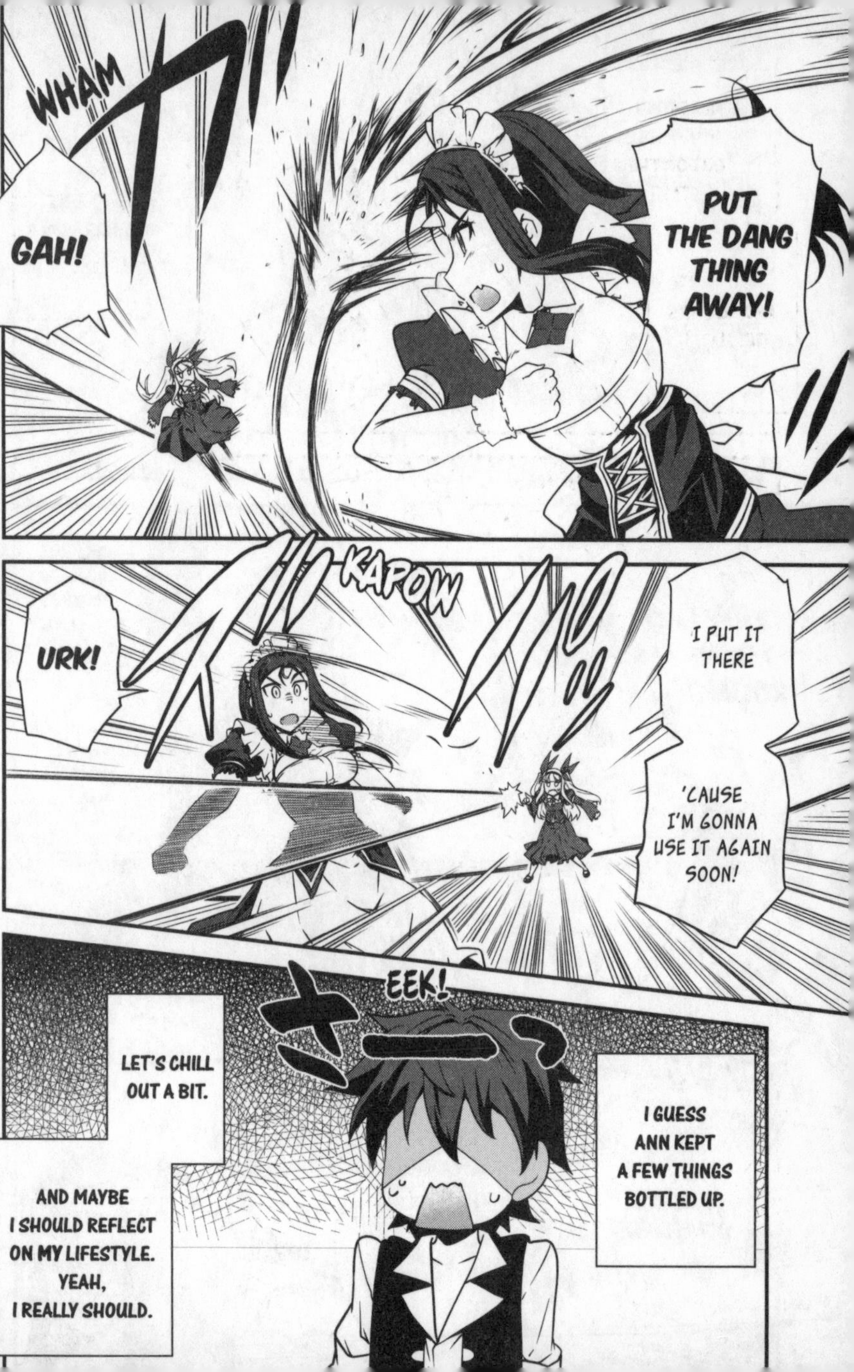
PUT THE DANG THING AWAY!
WHAM
GAH!
I PUT IT THERE
'CAUSE I'M GONNA USE IT AGAIN SOON!
KAPOW
URK!
EEK!
I GUESS ANN KEPT A FEW THINGS BOTTLED UP.
LET'S CHILL OUT A BIT.
AND MAYBE I SHOULD REFLECT ON MY LIFESTYLE. YEAH, I REALLY SHOULD.

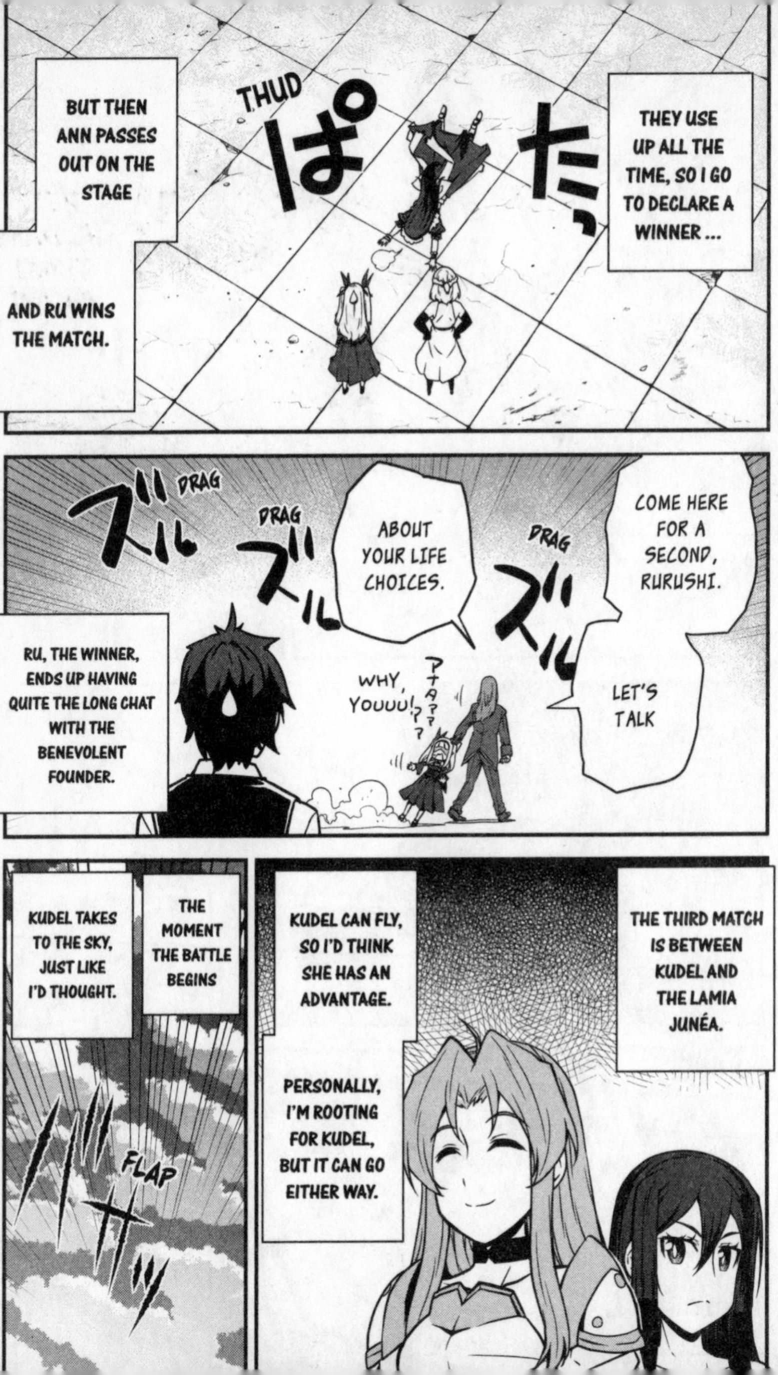
THEY USE UP ALL THE TIME, SO I GO TO DECLARE A WINNER ...
THUD
ぱた、
BUT THEN ANN PASSES OUT ON THE STAGE
AND RU WINS THE MATCH.
COME HERE FOR A SECOND, RURUSHI.
LET'S TALK
ABOUT YOUR LIFE CHOICES.
DRAG
ズル
DRAG
ズル
DRAG
ズル
WHY, YOUUU!?
アナタ???
RU, THE WINNER, ENDS UP HAVING QUITE THE LONG CHAT WITH THE BENEVOLENT FOUNDER.
THE THIRD MATCH IS BETWEEN KUDEL AND THE LAMIA JUNÉA.
KUDEL CAN FLY, SO I'D THINK SHE HAS AN ADVANTAGE.
PERSONALLY, I'M ROOTING FOR KUDEL, BUT IT CAN GO EITHER WAY.
THE MOMENT THE BATTLE BEGINS
KUDEL TAKES TO THE SKY, JUST LIKE I'D THOUGHT.
FLAP

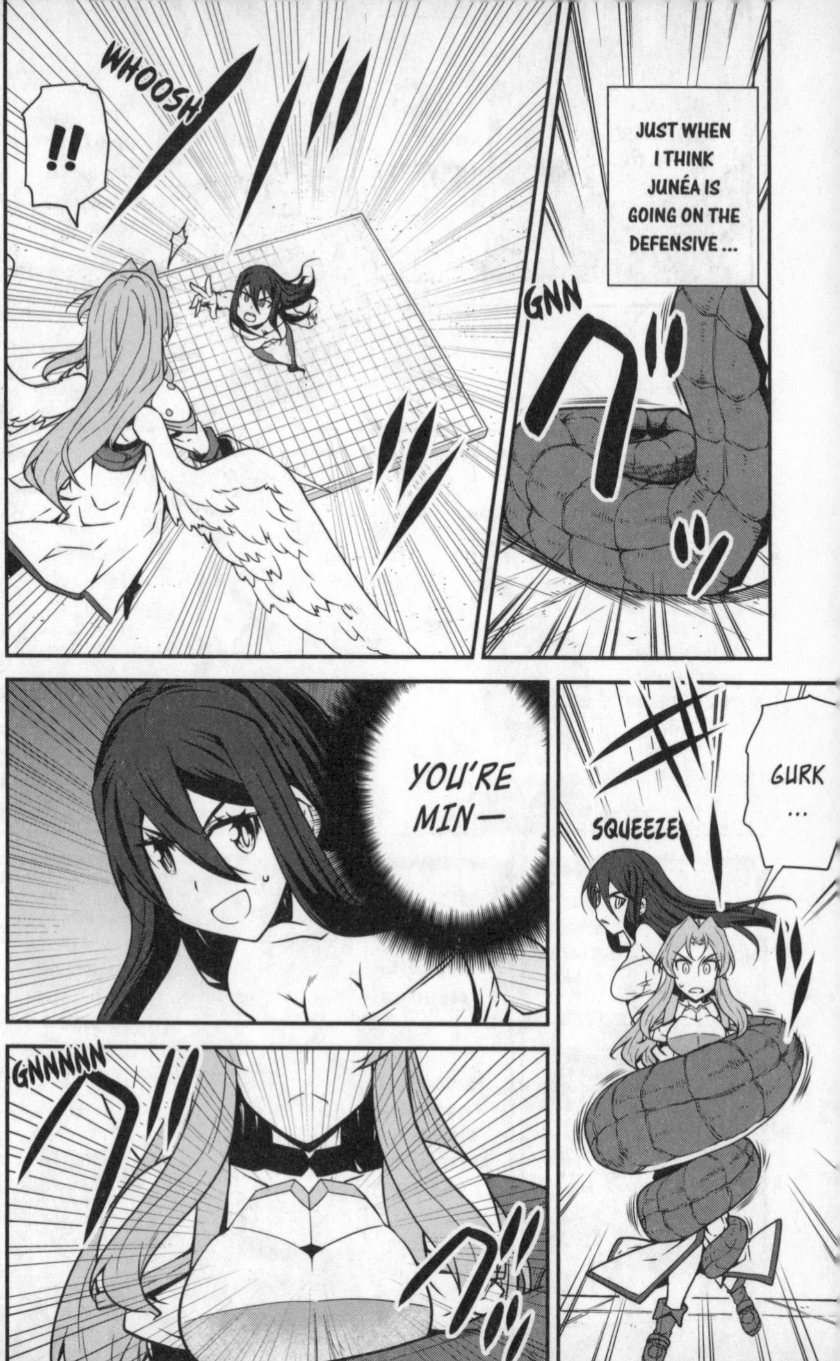
JUST WHEN I THINK JUNÉA IS GOING ON THE DEFENSIVE ...
GNN
WHOOSH
!!
GURK ...
SQUEEZE
YOU'RE MIN—
GNNNNN

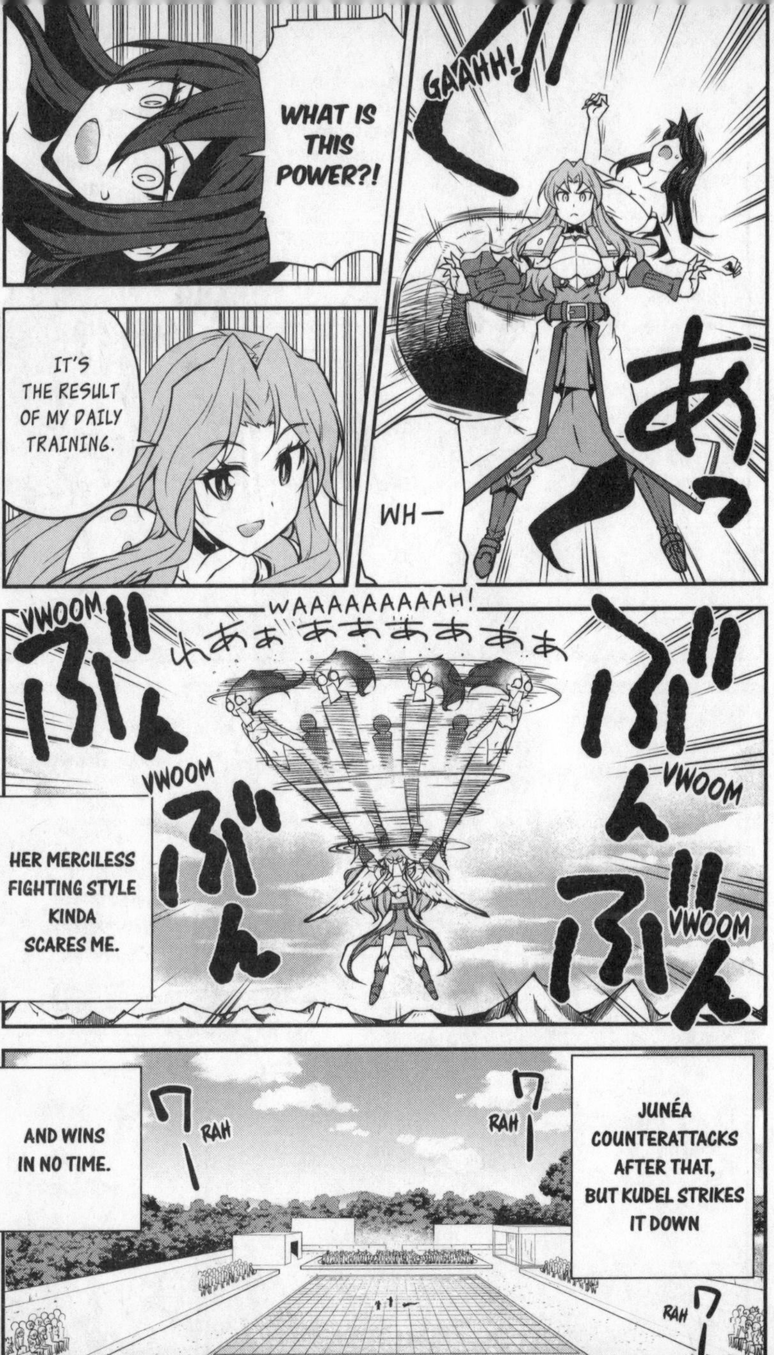
GAAHH!
あっ
WH—
WHAT IS THIS POWER?!
IT'S THE RESULT OF MY DAILY TRAINING.
WAAAAAAAAAH!
わあぁ ああああああ
VWOOM
ぶん
VWOOM
ぶん
VWOOM
ぶん
VWOOM
ぶん
HER MERCILESS FIGHTING STYLE KINDA SCARES ME.
JUNÉA COUNTERATTACKS AFTER THAT, BUT KUDEL STRIKES IT DOWN
RAH
ワー
RAH
ワー
RAH
ワー
AND WINS IN NO TIME.

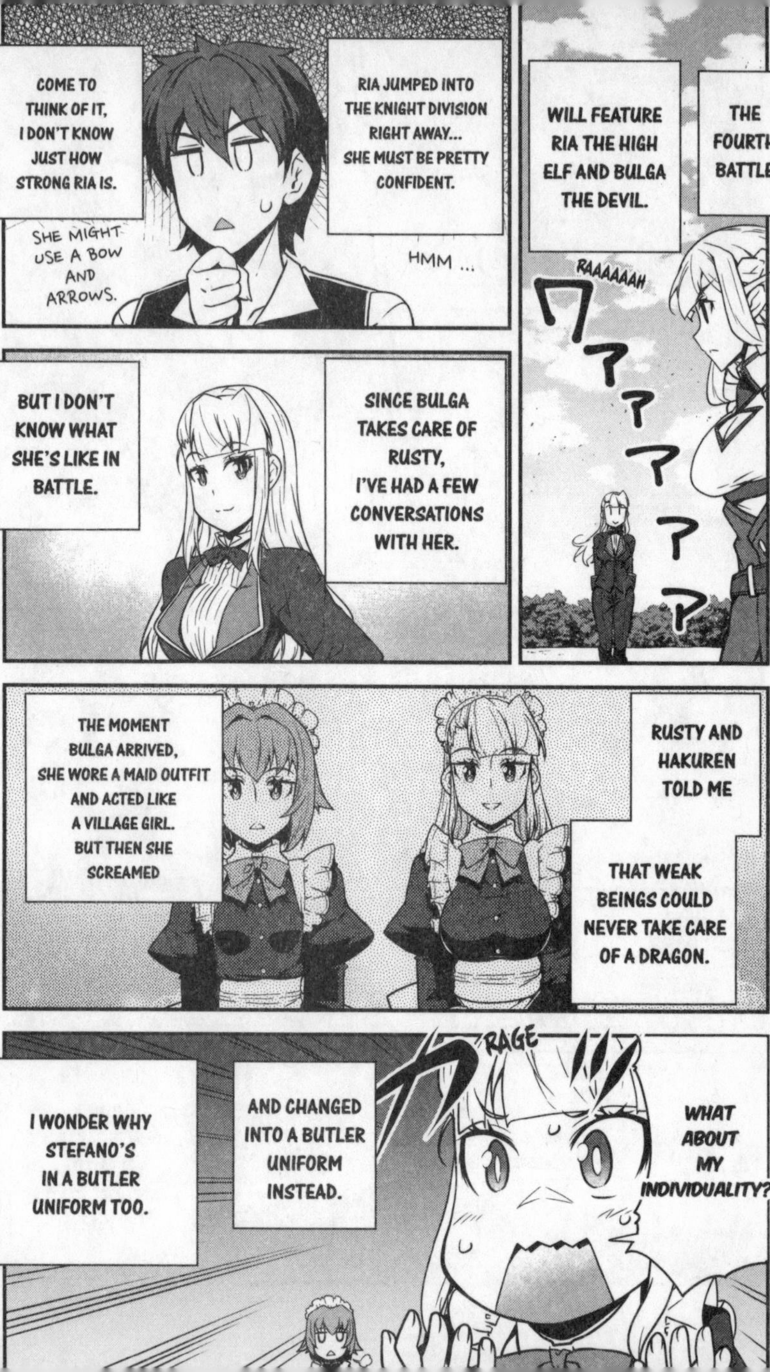
THE FOURTH BATTLE
WILL FEATURE RIA THE HIGH ELF AND BULGA THE DEVIL.
RAAAAAAH
ワアアアアア
RIA JUMPED INTO THE KNIGHT DIVISION RIGHT AWAY... SHE MUST BE PRETTY CONFIDENT.
COME TO THINK OF IT, I DON'T KNOW JUST HOW STRONG RIA IS.
HMM ...
SHE MIGHT USE A BOW AND ARROWS.
SINCE BULGA TAKES CARE OF RUSTY, I'VE HAD A FEW CONVERSATIONS WITH HER.
BUT I DON'T KNOW WHAT SHE'S LIKE IN BATTLE.
RUSTY AND HAKUREN TOLD ME
THAT WEAK BEINGS COULD NEVER TAKE CARE OF A DRAGON.
THE MOMENT BULGA ARRIVED, SHE WORE A MAID OUTFIT AND ACTED LIKE A VILLAGE GIRL. BUT THEN SHE SCREAMED
WHAT ABOUT MY INDIVIDUALITY?!
RAGE
AND CHANGED INTO A BUTLER UNIFORM INSTEAD.
I WONDER WHY STEFANO'S IN A BUTLER UNIFORM TOO.

KEEPING AWAY
FROM THE VILLAGE CHIEF ISN'T EASY.
THESE BEINGS QUIETLY PROTECT HIM
AT ALL TIMES:

TWO OR THREE OF MISTER KURO'S PUPS.
MANY SPIDERLINGS.
ONE HIGH ELF.

 I'LL KEEP AN EYE
ON THE VILLAGE CHIEF
SO NO ONE ELSE INTERFERES.

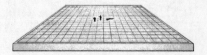
Farming life in another world.

CHAPTER 75: MARTIAL ARTS TOURNAMENT, KNIGHT DIVISION, ROUND 1 PART 3

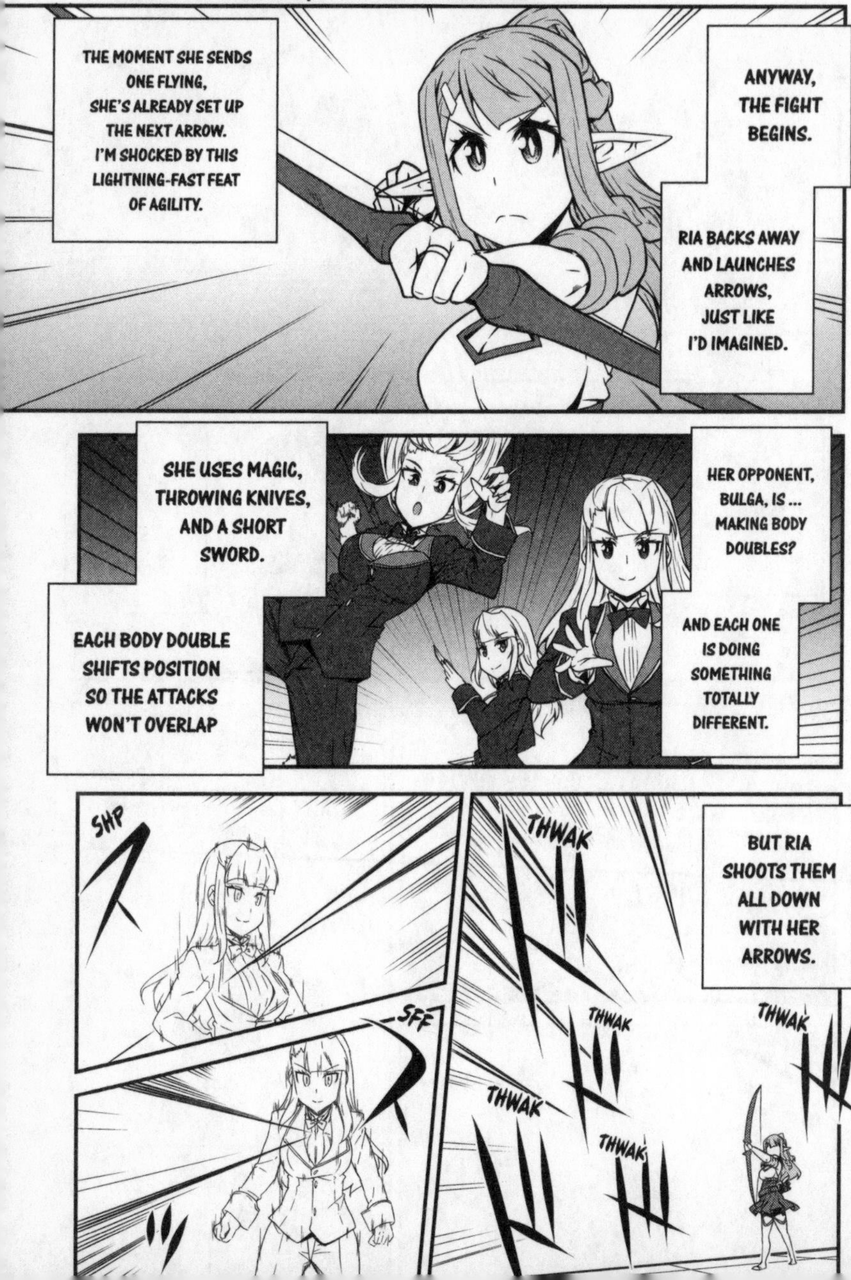
ANYWAY, THE FIGHT BEGINS.
RIA BACKS AWAY AND LAUNCHES ARROWS, JUST LIKE I'D IMAGINED.
THE MOMENT SHE SENDS ONE FLYING, SHE'S ALREADY SET UP THE NEXT ARROW. I'M SHOCKED BY THIS LIGHTNING-FAST FEAT OF AGILITY.
HER OPPONENT, BULGA, IS ... MAKING BODY DOUBLES?
AND EACH ONE IS DOING SOMETHING TOTALLY DIFFERENT.
SHE USES MAGIC, THROWING KNIVES, AND A SHORT SWORD.
EACH BODY DOUBLE SHIFTS POSITION SO THE ATTACKS WON'T OVERLAP
BUT RIA SHOOTS THEM ALL DOWN WITH HER ARROWS.
THWAK
THWAK
THWAK
THWAK
THWAK
SHP
SFF

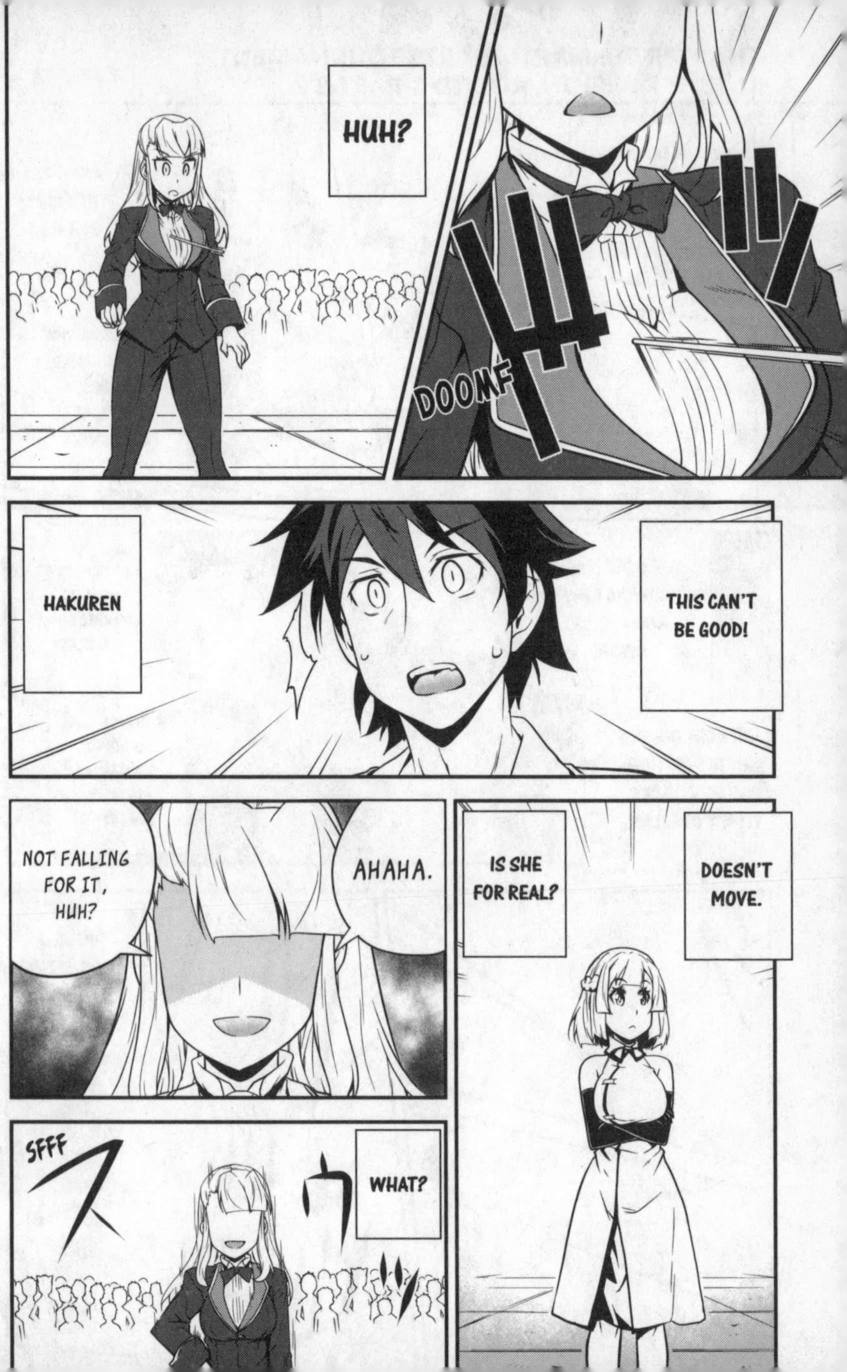
DOOMF
HUH?
THIS CAN'T BE GOOD!
HAKUREN
DOESN'T MOVE.
IS SHE FOR REAL?
AHAHA.
NOT FALLING FOR IT, HUH?
WHAT?
SFFF

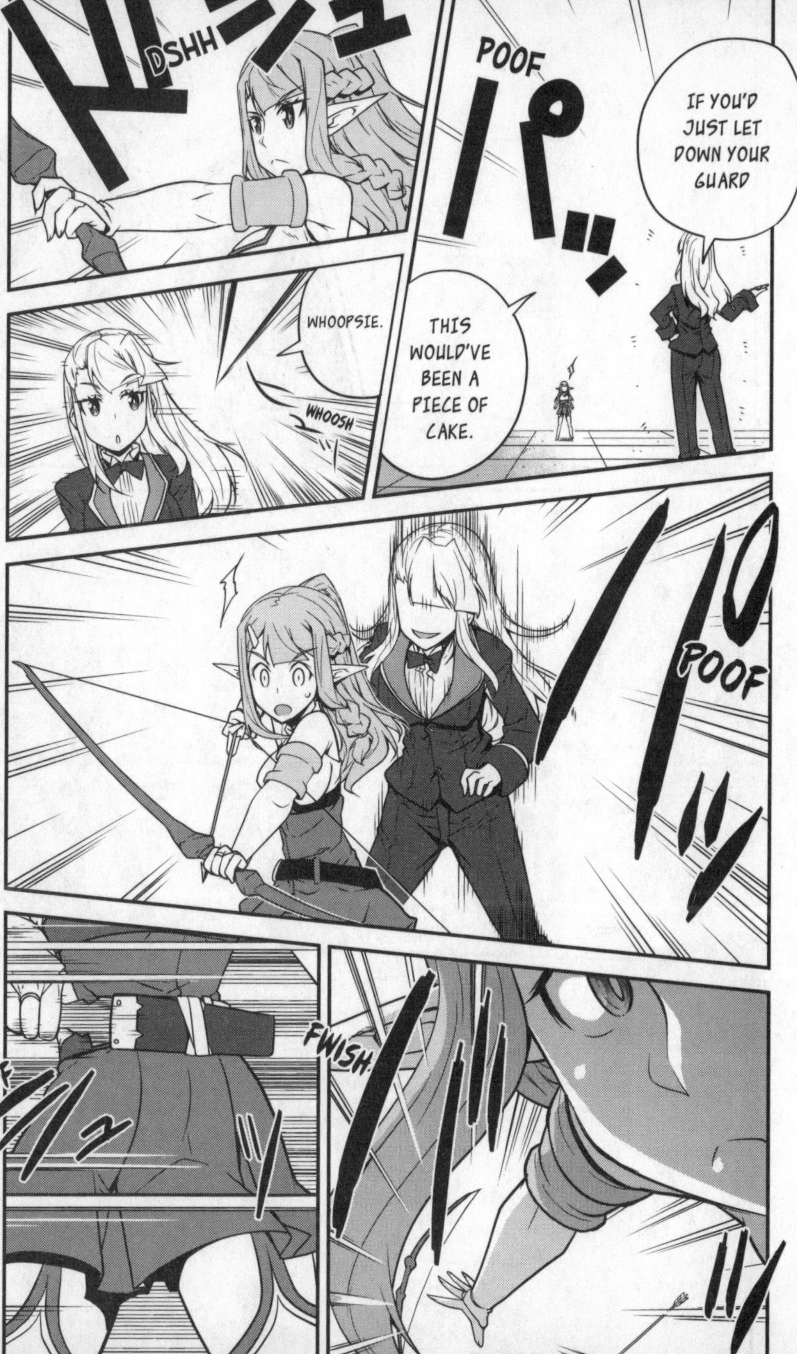
POOF
IF YOU'D JUST LET DOWN YOUR GUARD
THIS WOULD'VE BEEN A PIECE OF CAKE.
DSHH
WHOOPSIE.
WHOOSH
POOF
FWISH
SHFF

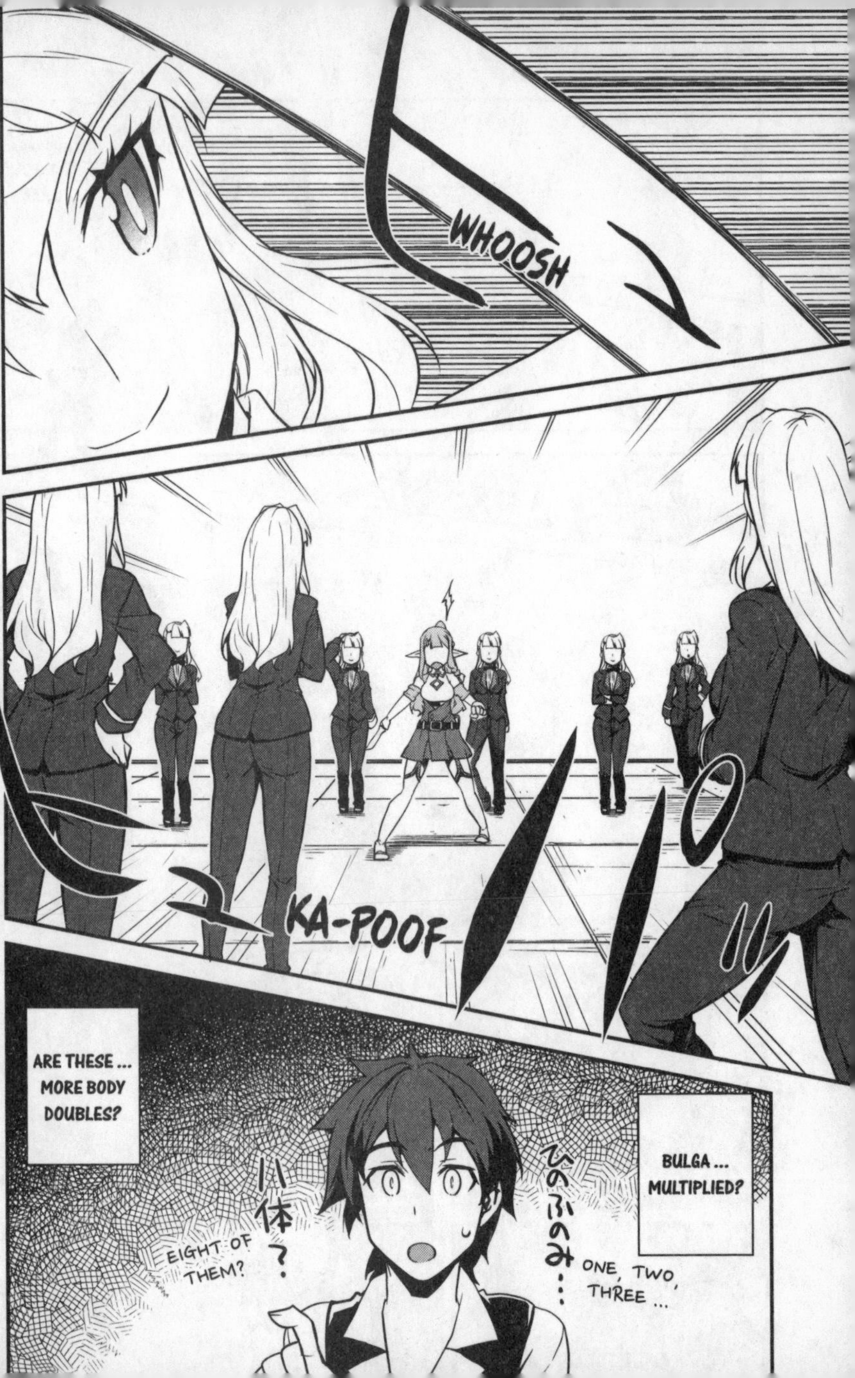
WHOOSH
KA-POOF
BULGA ... MULTIPLIED?
ひのふのみ…
ONE, TWO, THREE ...
八体？
EIGHT OF THEM?
ARE THESE ... MORE BODY DOUBLES?

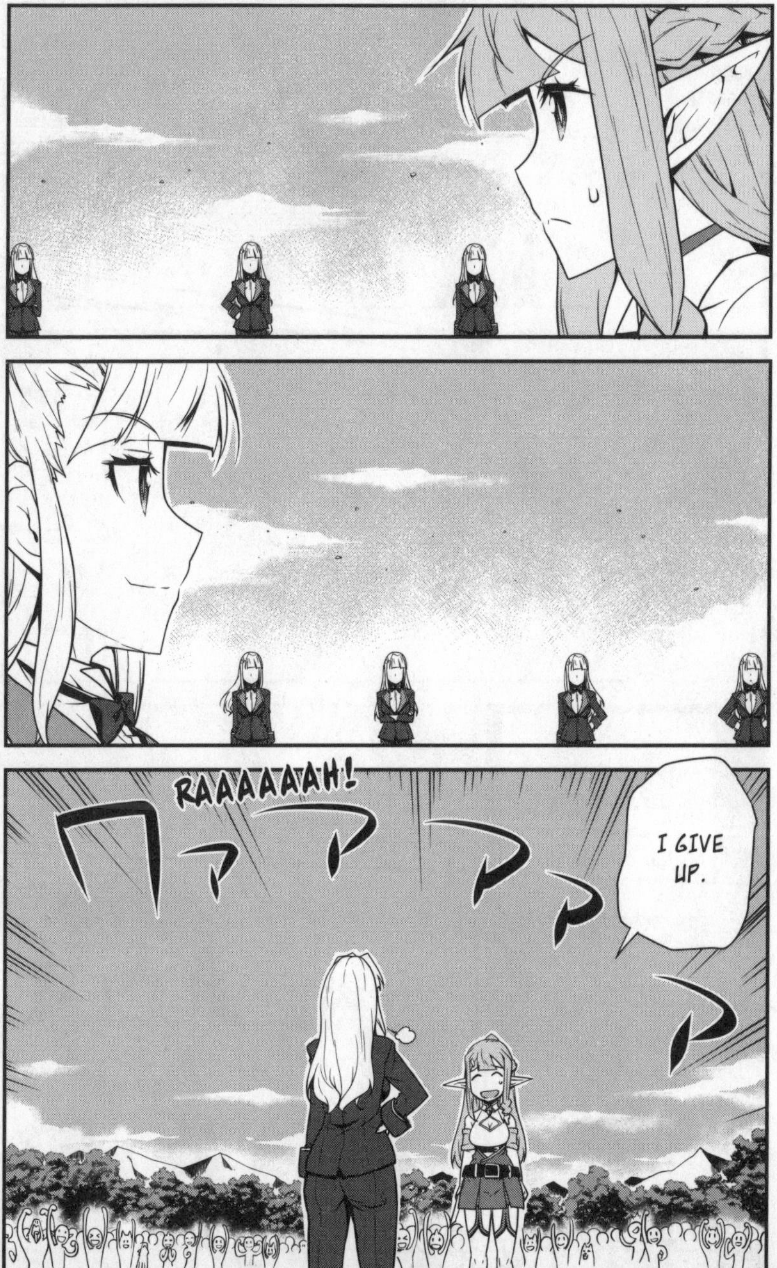
I GIVE UP.
RAAAAAAH!

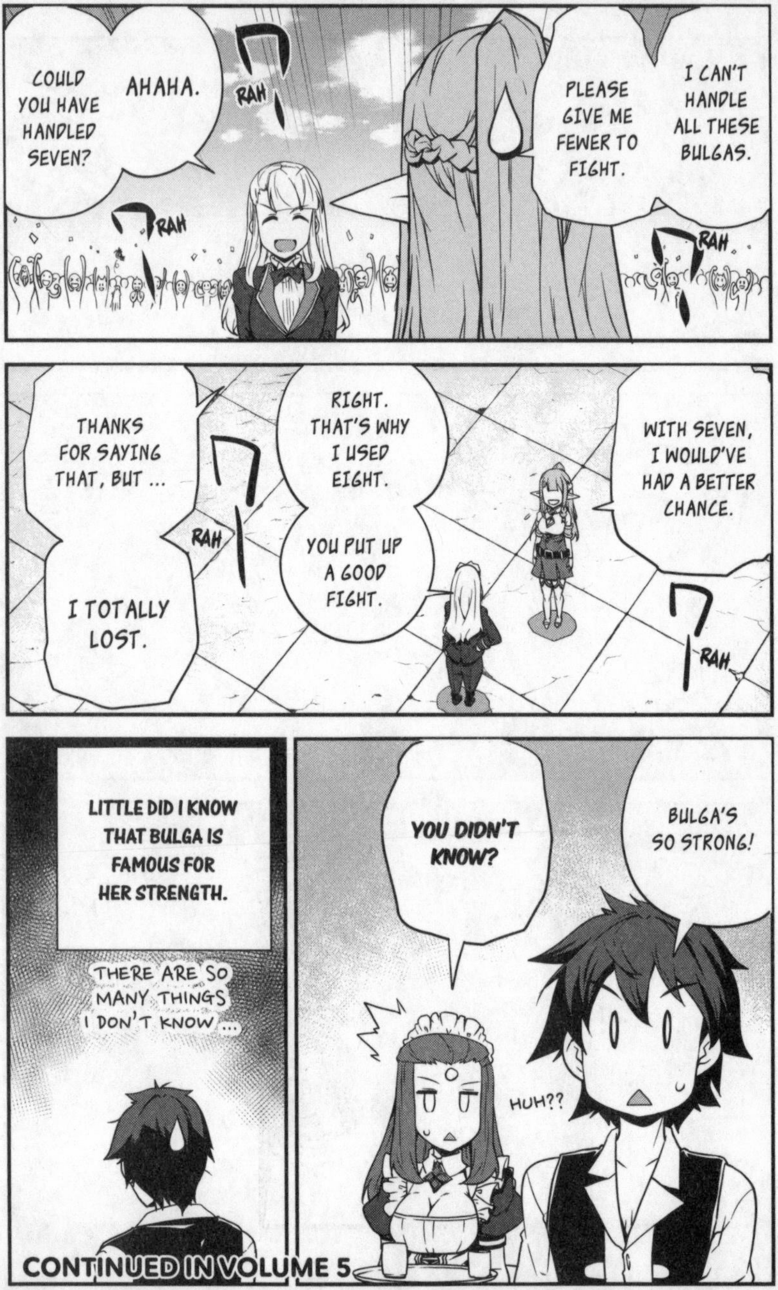
I CAN'T HANDLE ALL THESE BULGAS.
PLEASE GIVE ME FEWER TO FIGHT.
RAH
RAH
AHAHA.
COULD YOU HAVE HANDLED SEVEN?
RAH
WITH SEVEN, I WOULD'VE HAD A BETTER CHANCE.
RAH
RIGHT. THAT'S WHY I USED EIGHT.
YOU PUT UP A GOOD FIGHT.
RAH
THANKS FOR SAYING THAT, BUT ...
I TOTALLY LOST.
BULGA'S SO STRONG!
YOU DIDN'T KNOW?
HUH??
LITTLE DID I KNOW THAT BULGA IS FAMOUS FOR HER STRENGTH.
THERE ARE SO MANY THINGS I DON'T KNOW ...
CONTINUED IN VOLUME 5

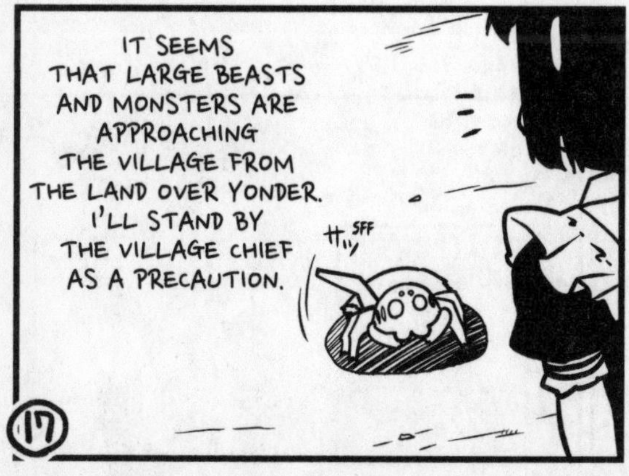
IT SEEMS THAT LARGE BEASTS AND MONSTERS ARE APPROACHING THE VILLAGE FROM THE LAND OVER YONDER. I'LL STAND BY THE VILLAGE CHIEF AS A PRECAUTION.
SFF
17

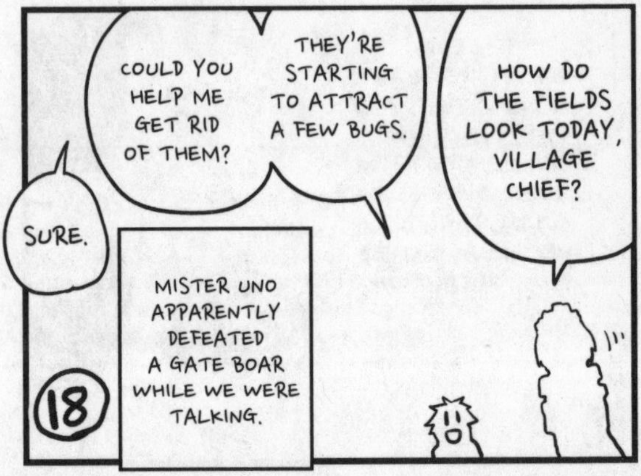
HOW DO THE FIELDS LOOK TODAY, VILLAGE CHIEF?
THEY'RE STARTING TO ATTRACT A FEW BUGS.
COULD YOU HELP ME GET RID OF THEM?
SURE.
MISTER UNO APPARENTLY DEFEATED A GATE BOAR WHILE WE WERE TALKING.
18

POSTSCRIPT

Hello! I'm Kinosuke Naito.
We're at Volume 4, where punches are thrown in the martial arts tournament. Where did all that "laidback farming" go? Not to worry. This, too, is a part of our laidback farming adventure.

-Original Author: Kinosuke Naito

I'm Yasumo, the person in charge of the character designs in this manga.
Reading the manga is always a blast!
This time, I'm going to read it and study the characters' facial expressions!

-Original Character Design: Yasumo

A DAY IN THE LIFE OF A CAMBION PART 2

THE VILLAGE CHIEF HAS COMBAT TRAINING AFTER LUNCH.
I CAN ALSO FIGHT PRETTY WELL, BEING A CAMBION AND ALL.
ALL RIGHT, IT'S TIME FOR ME AND THE VILLAGE CHIEF TO —
OH YEAH, I CAN'T PRACTICE WITH HIM. HE'S WAY TOO POPULAR.
I ALWAYS STAND BY HIM AS A MAID, SO LADY ANN TELLS ME THAT I SHOULD TAKE A STEP BACK.
SLUMP
OH WELL. I GUESS I'LL JUST TRAIN WITH ONE OF THE CIVIL SECRETARIES THEN.
LET'S PRACTICE.
SHE SEEMS IRKED FOR SOME REASON, BUT MAYBE IT'S JUST MY IMAGINATION.
I CAN'T BEAT A CAMBION!
NOOOOOOOOO!
AT LEAST SHE TRIED.

Nice to meet you! I'm Yasuyuki Tsurugi and I handle the illustrations. Thank you for reading Volume 3 and now Volume 4! In this volume, we suddenly find the villagers in a martial arts tournament. I've been enjoying all the action scenes, but the sketches I'm drawing are very different than usual. They're so different, in fact, that it sometimes feels like I'm drawing a different manga altogether. I had a tough time getting used to that style. Nowadays, I'm back to drawing a carefree village, but . . . I find myself grumbling that I can't get back to being used to that either. Manga is hard! In Volume 5, the battles end and we're back to our everyday village life. See you there!

-Yasuyuki Tsurugi

BEFORE THE MARTIAL ARTS TOURNAMENT

It's been decided that we'll hold a martial arts tournament.
The civil secretaries are making all sorts of preparations.
And so am I. More specifically, I'm making the stage.
But I won't be training. No way.
Because I'm not going to fight.
Am I gonna participate? Hah, real funny.
Just think about it for a second.
I've never used a weapon in my life, but everyone else is still alive because they know how to use weapons.
There would be no competition if I were involved.
So listen, Ria.
Don't try to make me participate in the tournament. Again, there'd be no competition.
That's not what I mean. It's not because I'm too powerful—it's because I'm too weak.
That distinction's really important, so please make no mistake.
Don't make that mistake either, Dagga.
I'm not gonna participate.
Like I said, it's not because I'm too strong, but because I'm too weak . . .
Hey, why are you making those faces?

In terms of sheer manpower, there's no competition.
I can only survive in the Forest of Death because I have the almighty farming tool.
I also have help from the Kuros, the Zabutons, Ru, Tia, and Ann's maids.
If you were to tell me to go back to my old, lonely lifestyle right now, I don't think I could.
It's not a matter of being able to live alone or not . . . It's more psychological. Plus, I have kids.
But I'm going off-topic.

People think I'm strong because I have the almighty farming tool.

For me, it feels like I'm just borrowing the tool, but everyone else thinks it's an extension of my personality.
On top of that, they expect me to participate in the tournament because they think the almighty farming tool's strength is my own.
Come to think of it, I've never fought Ria or Dagga. Not even Ru or Tia.
Should I fight in the tournament?
I'll ask Ru.
"Would you be able to go easy on them?" she asks.
No way.
I'm not going to fight in the tournament, like I'd planned.
I've made my decision.

That night, the almighty farming tool turns into a spear. It doesn't usually transform on its own. What could have happened?
Oh, I think it wanted to participate in the tournament.
Sorry, tool.
I apologize, so please don't go soft on me now.
Okay, okay.
I'll try to find an opponent I can attack at full power.

The next day, I ask Hakuren for a fight.
She turns me down with a smile.
I thought she'd want to battle the most, so I'm a little surprised. Why not?
She tells me it's because she hasn't finished the preparations she needs to win.
Huh.
Maybe she'll want to fight when she's done.

After that, I ask Rusty to fight.
She bursts into tears.
No, no, I don't hate you at all!
I comfort her and withdraw.

Hmm, I wonder what's wrong.
Doss is nearby. I'll ask him.
He tells me his lower back hurts and scurries away.

Drime . . . hands me cash.
I wouldn't be a decent man if I took it, so I give it back.

No one will fight me.
What do I do?
I won't be able to go easy on them, but maybe Ria or Dagga will fight me since they're the ones who asked me to participate in the first place.
I'll go ask Ria.
"I just want to see how strong you are, village chief, but I could never fight you," Ria says.
I also ask Dagga, but he says the same thing.
I see.
They want me to show off my strength, not battle me.
That makes sense.
It is what it is, so just throw in the towel, almighty farming tool.
What? You're telling me not to give up? That it'll be all over if I do? That there's still hope if I don't call it quits?
Stop talking like a character from a sports manga.
Some things are simply impossible.
But being persistent isn't bad. Maybe I just need to try a bit harder.

The Demon King's here, so I ask if he'd like to participate in the tournament.
Huh? I didn't misspeak, but for some reason he doesn't seem to understand what I said.
I wonder what happened.
Let's have a competition, a com-pe-ti-tion. Right, a competition.
Between you and me, Demon King. Yeah, a one-on-one match.
We'll take it easy, like we're still practicing.
See, I don't really want to fight. My spear is the one who's raring to go.
It's not a cursed blade, so no worries there. It's a lucky spear, if anything.
Yeah, maybe that's what it is.

In the end, no one accepts my request.
Sorry, almighty farming tool.
I know it might not cheer you up, but why don't we go hunt in the forest?
We're gonna use up lots of food at the tournament, so I'd like to hunt some

READ THIS PAGE LAST.

big game.
Hah! A wyvern would sure put us in a tight spot.
We want big game, so we'll get some grappler bears and bloody vipers.
That's when I turn the almighty farming tool into a spear and go hunting.

When I defeat an enemy with the tool's hoe, everything above it becomes dirt.
When I slay an enemy with the tool's spear, it scatters in every direction.
I had no idea this would happen.
What? Our enemies are too weak? Not much I can do for you there.
I'm glad my participation in the tournament didn't work out.
I shouldn't have been looking for an opponent.
That could've been dangerous.
I could have scattered my opponent. I'll try to be more careful from now on.
And listen up, almighty farming tool. I know it's not what you want to hear, but I want you to settle with martial arts practice.

On the night of the tournament, I practice martial arts onstage.
Honestly, I'm just hitting a rock with my spear.
It's a pretty simple show, but I'm glad the almighty farming tool got its time in the spotlight.
But I think I tried a little too hard.
There's a hole in the rock that goes all the way to the other side.
I'm glad I aimed the spear toward the sky.

End

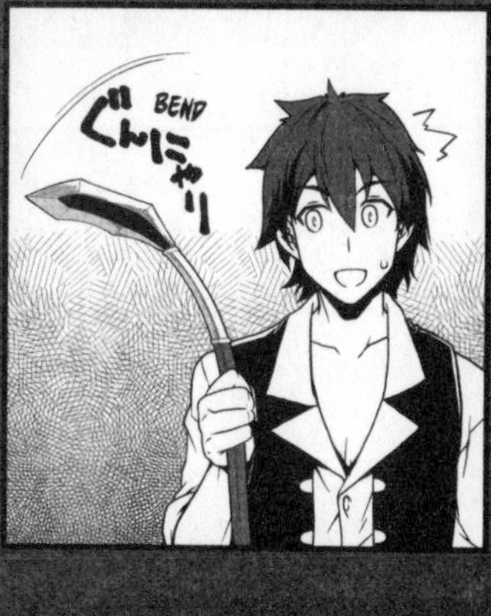
ぐんにゃり
BEND

Illustration
Yasuyuki Tsurugi

Farming Life in Another World Volume 4
(ISEKAI NONBIRI NOUKA Vol.4)
© Yasuyuki Tsurugi 2019
© Kinosuke Naito, Yasumo 2019
First published in Japan in 2019 by KADOKAWA CORPORATION, Tokyo.
English translation rights arranged with KADOKAWA CORPORATION, Tokyo.

ISBN: 978-1-64273-127-9

Story by Kinosuke Naito
Art by Yasuyuki Tsurugi
Character design by Yasumo
Translated by Kristi Fernandez
English Edition Published by One Peace Books 2022

Printed in Canada
1 2 3 4 5 6 7 8 9 10

One Peace Books
43-32 22nd Street STE 204 Long Island City New York 11101
www.onepeacebooks.com